D1570463

THE PROBLEM OF GENESIS IN
HUSSERL'S PHILOSOPHY

THE PROBLEM OF

GENESIS

IN HUSSERL'S PHILOSOPHY

Jacques Derrida

Translated by Marian Hobson

THE UNIVERSITY OF CHICAGO PRESS
Chicago & London

JACQUES DERRIDA is professor at the École des Hautes Études en Sciences Sociales in Paris and author of more than a dozen books published in translation by the University of Chicago Press, including most recently *The Work of Mourning* (2001).

MARIAN HOBSON is professor of French at Queen Mary, University of London and the author or editor of several books, including *Jacques Derrida: Opening Lines* (1998). Her previous translations include articles by Jacques Derrida, Jean-François Lyotard, and Werner Hamacher.

The University of Chicago Press, Chicago 60637
The University of Chicago Press, Ltd., London
© 2003 by The University of Chicago
All rights reserved. Published 2003
Printed in the United States of America
English language only
12 11 10 09 08 07 06 05 04 03   1 2 3 4 5

ISBN: 0-226-14315-5 (cloth)

Originally published as *Le problème de la genèse dans la philosophie de Husserl*,
© Presses Universitaires de France, 1990.

Library of Congress Cataloging-in-Publication Data

Derrida, Jacques.
    [Problème de la genèse dans la philosophie de Husserl. English]
    The problem of genesis in Husserl's philosophy / Jacques Derrida ;
translated by Marian Hobson.
       p. cm.
    Includes bibliographical references and index.
    ISBN 0-226-14315-5 (cloth : alk. paper)
    1. Husserl, Edmund, 1859–1938—Contributions in concept of genesis.
    2. Beginning—History—20th century. I. Title.

B3279.H94 .D3713 2003
116—dc21

                                        2002043560

⊗ The paper used in this publication meets the minimum requirements of the American National Standard for Information Sciences—Permanence of Paper for Printed Library Materials, ANSI Z39.48-1992.

CONTENTS

PART III

THE PHENOMENOLOGICAL THEME OF GENESIS: TRANSCENDENTAL GENESIS AND "WORLDLY" GENESIS

PART IV

TELEOLOGY. THE SENSE OF HISTORY AND THE HISTORY OF SENSE

TRANSLATOR'S NOTE

This is a translation into English of Jacques Derrida's *Le problème de la genèse dans la philosophie de Husserl,* Paris: PUF, 1990. The work, previously unpublished, was written in 1953–54 as a dissertation [*mémoire*] for the "diplôme d'études supérieures," as Derrida's preface of 1990 explains. The *mémoire*'s notes referred to the editions of Husserl's work available in German and French at the time of its writing. Again as the 1990 preface explains, these references were brought up to date by Elisabeth Weber, using Husserl's collected works, the *Husserliana,*[1] still in course of publication, and translations from the German into French which had become available since 1954. Her contribution is marked both in 1990 and in this present translation between angle brackets < >. The bibliographical and textual situation of the published dissertation becomes even more complicated when translated into English, because the published translations of Husserl in English are frequently different from the French. My remarks are between square brackets [ ].[2]

This translation has attempted at some points to advertise its complex linguistic situation. "Devenir," "originaire," and "vécu," for example, are common words in Derrida's French text, and ones that would have been more naturally translated by, for instance, "development," "original," and plain "experience" than as they have in fact been—as "becoming," "originary," and "lived experience." But Derrida himself chose words in French that referred directly to Husserl's German and to the distinguished translation by Paul Ricœur of Husserl's *Ideas.* These words in the French do not merge back into everyday common philosophical terms, but wear their side-on relation to ordinary language openly, and I have tried to keep that quality in the English. Philosophy written in English has a different history, and frequently different interests and different style from that written in French, not to speak of

German. If it is wished, and it is, for the translation to be connectable to the philosophic tradition of English, it is difficult to avoid the word "mind" sometimes, at least in relation to "psychique"; yet the English word has no clear-cut translation into either French or German and has a heavy philosophical past. Moreover, certain much-used words in French (and German) philosophy group senses in different ways to English: the interesting and important example of "unité" can translate the logical sense of *Einheit* in Frege, as well as the wider quality of "unity." In English, a choice has to be made between "unit" and "unity," which certainly have different areas of use at least, whereas French and German can leave the sense undivided. "Motif" in French is perhaps a similar example in Derrida's own text (see chap. 3). To my mind Derrida moves, without making this move explicit, between "motif = reason" and "motif = subject" in a way suggesting that a problem is surfacing that will figure in his much later work, the question of what happens when ideas are "thematized," that is, when ideas are turned into themes overtly itemized and expressed. Thence, they may harden into compacted constructions, semantic accretions that are no longer inquired into.

A striking thing about this *mémoire* is how intellectually rich it is, and yet how much it remains a thesis. It recognizably belongs to the genre, and yet, in a way to be discussed briefly below, it has extraordinary pointers forward, to the philosopher that Derrida is becoming. But, surprisingly, an inverse remark could be made about its style: it is straightforward—completely different from the way Derrida would write less than ten years later. Here the pointers forward in style are missing. The syntax used is at points even formulaic, building sentences out of syntactic molds that are repeated many times.

That may be so, but the overlaying of texts and languages, and even the interweaving of times, given the gap between writing and publication, is pretty complex in the present translation. This might seem a matter of inevitable accident, what happens when a work of philosophy is translated later into another language. But is it? And what did happen? Looking forward from the dissertation, into the 1960s and beyond, it seems crucial that Derrida began in this cross-lingual, cross-textual fashion, writing in French on a philosopher whose German was notoriously convoluted, with its own distinctive vocabulary; most of whose published works were unavailable in translation at that time, and a considerable part of which was actually unpublished. Derrida visited Louvain to consult the unpublished manuscripts in the Husserl archive and later translated into French *Die Frage nach dem Ursprung der Geometrie als intentional-historisches Problem* ["The origin of geometry as an intentional-historical problem," first published posthumously in German in 1939], published in 1962. His introduction to this work was his first extended publication, and in style and content it is part of the kind of work for which Derrida became rapidly famous in the 1960s. This turn in style, and possibly in what Derrida expected of philosophy, is clearly visible from upstream when reading this dissertation. Why it happened is another matter. Derrida has said that he prepared and wrote *Genesis* very fast, in the academic year 1953–54. There is among his papers at the University of California, Irvine, at least one essay written as a student at the *Ecole normale supérieure,* on the back of which there is a comment by his teacher, Louis Althusser. Althusser warns him, in friendly, indeed concerned, fashion that the style he is writing in is not obeying the rules of the academic genre he is working in: preparatory writing for the formidable French exam, the *agrégation* (year 1954–55). One can wonder whether the assembling of syntactic formulae noted above reflects not just the extreme urgency with which he wrote this *mémoire* but also a phase of heeding this warning, no doubt not the first of its kind.

Yet this dissertation, so remarkably abundant in ideas, clearly foreshadows his later work in several ways. First, it involved movement between Husserl's German and the existing translations, and must have made apparent the need to find adequate French versions of texts then untranslated from the German. Working on it must have heightened his awareness of the role of particular natural languages in philosophy. We are used to the idea that a poem is a different entity in different languages—but a piece of philosophy? I suggest here that Derrida at the outset of his philosophical work had to grapple with the question of language not just in general, but in relation to the different ways of generating philosophical meaning in two languages, French and German. This is not a question that can be subsumed under the word "translation" as commonly conceived, but one much wider and more fraught, one that points to fundamental questions about language.[3] Derrida has several times spoken of a "nonclassical dissociation of thought and language"[4]—that is, not one where thought is wordless, like the language of the angels, and then clothed in human language, not a match of thought with word or phrase, not an encoding. Instead, there is a molding of what is expressed both through the particularities of the natural language and through the constraints of the need to express in general; both of these play against the push of the new, of something being displaced from the past, as it irrupts into language. Language then brings with it not just the question of the possibility of sense in general, but of the possibility of sense in a particular language or system of languages.

Then, there is the relation to Husserl. Further to that, the dissertation shows a stratum of concern that was not easily visible before 1990, from the work Derrida actually published; this dissertation makes this concern more discernible. Husserl's first writings were on logic and on the philosophy of arithmetic; he corresponded with Gottlob Frege, the father of analytical philosophy, at a moment when, as Michael Dummett has pointed out,[5] two of the main strands in Western philosophy could meaningfully discuss questions of sense and reference with each other. Husserl's *Logical Investigations* (1900–1901) is still evidently working in a logico-mathematical context. *Ideas* (1913) is not. It is the problem of origin, and thus of genesis, the dissertation concludes, that acts as one of the drivers of Husserl's thought and yet is never fully clarified and rendered presuppositionless, that is, constituted transcendentally through reduction. ("Reduction" is the putting into brackets, the suspension of natural positings about the world, if a transcendental viewpoint is to be attained.) Derrida's introduction to his translation of the late Husserlian text, the *Origin of Geometry*, will show how it is language that is the object of Husserl's final attempted reduction. But the dissertation itself gives a detailed and sympathetic account of the earlier Husserl and his philosophy's relation to logic; this may come as a surprise to some, as may the understanding of the constant renewal Husserl felt philosophy demanded of him even on his deathbed (see the moving last words of the dissertation, quoted by Derrida from a report given by Husserl's sister).

In his 1990 preface Derrida picks out some of the themes that he sees as having been developed in his later work, in particular the question of origin and its synthetic *a priori* nature (a Kantian question, be it noted). He also picks out the name that served in the dissertation to cover the discussion of this origin: "dialectic." To this, one might add two further comments. First, the structure assigned to what is called dialectic is not one of balanced opposition; it limps:

> the question we will put to Husserl could become the following: Is it possible to ground, in its ontological possibility and (at the same time) in its sense, an absolute dialectic of dialectic and nondialectic? In this dialectic, philosophy and being would blend together the one in the other, without definitively alienating themselves from themselves. (p. xxix)

> This dialectic (at least that is the idea on which we want to throw light in this work) is at the same time the possibility of a continuity of continuity and discontinuity, of an identity of identity and alterity, and so forth. (p. xxi)

This structure, where one side of an opposition is prolonged into a tree-form by a repetition of that opposition, will prove to be fundamental for what is later called "differance." For the opposites in "differance" are not stable and cannot be held still; the process of differentiation is continuous. We do not stay with a pattern in which oppositions are recuperated in some way, as in Hegelian logic, but must face constant movement, continuous division and loss.

My second further comment is on the question of the infinite. Derrida matches different forms of the idea of the infinite to different stages of Husserl's thought (introduction, note 12). Later, he points out the essential role of the idea of the infinite for Husserl (chap. 3, note 73). The importance for Derrida of Husserl's struggle with the infinite that this note suggests is in fact glimpsed throughout the dissertation, and it throws light on what will be the end stages of the argument in his introduction to the *Origin of Geometry*. Note 89 of chapter 5 of *Genesis* explicates this problem for Husserl by contrasting it with a theme in existentialist thought. For the intuition of the infinite in the form of the indefinite is impossible, but the idea of the infinite can still be seized because its form is finite; yet Husserl does not explore this contradiction. Derrida will.

PREFACE TO THE 1990 EDITION

Was it necessary to publish this writing dating from 1953–54? In truth I must say that even today, though it is over and done with, I am not sure.

In the months preceding this publication, the idiomatic quality of the French expression "to listen to oneself" [*s'écouter*] seemed to me more unstable than ever, even threatening sometimes. To listen to oneself, can that be pleasant? Can one find that pleasant without the nasty taste of a poison, or the foretaste of an illness? I doubt that more and more. Certainly, in giving in to the temptation to publish, one is always listening to oneself. How can that be denied? Or to put it differently: How can one do anything else than deny it? One is listening then to one's desire, that's right, and one is still listening to, at least one accepts hearing, the voice which speaks in the text resound again for a while. But is that still possible after nearly forty years?

In rereading this work, along with the worries, the reservations, even the objections which multiplied in me, along with the bouts of ill-ease that I felt then, I was most disturbed by the listening to myself, in the experience that consists of hardly hearing myself, with difficulty, as on tape or on screen, and of recognizing without recognizing, I mean without accepting, without even tolerating, through the memory of shifts in philosophy, in rhetoric, in strategy, a way of speaking, hardly changed perhaps, an ancient and almost *fatal* position of a voice, or rather of tone. This tone can no longer be dissociated from a gesture that is uncontrollable even in self-control: it is like a movement of the body, in the end always the same, to let itself into the landscape of a problem, however speculative it may seem. And yes, all that seems like an old roll of film, the film is almost silent, above all one can hear the noise of the machine, one picks out old and familiar silhouettes. One can no longer listen to oneself at such a distance, or rather, if one can, on the other hand alas, begin to hear a bit better, it is also because one has the most trouble in doing it: pain in front of a screen, allergy at the authoritarian presence of an image of oneself, in sound and in sight, about which one says to oneself that in the end, perhaps, one had never liked it, not really known it, hardly run across it. That was me, that is me, that?

I had not reread this student essay for more than thirty years. The idea of publishing it had, of course, never crossed my mind. Since here I am not worried about saving appearances, should I say that if I had only listened to myself, I would not have listened to my friends? Should not I have resisted more firmly the advice of certain readers (notably that of certain colleagues in the Center for the Husserl Archives in Paris, first of all Françoise Dastur and Didier Franck) as well as the generous proposal of Jean-Luc Marion, director of a collection in which I had already published other Husserl studies while it was directed by its founder? For Jean Hyppolite had also read this work with his usual solicitude and had encouraged me in 1955 to get it ready for publication. Whether I was right or wrong in the end to let myself be persuaded, this remains: I alone retain all the responsibility for taking the risk, that goes without saying. But in remembering what this publication owes them, I want to thank these friends for their confidence, even and especially if I hesitate about sharing it.

This work corresponds to what then was called a dissertation for the diploma of advanced studies. I prepared it in 1953–54 under the vigilant and kindly direction of Maurice de Gandillac, professor at the Sorbonne, when I was a second-year student at the *Ecole Normale Supérieure.* Thanks to M. de Gandillac and to Father Van Breda, I had been able to consult certain unpublished Husserl material in the archives at Louvain.

If someone approached this old book, I ought now to leave him alone, not anticipate in any way his or her reading, and immediately tiptoe away. In particular, I ought not to allow myself philosophical interpretations, nor confidences. I ought not even to mention the thing which has seemed to me in the end the most *curious* in this document, namely, to answer a kind of *concern* as a *concern for knowledge,* what confers on this work today some *documentary* significance. That is my only hope, and I hope I will be forgiven for saying a couple more words about it.

1. This panoramic reading, which here sweeps across the whole work of Husserl with the imperturbable impudence of a *scanner,* refers to a sort of law whose stability seems to me today all the more astonishing because, *since then, even in its literal formulation,* this law will not have stopped commanding everything I have tried to prove, as if a sort of idiosyncrasy was already negotiating in its own way a necessity that would always overtake it and that would

have to be interminably reappropriated. What necessity? It is always a question of an originary complication of the origin, of an initial contamination of the simple, of an inaugural divergence that no analysis could *present, make present* in its phenomenon or reduce to the pointlike nature of the element, instantaneous and identical to itself. In fact the question that governs the whole trajectory is already: "How can the originarity of a foundation be an *a priori* synthesis? How can everything start with a complication?"[1] All the limits on which phenomenological discourse is constructed are examined from the standpoint of the fatal necessity of a "contamination" ("unperceived entailment or dissimulated contamination"[2] between the two edges of the opposition: transcendental/"worldly," eidetic/empirical, intentional/nonintentional, active/passive, present/nonpresent, pointlike/non-pointlike, originary/derived, pure/impure, etc.), the quaking of each border coming to propagate itself onto all the others. A law of differential contamination imposes its logic from one end of the book to the other; and I ask myself why the very word "contamination" has not stopped imposing itself on me from thence forward.

2. But through these moments, configurations, effects of this law, the originary "contamination" of the origin then receives a philosophical name that I have had to give up: *dialectic,* an "originary dialectic." The word comes back insistently, page after page. A "dialectical" escalation claims to go farther than dialectical materialism (that of Trân Duc Thao, for example, often quoted and deemed insufficiently dialectical, still a "prisoner . . . of a metaphysics"[3]), or further than the dialectic that Cavaillès thinks he should invoke against Husserl in a phrase that was famous at that time ("the generating necessity is not that of an activity, but of a dialectic"[4]). That in the course of a very respectful critique, this hyperdialecticism often takes issue with Trân Duc Thao or with Cavaillès (rather than with other French readers of Husserl: Levinas, Sartre, Merleau-Ponty, Ricœur);* that several years later, even when in the introduction to [Edmund Husserl's] *Origin of Geometry* (1962) and in *Speech and Phenomena* (1967) I was pursuing the reading started in this way, the word "dialectic" finished either by totally disappearing or even by designating that *without which* or *separate from which* difference, originary supplement, and trace[5] had to be thought, all these are perhaps a kind of road sign:

---

* Jean Cavaillès, Emmanuel Levinas, Jean-Paul Sartre, Maurice Merleau-Ponty, and Paul Ricœur. *Trans.*

about the philosophical and *political* map according to which a student of philosophy tried to find his bearings in 1950s France.

One rule was a matter of course for such a publication, and allowed of no exception: that the original version should not be modified in the slightest way. This rule has been scrupulously respected,[6] every kind of imperfection could, alas, bear witness to this, in particular in the translations of which I am the author.* Where it was a question of translations and reference to the works of Husserl in general, it was at least necessary to bring up to date the bibliographical indications; since 1953, the publications of the works of Husserl have multiplied, in German and in French, as is well known.

Elisabeth Weber is the author of the notes which she judged necessary to add and to indicate by brackets [angle brackets < >].† She also checked the references, brought the bibliography up to date, and checked the proofs of this book. I should like to express here my deep gratitude to her.

Jacques Derrida
June 1990

---

* This present translation has referred to the Husserl translations into English generally available. See the list of Husserl translations following the bibliography. *Trans.*

† Notes or remarks for this present translation are in square brackets. *Trans.*

PREFACE TO THE 1953/54 DISSERTATION

The Theme of Genesis and the Genesis of a Theme[1]

"History of Philosophy and Philosophy of History"

Running throughout this work, there will be two sets of problems that will continually mix with and imply each other. Were these to be susceptible of distinct definitions that could be strictly placed side by side, we would have to speak here of a "historical" set of problems and of a set of problems that is "speculative" or philosophical in a very wide sense. But from the start we must say that we shall finish by adopting a philosophy of genesis which precisely denies the possibility of such a distinction; both through its conventions and its method, this philosophy will reveal to us [what are] the radical implications of this essential inseparability of these two worlds of meanings: history of philosophy and philosophy of history.

On the one hand, indeed, we will seem to be working on the philosophical problem of genesis, considered as such, that is to say, as essentially lifted out of the historical soil in which it was able to take life; the Husserlian texts will then take on the shape of pretexts. They will, in their historical outline, be the singular routes of access to a problem treated in its philosophical specificity and extension: with it, we will be at the heart of the great classic questions of objectivity, of the validity of foundations, of historical becoming,* of the relations of form and matter, of activity and passivity, of culture and

---

* The present translation keeps particularly close to Derrida's French in two cases, "originarity" and "becoming," which both refer to Husserl's German. Derrida has adopted the translations used by Paul Ricœur, which deliberately do not naturalize the terms into the more straightforward "originality" and "development." *Trans.*

nature, and so forth. Questions which it is enough just to evoke in order to unveil the horizon of philosophy in its totality.

On the other hand, the interest that we will take in the problem of genesis, in its philosophical significance, will in one sense appear as secondary and mediate; it will be used as a line of approach; it will be what links together research of a more immediately historical style: Should we conclude that there is a unity or a discontinuity in Husserlian thought as we find it presented to us in its becoming? How should the one or the other of these hypotheses be understood? What is the meaning of what is at least apparently a transformation of these Husserlian theses and themes?

The notion of genesis is thus at the center here in a double way: first, it puts into question the relations of philosophy and history. In a very general way, in its universal as well as its individual sense, history[2] in describing the successive appearance of rational structures, of "consciousnesses" (in the sense in which Sartre uses this word), of systems of original meanings, seems to imply that all knowledge or all philosophical intention is dependent in relation to the reality of its historical moment. Thus it seems to disappoint every claim to an objectivity which is absolute, to a foundation which is autonomous. By situating Reason and philosophical consciousness in a time which is natural and objective, genesis seems to pose the problem of the possibility of philosophy as a search for autonomous foundation, along with the problem of philosophy's relations to the physical and anthropological sciences, which, before any philosophy, seem to give us the spectacle of real geneses.[3] But is not this spectacle originarily possible for and through a philosophical consciousness that not only founds its scientific value but also makes itself arise there, be engendered there, comprehend itself there? It is the whole of philosophy which seems to be asking itself here about its own sense and dignity.

It might seem interesting to look at the way Husserlian thought studies the posing or the treatment of this problem, through this philosophy which simultaneously takes as a theme the demand for absolute beginning[4] and the temporality of lived experience[5] as the ultimate philosophical reference; which at the same time claims for philosophy a new scientific rigor[6] and refers it to the purity of concrete lived experience; which, having torn absolute subjectivity away from the constituted sciences, be they psychology or history,[7] tries to found a philosophy of history[8] and to reconcile in a certain sense phenomenology and psychology.[9]

Now it is indeed the theme of genesis that drives all Husserl's concern, which looked at superficially in its main methods of approach, seems to follow two vast movements, one forward, one back: first, the refusal of psychologisms, of historicisms, of sociologisms; the logical and philosophical ambitions of the natural or "worldly" sciences are illegitimate and contradictory. In a word, the existence of a "worldly" genesis, if it is not denied as such by Husserl, nevertheless does not attain in his eyes either the objectivity of logical meanings or, correlatively, the being or the dignity of phenomenological or transcendental consciousness. It is this latter which is the constituting source of all genesis; in it, originary becoming makes itself and appears to itself. The "transcendental" reduction, end and principle of this movement, is the reduction, the farewell to every historical genesis, in the classical and "worldly" sense of the term. But after this retreat to a philosophical purity of an idealist style, there are announced a kind of return, the outlines of a movement of broad reconquest:[10] it is the notion of transcendental genesis[11] which, resistant in principle to every reduction, revealed perhaps by every reduction properly understood, will oversee a kind of philosophical recuperation of history and allow a reconciliation of phenomenology and "worldly" sciences. The first will be the foundation of the latter. For from the beginning of his career, Husserl had formulated the demand for such a synthesis. How did he safeguard the unity of his search during his maneuvers of approach, with their movement that was, at least apparently, uneven or oscillating? In a word, if the theme of transcendental genesis appeared at a certain moment in order to understand and found the theme of empirical genesis that preceded it in natural time, we need to ask ourselves about the meaning of this evolution. How was it possible? We want to show here that this is a question that does not belong to the pure history of philosophy, but rather one that in its historical specificity refers with the greatest precision to the meaning of every genesis.

Duality and Dialectic

It could indeed be objected that our set of problems is dual, that when put forward in its most schematic and abstract form, it is of a piece with the method of any history of philosophy; for is not the latter, being at the same time history and philosophy, by definition destined to be caught in an oscillating dialectic, in an original and insurmountable reciprocity of referrals and references between the historical singularity of someone's thought, taken at the root of their discourse and their writing, and philosophical universality, considered here as its claim and its intentional significance? The idea of this dialectic, set out in this way, is not only banal and vague; it is insufficient and

false as well. It is not a question here for us of obeying a fatality, of applying
the laws of a history of philosophy constituted as a science, of following
through to its conclusions a problem that will have been discussed elsewhere:
this problem will be our problem. We already need to put into practice a
Husserlian attitude in placing ourselves before or beyond the specific problems of a constituted science in order to test its dependence in the very experience of its original constitution. The dialectic whose idea we are underlining here will not be a "method," a viewpoint, a praxis; we will try to show that
it is "ontological" insofar as ontology is not an already constituted worldly
science; it is precisely transcendental in the Husserlian sense of the word
(which we shall have to distinguish from the scholastic sense or the Kantian
sense). This problem will be the unity of the problems evoked above. What
this introduction would wish to foreshadow is that this unity will be a dialectical unity: it will distinguish itself first from a formal or artificial unity that
could be imposed from the outside on the real content of the work, an accidental unity of two perspectives or two lines of research conducted in parallel. Nor will this unity be an analytical identity that would reduce the historical content of Husserl's philosophy to its philosophical meaning, or
conversely. A philosophical examination of Husserl's thought will impose on
us a conception of genesis that, in return, will itself oblige us to adopt a certain understanding of Husserl's philosophy in its process of becoming. The
expression "in return" this time has only a methodological sense. It will be
constantly impossible to determine the real beginning of this dialectic; one
could affirm at the same time the distinction and the solidarity of the two
movements without ever being able to reduce this simultaneity and this complexity to a pure and simple succession. In the last resort, one will not be able
to give to either of the terms a value according to principles, be they chronological, logical, or ontological. The ultimate sense of the philosophy of genesis that we will try to define in the conclusion to this work will be the impossibility of all real determination of a real beginning; though we will still
have to show that this impossibility, as the ultimate philosophical conclusion,
is a formal and not a transcendental conclusion, that is, that it does not immobilize dialectic and that it allows us at the same time to remain faithful to
Husserl in his reference to an originary absolute[12] and to go beyond the interpretations of phenomenology that would determine these dialectics in a
metaphysical sense, be it materialist or idealist.

The way in which we will understand the successive connection of the diverse moments of Husserl's thought, their correlation and their mutual implication, will thus simultaneously presuppose and call for a philosophy of

genesis. It will not be in any sense a question of a conclusion, or a deduction, or again of a putting into action, of a technical exercise of a method given by one or the other of these approaches. It is always an application, a dialectical making-complex of a principle that is revealed as formally primordial and simple, as really ambiguous and dialectical. The two terms will put each other in question at each moment without allowing us to conclude that there is a real secondarity in the case of the one or the other. Better, we propose to show that it is only from Husserl on, if not explicitly with him, that the great dialectical theme which animates and motivates the most powerful philosophical tradition, from Platonism to Hegelianism[13] can be renewed, or if not renewed then at least rounded, authenticated, and completed.

The Contradictions of Genesis

How does the irreducibility of this dialectic present itself in its most general form in our work? First of all, genesis, when it is examined naively and in the most formal way possible, brings together two contradictory meanings in its concept: one of origin, one of becoming. On the one hand, indeed, genesis is birth, absolute emergence of an instant, or of an "instance"[14] that cannot be reduced to the preceding instance, radicalness, creation, autonomy in relation to something other than itself; in brief, there is no genesis without absolute origin, originarity if it is envisaged ontologically or temporally, originality if it is envisaged axiologically; any genetic production makes its appearance and takes on meaning by transcending what is not it.

But at the same stage, there is no genesis except within a temporal and ontological totality which encloses it; every genetic product is produced by something other than itself; it is carried by a past, called forth and oriented by a future. It only is, it only has its meaning, when it is inscribed in a context which on the one hand is its own, that is to say, to which it belongs and in which it participates, with which it is in continuity, which in a certain sense it implies and at the limit entails, comprehends, knows, but which, on the other hand, goes beyond, which envelopes it from all sides. Genesis is also an inclusion, an immanence.

The existence of any genesis seems to have this tension between a transcendence and an immanence as its sense and direction. It is given at first both as ontologically and temporally indefinite and as absolute beginning, as continuity and discontinuity, identity and alterity. This dialectic (at least that is the idea on which we want to throw light in this work) is at the same time the possibility[15] of a continuity of continuity and discontinuity, of an identity of identity and alterity, and so forth. This identity and this continuity are neither

absolutely formal nor absolutely real; the opposition of formalism and realism is here formal, in antithesis not to the "real" but to the "transcendental";
in a word, it is "worldly." Or, if it is preferred, the formal absolute of the absolute and the relative is neither absolutely formal nor absolutely real, that is
to say, already constituted in some way. The dialectical logic of this dialectic
is a constituted "formal logic" referring to the genesis of a constituting "transcendental logic" at whose level, we will see, the word "dialectic" has only an
analogical sense. The weakness of the great dialectics and the great classical
philosophies of becoming might be said to be their formalism, their "worldliness": they are said to have always instituted themselves on the basis of an
already formalized "secondary" opposition between form and matter, sense
and the sensible, and so on, so that genesis, as it is presented in traditional
metaphysics, under pretext of being perfectly intelligible or meaningful
(within a Platonism or a Hegelianism), perfectly historical or effective (within
a dialectical materialism), severs the link that attaches it to transcendental
genesis; this, being "originary," is dialectic only in its constituted products.
But so that a "nondialectic" may constitute a "dialectic," without this constitution being a pure creation *ex nihilo* or a simple construction through association, does it not "already" have to be dialectical? This is the question that
we will set ourselves about transcendental genesis as Husserl conceives it. If
the "origin" is dialectic, is not it secondary in relation to a "primitivity"? The
distinction between the transcendental and the worldly would collapse and
with it the possibility of any radical foundation of philosophy; phenomenology would become phenomenism. But we already know that Husserl would
have considered this dialectic of the nondialectic with dialectic as a formal and
"empty" meaning, a hypothesis that has been derived, a concept not referring to any essence, to any originary presence, as an inauthentic intention. It
will often be difficult to grant this to him, but the problem is an important
one, and it remains posed. It is at one with the second ambition of the present work: to show that the originary movement constituting this dialectic,
as it is described by Husserl, dictates to us at the same time a "dialectical"
comprehension of the development of Husserl's philosophy; in a word, this
infinite contradiction would be at the same time the motivation and the final
sense of the phenomenological enterprise.

Anticipation and "A Priori" Synthesis

It is no matter of chance if we need to give the ultimate sense of these reflections right from the beginning. It is not here a question of a necessity of

method or of technique, of a constraint of an empirical order; for it really is true that, as we were saying, the shape that we will give to our account is intimately and dialectically linked to an answer to the problems posed speculatively; this constant anticipation is not artificial nor accidental. For every genesis, every development, every history, every discourse to have a sense, this sense must in some way "already be there," from the beginning, without which one would fail to make comprehensible to oneself both the apparition of sense and the reality of becoming; a certain anticipation[16] is thus faithful to the sense of every genesis: every innovation is a verification, every creation is a fulfilling, every emergence is tradition. Let us pause an instant at this series of pronouncements. It can be seen straight off that, without one or other of these terms, no human becoming is possible either in its content or in its significance. An invention without verification could not be assimilated; it would be pure accommodation; at the limit, it would not even be "for a consciousness." There is no consciousness that does not perceive every sense as a sense "for self" (this "for self" being one of a transcendental subjectivity, not a psychological one). Every sense being for a consciousness, by definition not being able to make itself a stranger to a "transcendental ego," an intentional ego, it always reveals itself as "already" present. At the limit, an invention without verification would deny the intentionality of consciousness; it would be invention "of" nothing or invention (of) itself (by) itself, which would destroy the very sense of any inventions, which is a synthetic sense. The paradox and strangeness of transcendental intentionality[17] reappear at the core of every invention, symbol of genesis: it is through a "synthetic" value that a becoming and a temporal act are acts of verification and at the limit analytic. But just as invention without verification is only conceivable in the myth of consciousness without intentionality, of thinking torn from the world and from time, so verification without invention is not verifying anything by anything, is a pure tautology, an empty and merely formal identity, a negation (of) consciousness, (of) world, (of) time, where every truth appears; it is thus through the "analytic" essence of every verification, of every aiming at sense, that this latter must refer out in a synthetic act to something other than itself. It is in the same sense that the solidarity between every creation and every fulfilling, every arising and every tradition, can be experienced. However, from the point of view of a formal logic or of an absolute logic, these judgments bear within them an irreducible contradiction. For it is not a question of attributive judgments of the type "A is B," in which B is the predicate of A; here the very sense of each of these terms is such that the subject and the predicate are given together in each of their respective moments. Even before these are attributed one to the other, from an apparently analytical point of view, invention is "already" verification, verification is "already" invention. It is thus an *a priori* necessity that the two terms of these judgments be interchangeable; both are at the same time subject and predicate. The necessity that links them is absolute. But at the same time the obviousness of these judgments is not analytic; if it were, it would be in contradiction with each of its terms; indeed, both have a genetic or synthetic value; both aim at, take in, produce something other than themselves. The explanation, that is, the unveiling, the explicitation that would be held to be an analytic act in a logic is here a synthesis in the ontological or transcendental sense that founds logic. But to the degree that this synthesis is revealing, it is made *a priori*. For this synthesis to be synthesis, it must be productive, generative; so that it appears to us as a meaningful synthesis, it must be *a priori*. Without that it would present no sense and would not be knowable as such. Every passage from one moment to another would take on the figure of a miracle, of an exception to history, of an unheard of novelty; genesis or synthesis would not be real stages of becoming, but explosions and expropriations of time. Kant, in refuting Hume, showed convincingly that without the intervention of an *a priori* form of the understanding, any judgment loses its necessary character. We will not here go into historical analyses; let us just note that Kant called "synthetic *a priori*" judgments only those of a mathematical order. These judgments are precisely those which escape from genesis. Their synthesis is not "real,"[18] at least not in the eyes of Kant. Insofar as they are not born in effective historical experience, insofar as they are not "constituted" by this, they are *a priori*.[19] In a sense, for Kant, the empirical and the *a priori* are mutually exclusive. The sense of every genesis is a phenomenal one. Invention is not absolute verification. Hence it is not real invention. The sense of every empirico-genetic judgment is the object of a construction, thus by definition dubious. On this point at least, it is surprising to see the precision with which Hegel's[20] criticism of Kant points to Husserl's perspective: far from the experience of the real which is called "phenomenal," excluding *a priori* synthesis, it is *a priori* synthesis[21] (of thought and the real, of sense and of the sensible, for example, and in a very general way) which makes experience possible, and every meaning of experience. It is too obvious that the idea of this originary synthesis, as a real principle of every possible experience, is closely linked with the idea of the intentionality of transcendental consciousness. We shall often have to test the strange depth of certain resemblances between Hegel's and Husserl's thought. For the moment, it must suffice to remark that it is only in the perspective of these two thinkers that the problem of real genesis can be posed;

this latter is a synthesis; while, with Kant, it could as such only be, on occasion perfectly intelligible, *a priori* necessary, but "irreal"[22] and atemporal in the world of mathematical rationality, on occasion effective and temporal but *a posteriori*, contingent, and doubtful in empirical becoming, when the indubitably originary and fundamental experience of intentionality reverses the "critical" attitude, it inscribes the *a priori* synthesis into the very core of historical becoming; such an *a priori* synthesis is the originary founding of every experience, which is delivered in and through experience itself. This is the interest and the difficulty of the problem of genesis, considered as synthesis: How can the absolutely originary foundation of sense and of being[23] of a genesis be comprehended in and by this genesis? For if it is true that any synthesis is founded on an *a priori* synthesis, the problem of genesis is that of the sense of this *a priori* synthesis; if an *a priori* synthesis is at the source and foundation of any possible judgment and any experience, are we not referred to an indefinite dialectic? How can the originarity of a foundation be an *a priori* synthesis? How can everything start with a complication? If any genesis and any synthesis refer to their constitution through an *a priori* synthesis, then has not the *a priori* synthesis itself, when it appears to itself in a constituting, transcendental and supposedly originary experience, already taken on sense, is it not always by definition "already" constituted by another synthesis, and so on infinitely? How can a phenomenological originarity lay absolute claim to the first constitution of sense if it is preceded by what could be called a historical "primitiveness"? a primitiveness which, it has to be said, only "appears" as such through an originary constitution. Is there not some trick in any going beyond of this dialectic? Does one not fall back into the formalism that one claims to be going beyond, by referring the philosophical thematization[24] of this dialectic to the originarity of its transcendental constitution, to intentionality, to perception? Is not phenomenological temporality, at once transcendental and originary, "temporalizing," constituting, only in appearance and starting from a "natural" time, indifferent to transcendental consciousness itself, preceding it, enveloping it? Husserl, especially in the last years of his life, would not perhaps have absolutely disputed this; perhaps all his last efforts were for saving phenomenology by assimilating to it this new relation. However that may be, it is clear from now on that it is always through an "anticipation" which is at least formal, that any signification, founded on an *a priori* synthesis, appears, and appears to itself originarily. Let us leave open the question of how the absolute sense of genesis can be at once "originary" and "anticipated"; whether this anticipation occurs about the future as such, or about a past always reconstituted by the originary present and by the anticipated future, it is always indispensable for the appearance of every possible meaning, whatever may be its sense. Without it, to keep to our initial argument, any research in the history of philosophy would wear itself out and be scattered in a multiplicity of textual points; at the limit, this multiplicity could not even appear to itself as a multiplicity, that is to say, as relationality, but only as an opaque literalness, as a confusion. Any intelligibility is, in a certain sense, relation and going beyond toward something other than itself. But, conversely, any anticipation occurs from the historical textuality of Husserl's discourse or from an initial philosophical meaning. It is in the impossibility of determining the real beginning of our research that all the difficulties of a philosophy of genesis appear in outline.

Indeed, if some anticipation is always necessary, if the future in some way always precedes present and past, hence if some implication always remains hidden, then the intelligibility and significance that depend on it essentially, being always referred toward the indefinite of a past, of a future of the past, and of a past of the future, and thus stripped of their absolute foundation, of their radical and originary validation, run the risk of being definitively compromised by this. A phenomenological philosophy must be genetic if it wishes to respect the temporality of the originary lived experience. Now a philosophy of genesis must lay claim to the dignity of philosophy to arrive at an unconditional foundation; but in order to be authentically genetic and phenomenological, it must also describe the conditions of the founding without deforming them, that is to say, it must describe the arising of meanings in the becoming of experience, conceived in the largest and most originary sense as including the experience of the founding itself. The immense difficulty of a transcendental genesis is glimpsed: the absolute founding itself must be described in its genetic appearing; implying its past, implying itself in its past, it must not reduce itself to that nor be dependent on that in the sense in which it is said that a conclusion depends on its premises or that an effect depends on a cause. Here, it is the effect that constitutes the sense of the cause as such. A genetic conception wrecks the foundations of any intelligibility in general, of its own in particular, if it comes back to being a causal explanation and analysis in which temporality is supposed to be integrated as a simple "element"; for the same reason, such a conception cannot be purely inclusive, for then it would neglect the creative and synthetic character of its own genetic becoming. In both cases, the mistake would be a reduction of genesis to simple unfolding and pure unveiling, to a constant and continuous explicitation in the series of nature or in the series of essences; facing a purely inclusive attitude, history would become a pure ideality, or a pure finality; in the face of an explicative attitude, it would only be a material facticity. To take an example: at a certain moment of history, of natural time, man accedes to one or other power of objectivity; this power, to be integrated into a genetic philosophy, must on the one hand appear as an uninterrupted continuation of what is not it, for example, of the attitude called "participating" or "animist,"[25] and so forth; it must be grasped in its historical rootedness, and the historical passage from an absence of objectivity to its opposite must be made historically intelligible; but to attain this intelligibility, one must on the other hand use this power of objectivity which itself would be fitting for its phenomenological meaning only if it is given as transcendental freedom, radical autonomy in relation to history; without such an autonomy, the value of its objectivity would be rendered doubtful precisely by its historical determinations. How can an authentically genetic phenomenology go beyond the two temptations between which any philosophy of history oscillates? On the one hand, the past of this objectivity is described as a simple pathway toward it or as one single "appeal" from this objectivity; this will be, since forever, "already" present in history; active in a quiet way, it will be seen to precede and prepare its [own] phenomenological advent. It is in order to avoid introducing *a priori* rational finality and sense in history that one succumbs to the other temptation: to distinguish into an absolute opposition the phenomenological advent of objectivity and the historical event of its appearance; starting from this separation, there is an oscillation again between two types of reduction of genesis to a pure accident stripped of all phenomenological meaning: at some points, under the pretext that objectivity presupposes freedom in relation to historical determination, and thinking thus to be respectful of its phenomenological signification, its advent is held to be the only essential thing; at other points, considering that this liberty is nothing without the historical act of liberation that produced it and produces it at each instant, and that objectivity and freedom are "constituted" in and through the history of a nature, the event is made into the only effective reality. In both cases, is there not infidelity to the most authentic intention of Husserl's phenomenology? On the one hand, one encounters the stumbling block of "worldly" philosophies, of psychologisms and historicisms, making a constituting nature out of a constituted nature. On the other, a pure and simple negation of existence is made out of the transcendental reduction and intuition of essences. Does Husserlian phenomenology offer us the real possibility of going beyond this alternative? Is it not, on the contrary, just a constant oscillation between these two poles? We shall have cause to debate this. Henceforward we know that such an oscillation can be escaped only by assuming and going beyond this paradox or this dialectic: the power of objectivity (to keep to our example), faithfully described as it appears to us in history and according to its true sense, is nothing but a genetic product that escapes from its genesis, that radically transcends it and is essentially untied from it. Its rootedness and its novelty are irreducible one to the other. In wider terms, a philosophy of genesis must convert itself immediately into a genesis of philosophy without falling into a historicism or a psychologism. In this genesis it must found itself as philosophy, that is, avoid all the skepticisms which from the historical dependence of philosophy might draw the conclusion that it is eternally powerless.

But the problem is posed here formally and a dialectic description has never resolved a difficulty. Does not this dialectic put itself together from concepts that are elaborated and from a world already constituted that would refer itself back, in the last instance, to the simplicity of an originary constitution? How can philosophy, if it is engendered by something other than itself, lay claim to an originary autonomy? To save philosophy, must not this be a genesis of philosophy by philosophy? But in this hypothesis, would we not end up at a "panphilosophy" which, close to a "panlogism," would reduce real history to being no more than the handmaid of philosophical teleology and would make an illusory appearance out of the originary experience of intentionality, of the world's transcendence, of alterity, of effective temporality, and so on? But dialectic is only reborn in a slightly different form. For if the antinomy of every genesis is naive or "worldly," that is to say, already constituted by the act of a transcendental consciousness to which it refers and which in this way suspends the dialectic, then transcendental genesis itself, toward which we are thus carried, even if it is not itself conceived in terms of constituted formal logic, even if it is not the production of an "understanding" or of a pure "reason," must *really*[26] mingle with the ontology that is being constituted within it. Indeed, as soon as one makes something other out of the genesis of transcendental consciousness, something other than the genesis of being through itself (in its transcendence to consciousness), then a reality which is itself thematized and constituted over against being is made out of the transcendental consciousness: the intentionality of consciousness is denied; [the argument] collapses back again into psychologism and worldly philosophy. But, conversely, if it is being that engenders itself through transcendental consciousness and its productions, if the dialectic takes place in being before presenting itself to consciousness (we are here quite close to an intentionality-reflection[27] and to its contradictions), we fall back into the sort of aporia of genesis that we mentioned at the beginning: in this perspective, there can only be promoted a scientism by which every access to the original sense of genesis would be forbidden us, or a hypothesizing of a supposed originary sense, which, cut off from its historical effectivity, would no longer be the sense "of" genesis but one or other meaning just happened upon; whether it may be "naive" scientism or substantialist metaphysics, the same result is arrived at; and this is not something that happens fortuitously but the direct consequence of a common implication: it is the same negation of transcendental intentionality that leads by two different paths to the same psychologism. In order to make a historical content pure and simple out of consciousness and meanings, the intentional originarity must have been ignored beforehand; what being aims at (and to which it was hoped to reduce the transcendental consciousness) must have been shut away, together with its "evidence," in the natural psychological content of subjectivity. To make out of an apparently originary sense an absolute that is self-sufficient and that does not refer to any objective natural history, it has to be turned into a "content of consciousness" with all the plenitude of an "in itself" closed up on itself. The problem is difficult. It is a question of reconciling transcendental intentionality, which is by its essence dialectic since it unites in one single act the originary transcendental subjectivity and the transcendent "sense of being" that it constitutes,[28] with, on the other hand, that absolute which is of a piece with every originarity. In a word, the question we will put to Husserl could become the following: Is it possible to ground, in its ontological possibility and (at the same time) in its sense, an absolute dialectic of dialectic and nondialectic? In this dialectic, philosophy and being would blend together the one in the other, without definitively alienating themselves one in the other.

The Genesis of the Theme: Two Inadequate Interpretations

So as to prefigure the main lines and main approaches of our problematic, we have just made some schematic and dogmatic allusions to the difficulties that any philosophical understanding of genesis brings up. Are not these difficulties going to reappear at the core of research that would like to follow the evolution of Husserlian thought closely, in its very historical uniqueness? Seen in this way, this singularity presents itself to us as a philosophy that "becomes" at the same time as it approaches "becoming" ceaselessly, and as it understands it better and better. Now there are two interpretations of this becoming, which are two reductions of genesis in its veritable signification.

In a perspective that we will first define as purely "analytic," there is a temptation to insist on the radical side of genesis. Husserl's progressive thematization of the notion of genesis, the passage from empirical to transcendental genesis, in a word, the whole genesis of the genetic theme, would be reduced to a discontinuous series of coups d'état, to a succession of absolute moments where the preceding moments would be overtaken and abandoned. Thus, for example, the return to the lived experience of transcendental subjectivity, the "constitutive" researches, the transcendental reduction, in short, everything that it is agreed to call the idealism of *Ideas* would overturn the claimed logicist and "Platonist" realism of *Logical Investigations;*[29] a logicism that itself was a pure and simple negation of the psychologism of the *Philosophy of Arithmetic.*[30] In the same way, researches of a more historical kind, the thematization of transcendental intersubjectivity, of transcendental genesis, of "the lifeworld," of the antepredicative, and so on would utterly condemn the doctrine of the "ego" as absolute monadic subjectivity. There is something caricatural in this hypothesis. But even if it is aberrant, nonetheless it has been formulated or implied in many cases; this example, though it is fictive and forced in its real content, yet delivers us the eidetic meaning of a certain conception of genesis that, in order to safeguard the specific purity of a genetic product, its purely phenomenological meaning, isolates it from its historical past, cuts it off from the act of its production, makes of it a negation that, at the limit, would not even pose itself as a negation "of" something, would become "forgetting." We find ourselves then in the presence of a pure ideal residue, stripped of all the empirico-historical facticity of its real genesis; we no long perceive that, at the limit, this pure intelligible product, dislodged from any temporal lived experience, from any correlative act, unbound from its context, no longer referring to anything except itself, reduced to an abstraction, to a transparency behind which nothing appears, turns into pure opacity or into appearance without density; it is pure meaning, and it is precisely to that extent that it is meaning of nothing. The absolute of purity is always transformed into its opposite, or more exactly, it is the analytical identity of the two contraries; totally indeterminate, it is at the same time form or pure signification, intelligible absolute and pure opacity, integral absurdity. For example, in order to be totally intelligible, the transcendental reduction, reversal, and recommencement of the naive attitude must cancel or remove from its effective existence the whole history that has made its way toward it; the transcendental reduction, to live up to its phenomenological value, to appear to itself as the act of a transcendental freedom, must suspend everything which could have seemed to have "motivated" it.[31] But the paradox is that in order to be intelligible in its very "demotivation" and to give itself as intentional originarity, it is, in its very actuality, reduction "of" something which was and still is effectively "already there." On the one hand, the existence of a world that precedes transcendental consciousness must be put into brackets; on the other hand, in this reduction one must convert a naive attitude, an attitude that, chronologically at least, always seems anterior to the phenomenological attitude (the sense of this anteriority and of this chronology will determine, as we will see, our whole problematic of genesis). It will be asserted, certainly, following Husserl,[32] that the natural attitude cannot be understood as such until after the reduction. But is not this recognition exactly a recognition of a historical anteriority which is irreducible? And even if we were to make of the reduction a pure possibility of the naive consciousness, a virtuality present right from the origin of consciousness, would we not still have to make clear what is understood by natural origin of the consciousness? Would it not be necessary to make more precise the way in which a "pure possibility" can be carried by the actuality of natural consciousness? One might say again that this natural consciousness is "primitive" in relation to the "originary" attitude of the reduction. Now it seems that the transcendental reduction, as Husserl has always understood it—in spite of all the misunderstandings—has never aimed at the negation of this "primitivity"; it simply "suspends" it in its existence in order to have access to its essence; but what essence is in question here? Is there an essence of existence as such? In our argument, what would be an essence of real genesis that would not merge itself with the very existence of this genesis? Just as it is difficult to seize what can be the essence of a pure and simple existence[33] as such, so it seems that every essence of becoming may be in a certain measure the contrary of this becoming. That is a very classical view, and it will impose itself on us frequently. To understand the "sense" of the genesis of the Husserlian themes, is it not in a certain way to deny the becoming of these themes in order to let the continuous unity appear, the stable permanence, or even, inversely, the discontinuity, the series of interruptions, of breaks or of revolutions that appear as such only to the degree that they escape from the unalterable continuity of primitive time? Without the mysterious and primordial dialectics of the primitive and the originary, we must envisage either a reduction of the primitive to the originary and a genesis of the naive attitude starting from the phenomenological attitude (which would carry us toward the form of idealism which is the least acceptable)[xlv] or a simple inverse "evolution" that would remove all dignity from the originary. In both cases the distinction between the transcendental and the empirical escapes us and with it every hope of an absolute foundation. It seems that the sense that we can gain from examining Husserlian thought in its becoming can only be dialectical.

From this example it can be seen that, like every genetic interpretation in general, the genetic interpretation of Husserl's thought which would attach itself only to the creative or "radical" aspect of genesis would disperse it in an infinite multiplicity of absolute beginnings that are neither temporal nor atemporal nor historical nor suprahistorical. This interpretation suppresses what every genesis constantly implies and what it refers to as to one of its foundations: the essential rootedness in the continuity of being, in time, in the world.

Such a point of view, which is purely analytical at the origin, since it reduces the whole dynamic continuity of someone's thought to a series of points, of ideally original significations, ends up, when it is confronted with the real movement it is analyzing, in a cascade of pure and unintelligible syntheses, adding and juxtaposing some to the others in a mechanical fashion. Pure analysis—that is to say, *a priori* since it is uniquely founded on the necessities of essence which are already given to it—and pure synthesis—that is to say, *a posteriori* since it only sticks together afterward moments which are first given to it in their mutual exteriority—join up and become identified in the same abstract indetermination and the same lack of recognition of effective genesis.

In one sense, this analytical method might appear faithful to Husserlian principles. It is claimed that it is being closed off into a dialectic, but does this not suppose an originary seizing of dialectical meanings that frees us from any conceptual dialectics? Is not the aiming at meanings and essences done beyond or beneath any opposition of analysis and synthesis? Indeed, it is in order to avoid spoiling the originality and the ideal objectivity of an essence that one fears confusing it with a concept or with a "fact" by rooting it in what is not its own purity. The distinction[35] between pure facticity, constructed concept, or even essence is fundamental in Husserl's work. Thus it would be necessary here to remain faithful to the phenomenological appearance of "sense"; to explain it by a conceptual construction is to assume already what it is claimed is being constructed; to explain it through a genesis of simple facticity is to denature sense, to make impossible the appearance of the fact "as such." Reducing every sense to a concept or making of it the product of a purely material genesis, those are two similar attempts that deny intentionality in favor of a psychological[36] subjectivity or of a physical facticity. At the limit, to think that such a transformation of Husserlian thought has been imposed on him by the architectonic necessity of a conceptual system or by the empirico-historical determinations that attack it from the outside, is not that to be bogged down in all the incoherences found in psychologistic and historicist constructivisms?

Thus, to the extent that the primary intention of the so-called "analytic" attempt refuses to describe "sense" as the product of a pure historical materiality or as the construction of a psychological activity, to the extent that it recognizes and respects the absolute originarity of such a sense, it could seem faithful to the fundamental intention of Husserl. But it is not so easy to go beyond constructivist empiricism; by trying to strip it out absolutely, one even more nearly runs risks of contamination. For one is thus condemned to the impossible "conception"[37] of an absolute plurality of absolute beginnings that alienates any unity of intention and of sense. Is there not, then, a kind of condemnation to an associationism of very shabby sort? Husserl, in his anxious patience, incessantly taking up and reworking his first writings, secures a continuity to all the developments of his research, and one has no right to neglect this as if it were a psychological accident. To do this would be to make the "real" distinction of "content," which Husserl has always refused to recognize, fall between the transcendental and the empirical. Absolute fidelity meets up here with absolute infidelity.

So, this present work will reverse completely the perspective and, in a treatment that is purely "synthetic" in its origin, in order to avoid the parceling out and setting side by side typical of constructivism, would aim at seizing and assembling the totality of Husserlian thought in one single movement. To do this, it will be necessary to start off *a priori* from a unity of sense that might also be a unity of intention, such that the whole development of Husserl's meditation, for nearly half a century, would have only unrolled, revealed, brought progressively to light a disquiet or a demand, an implication or a project animating the whole work, from the *Philosophy of Arithmetic* to the last manuscripts. For example, the theme of the historico-intentional genesis, the theories of "sedimentation" and of "reactualization" *(Reaktivierung)* presented in the *Origin of Geometry* would only make explicit the dialectic of "protention" and of "retention" described in the lectures on "internal time consciousness." The genesis would be an unveiling. Such a unity of sense, if it was absolutely real, would guarantee the transparency, the absolute intelligibility of Husserlian thought. But at the limit, it would no longer give an account of the very existence of this thought; it would no longer give an account of its progressive character, of its exposition, of its discourse. For that, it [such a sense of unity] would have to reduce the discursive manner of proceeding to an accident, one essentially exterior to an intuitive unity. But such an exteriority would stop us from understanding how the one can refer to the other. There Husserl's real language would be imposed from the outside, by a purely factitious contingency, by a fortuitous pedagogical or methodical need or again by an empirical necessity, that of a psychological time, for instance. In its essential logic, the slow passage from a certain psychologism in the *Philosophy of Arithmetic* to a clear logicism in *Logical Investigations*,[38] the return to a subjectivity, no longer psychological but transcendental, in *Ideas* I would then be independent of this necessity. Situating the transcendental reduction at any particular determinate moment of objective time, in which one has to "begin" in a certain sense at least by encountering Husserl's discourse, would be attributed to mechanical chance or—which comes to the same thing—to a purely rhetorical necessity. Ideally (if this word can have a pure sense) the transcendental reduction would be constantly and essentially present in the implications of all Husserl's ways of proceeding. In the same way, the thirty years of anxious and personal meditation that separate the rejection of a genetic explanation in the "worldly" sense and the explicit recourse to a genesis that is transcendental would ideally be suppressed. The historical path, which goes from the idea of absolute subjectivity, as "ego" to the intervention of the "alter ego" in the transcendental intimacy of the "ego" would definitely be put in brackets. Under a hypothesis of absolute continuity, the real movement that goes from objectivity as conceived in *Ideas,* as linked to the intentionality of a pure "ego," right up to objectivity as described in *Cartesian Meditations,* which makes of transcendental intersubjectivity the last condition of access to the sense of the object, is suppressed.[39] In the same way, after he has dismissed historicisms, Husserl is obliged, merely by the internal logic or the mere phenomenological requirement of continuous unveiling, to undertake a description of the historical world of the spirit, of the "objective spirit," and so forth[40] in an attitude that is renewed and that presents itself as purely transcendental. Finally, it is a simple laying bare of the foundations that links in a continuous web the successive thematizations of transcendental temporality and of historical time, of the pure flux of essences and of the antepredicative world, or of antinaturalism and of the "life-world." The absolute sense of genesis is so well known and assimilated that the uselessness of genesis itself, in its real content, becomes blatantly obvious.

   This view is strangely like the preceding one, however opposed to it it was at the origin. Their absolute difference is an absolute resemblance. There is here a classical dialectical movement and principle that we will verify at every instant in this work. All the absolutes meet in the same indetermination. Absolute alterity is absolute identity. The more identity deepens and affirms itself, the more it gives itself being and expands, the more it determines itself; in differentiating itself, it alters itself. The more alterity is verified and authenticated in its essence, the more it "alters" itself; in altering itself, it tends toward identity.

Here the enterprise of understanding Husserlianism in a completely synthetic manner has had *a priori* to reduce the whole discursive complexity of his thought to the intuitive simplicity of a unique meaning, and his whole enriching and synthetic development to an analytic series of points [*ponctualité*]. The initial idea of this conception was also to arrange for access to and complete intelligibility of a historical movement: that of Husserlian phenomenology. Once again, to do that is to deprive a movement of its dialectical sense. Just now, in order to place the whole "genesis of sense" of a thought in the simplicity of a single concept, genesis was suppressed by making of "sense" an absolute source springing up out of temporality at every moment. Now, genesis is expelled by making it be preceded absolutely by a sense that it adds itself onto, as if it were some instrument come by afterward to inscribe it into history. As in the first attempt, one is a long way from escaping from dialectic in this way. On the contrary, by trying to put dialectic in brackets arbitrarily, one is all the more determined by it. Perfect intelligibility is turned into total absurdity: pure synthesis, that is, *a posteriori* synthesis, comes back to pure analysis, that is, *a priori* analysis. In both cases, intelligible sense or form, here the original intuition or infinite diversity of absolute beginnings, is separated from their material and historical correlatives; and comprehension of both of them ceases because they have been made too determinate in their formal originality. Starting from an analytic sense given in one go, the juxtaposition of absolute syntheses becomes incomprehensible, as does the real synthetic historical development.

But the resemblance between these two attempts is even more striking. In the first, in trying to avoid constructivisms, at the end one was obliged to end up there; meanings described in their irreducible autonomy had to be associated and understood in their multiplicity. The whole historical thought of *Husserl* had to be reconstructed starting from its "elements"; these, because one wanted them to be fully intelligible in themselves, have become closed and opaque to each other. [Yet] in the "synthetic" interpretation, the original unity of meaning was not historical. It was not by definition confused with the chronological point of departure of Husserl's thought; so a meaning had to be discovered which, emerging at a certain moment in the work, might be the appearance, second in chronology, of an originary intuition. From this, it is claimed that a meaningful totality is being reconstituted. Now, on the one hand, this reconstitution presents all the dangers of a reconstruction *a posteriori*. On the other hand and especially, it can be done starting from any moment of Husserl's evolution. Whether appeal is made to one or other theme, that of category-specific intuition, of the intuition of essences, of eidetic reduction, or of transcendental reduction, it is always possible, by the unveiling of implications and consequences, to find the totality of the meanings of Husserlian phenomenology. But this operation can be done starting from any chronological point; the choice is arbitrary. Why is this so? Because, by claiming that the "chronology" of natural time is constituted and secondary in relation to its "originary" meaning, it is thought that the latter is independent; thus, it is forgotten that, in Husserl himself, the "originarity" of essence is founded on the "primitivity" of the "antepredicative" world, substrate of the appearing of sense.[41] By arbitrarily choosing one or other Husserlian theme, by enlarging it in every direction to define the totality of Husserl's "system," there is not an essence facing us, but a concept; this no longer refers back to a real substrate—here a chronological moment of the work—but to a logical or psychological construction. Essence is no longer an essence of something but an abstract concept; thus, since the facticity of a precise moment no longer imposes "its" sense, how is an arbitrating choice going to orient itself? For choice is indispensable and so is reference to some point of historical materiality, even if these were claimed to be contingent and artificial. The antepredicative, the infraconceptual, or the "inessential" cannot not make an appearance at first, however short and unperceived it may be, without running the risk of making the boldest essentialisms collapse. It is there that the claim to absolute free will in the face of history lets itself be determined as the worst slavery: not wishing to give any essential privilege to one or other historical moment of Husserl's thought, in the end it is seen that the best point of departure is the "last" state of this thought. And thus one gives in "absolutely" to a factitious chronology that one wanted to essentialize "absolutely." From this moment on, there is nothing to be done but give way to the rules of a conceptual exercise: the recomposition of a system, the *a posteriori* reconstruction of a real movement.

To be sure, such an attitude can in a certain sense also claim to follow Husserl. Does not Husserl himself indeed claim in *Origin of Geometry* to exercise a historico-intentional method and to "reactualize" the "first" historical acts *(Leistungen)* of consciousness in their original meaning? In the *Crisis of European Sciences and Transcendental Phenomenology* does he not claim to neglect the historical facticity of philosophies in order to discover their hidden "motive,"* their dissimulated, latent sense? Does he not concentrate uniquely on their rational intention, at the same time veiled and present in

---

* *Motif* in French, like *Motiv* in German, has the meaning of a "content that distinguishes" as well as that of "incitement." *Trans.*

the whole route toward transcendental philosophy? No doubt, such a perspective escapes the danger of those historicisms that, while claiming a rigorous fidelity to the letter and textuality of a doctrine, would deprive the latter of any meaning and would transform it into a collection of abstract elements engendering each other through some mystery or other; in this sense, if it were not decided "first" to assume the "intention" of a philosophy, under the pretext of realism and objectivism, a whole scattering of empirical accidents would be met with, which would tend indefinitely toward an inaccessible essence.

It is to obviate such a danger that we are trying to understand Husserl's thought synthetically, starting from a pure and "pregiven" meaning. Such a "method" might seem fertile. It gives us access to the "pure" continuity of Husserl's thought, to its essential logic. From a very perfunctory point of view, it teaches us how the objectivity of logical significations cannot be founded by an autonomous logicism without being limited to inertia and to the secondariness of a formal logic; a return to lived experience was from then on necessary, one that could not be a falling back into a psychological lived experience, getting caught in the same aporias, but a working back toward the "pure lived experience," originary and transcendental.[42] Thus, the transcendental reduction was invoked or implied from the start. On the other hand, transcendental intersubjectivity, before it was thematized, had to be present from the first allusions to reduction; without this, one could not understand how it was still possible to escape solipsism and how the "transcendental" constitution of the world could happen, since the world had to give itself to consciousness in its strangeness, in its otherness, and in its transcendence of consciousness. Indeed, without the originarity of the transcendental constitution of the other as such in consciousness, would one not stay with psychological intentionality, incapable of "transcending" oneself originarily toward the world and toward objectivities in general? How would a genesis be possible for a "worldly" consciousness closed on itself? Temporality itself would no longer be creative or synthetic; it would be indefinite analysis of itself as already constituted nature. Through this, duration "for consciousness" would become impossible; transcendental genesis would be referred back beyond any possible experience.

But at the same time, one escapes from analytical identity, from which it was claimed to start out. To conquer its fullness, to complete itself, this [the egological lived experience in time*] must have lost itself and found itself in

---

* The square brackets are in the 1990 French text. *Trans.*

historical discourse. This could not be assimilated to the genetic synthesis that bore it or that seemed to emanate from it, any more than it could be reduced to the historical content of its evolution. The originary dialectics of sense and of the antepredicative substratum has not been able to be either interrupted or overcome.

Genesis and Reductions

What the two great attitudes evoked above have profoundly in common, what makes them so similar in their approach and in their failure, is the reduction of effective genesis to its phenomenological sense, the reduction of singular historical existence to a supposed universal essence which is no more than a concept in disguise. In the intention of escaping the insufficiencies of a "worldly" genesis, and to avoid any risk of contamination, the "world" has been *definitively* put into brackets. The transcendental constitution itself became impossible, since it comes into operation originarily on the foundations of an antepredicative world. In place of a transcendental genesis, there remained only a formal and empty "notion," already constituted, more "worldly" than ever. Instead of an authentic transcendental reduction, an eidetic reduction, which was the most inconsistent and the most secondary, was proceeded to. It is only too obvious that these two attempts at reduction are at the same time faithful and unfaithful to Husserl. They are faithful to him to the degree that they force themselves by means of a reduction toward a purity of meaning, to the degree that this reduction is that of a genesis that one would like to be merely "worldly" and that this purity is that of an originary lived experience. But the attempts are unfaithful to him to the degree that these reductions end in a pure and simple expelling of existence, in the methodical destruction of empirical facticity. This error was often committed in relation to the reduction.[43] Now it is known that Husserl claimed only to "suspend" the position of existence, but to preserve the whole content of real experience by "neutralizing" it. The problem is now to know whether this neutralization is transcendentally possible in the face of the actuality of the genesis. Does not a perfect transcendental reduction, congruent with the deepest intentions of Husserl, fail when faced with the irreducible existence of genesis? Perhaps a "worldly" genesis, psychological or otherwise, can be easily bracketed; it would be "second" and already constituted. Phenomenological reduction cannot by definition be inscribed in constituted nature. But to the degree that the act of this reduction belongs to the originarily constituting sphere, it must, if it is not to be an abstraction, a logical operation starting from formal concepts, also appear to itself as an originary "lived experience." This lived experience is temporal. In its originarity, is it not time itself, constituting itself and temporalizing itself? In reducing empirical genesis, we have only pushed the problem farther back, and it comes back again with transcendental genesis in a form that is hardly different. As such, it seems that the transcendental genesis must not be the object of a reduction. For if, according to its sense, transcendental genesis remains indeed originary becoming, empirical (in the nonworldly sense of that term), what subject will absolute meaning appear for? How can an absolute and monadic transcendental subjectivity be at the same time a becoming that is constituting itself? In this radical autonomy of time, is not absolute subjectivity "constituted" and no longer constituting? Far from being reduced or, on the contrary, revealed by the phenomenological reduction, is not transcendental genesis something which, originarily, makes possible the reduction itself? The latter would then no longer be the ultimate foundation of the absolute beginning of meaning; absolute sense or philosophy cannot, it seems, be reconciled with pure becoming, and we would thus be referred to a new reduction that would "suspend" transcendental genesis itself. But on the one hand, we would thus only push back the problem to another originary temporality; on the other, we would run up against the most authentic and the most "serious" motives of Husserlian phenomenology. We would fall into the weaknesses of an abstract logic.[44]

So, when on the one hand, reflection shows that all the meaning of phenomenology depends on the pure possibility of a transcendental reduction as absolute and "unmotivated" beginning, but that on the other hand, not only does the reduction not get to transcendental genesis (and that essentially) but is in addition constituted by it and appears in it, the problem is seen not to be lacking in difficulty. If there is a transcendental genesis, if there is an originary temporality that founds all intentional acts, if correlatively a transcendental intersubjectivity is originally present at the heart of the ego, how can the latter absolutely suspend the existential thesis? Does this latter not blend itself originarily with that temporality which is at the same time the "primitive" substrate from which every transcendental constitution is effected, and the "originary" movement of intentionality, of the moving beyond to something else, of the protention toward another moment?[45] Does this irreducible alterity not make the purity of meaning explode? To say that the transcendental genesis not only resists reduction but reveals itself in it, is that not to reintroduce in the guise of the pluri-dimensionality of time a whole dialectic of the Same and the Other at the heart of an originary that appears to itself as such only when it refers to an originary past or in projecting itself toward an originary future? The absolute of sense would appear to itself as such only in alienating itself and in putting itself in relation with what is not it; better, this alienation would be the condition of possibility of its appearance. It is not an accident that the themes of transcendental genesis and of transcendental intersubjectivity appeared at about the same moment in Husserl's meditation: transcendental intersubjectivity, originary presence of the "alter ego" in the monadic "ego," is, it seems, the impossibility of an originary that is absolutely simple; is that not also the kernel of a primitive existential thesis on which no reduction can get purchase, what not only cannot be "suspended" but which must be admitted at the very origin of the act of reduction and of its condition of possibility? So, under the appearance of an autonomous transcendental reduction "of" existence, which drew its value only from its freedom and from its lack of rootedness, it would be existence itself, in its most originary form, that of time or that of the other [*autrui*], those foundations of all the other [forms], which in a real movement of abstraction (logical or psychological in its constituted form) sketches out symbolically a real act or a real maneuver of retreat or of absence.[46] After which, there would no longer remain an originary lived experience but an already constituted sense, or a concept. If, under the form of time or of other [*autrui*], existence is at the very heart of the transcendental "I," can there be no danger of lack of logic, of unperceived entailment or of dissimulated contamination, in making a distinction between worldly genesis in which primitive existence is invested with a sense by a transcendental act and a transcendental genesis in which there is still existence that gives "itself" sense?[47] Are not temporality and alterity, if they have a status that is originarily transcendental in irreducible fashion, always "already" constituted as pure existence at the moment when they appear as constituting? Was not the reduction then an abstraction? Which would signify the collapse of the phenomenological enterprise.[48]

Has Husserl succeeded in dominating and going beyond the alternative and beyond the dialectic between a purely empirical genesis which would be bereft of sense, and of which, at the limit, one could not even "speak" and a transcendental genesis, which itself oscillates between empirical sense and abstract sense?[49] The absolute of originary sense would be tainted in both geneses. Has Husserl got to an originary comprehension of the dialectic of originary sense and primitive existence? At the point we have got to in this, the originary seems more primitive than the primitive of which it is the sense and of which it allows the appearance, but the primitive is more originary than the originary itself since it is *at the same time* the transcendental foundation and the ultimate substrate of sense. To what extent does "existence," when re-vealed by every transcendental genesis in its purest forms, time and the other, not install contradiction in the act of reduction, whose radical "simplicity," whose absolute originarity ought to found the initial and final meaning of phe-nomenological philosophy? How far and in what way has Husserl assumed this apparently irreducible dialectic? This is the question we will try to ask.

Inextricable Implication and the Difficulties of a "Method"

The initial intention of these preliminary remarks was to underline at one and the same time both the essential solidarity of the historical and philosophical problematics and also the impossibility of a total assimilation of one to the other. Husserl's philosophy, in fact has not served us only as an example, because a phenomenological attitude has [in fact] been adopted constantly from the beginning: it can even be said that the problem of genesis has only been able to be posed by returning to that attitude. Indeed, we have seen that the primary sense of genesis, its authentic problem, arose only in mutilated form, when a start was made from an empirical or "worldly" attitude, be it that of a supposed philosophy or of a psychological or biological science, in the same way as in a metaphysical or transcendental perspective (transcen-dental in the formal or abstract sense of the word). The terms in which this sense was presented were inconsistent. But if Husserl's thought has been more than an example for us, more than a pretext or a universe of discourse, it is not exactly the endpoint of this research.

Indeed, while trying to show that the phenomenological project of Husserl is indissociable from a purely dialectical philosophy, with all its con-sequences, we will willingly recognize that very probably Husserl would have contested the well-foundedness of such an interpretation. Dialectic as gener-ally conceived is the very opposite of philosophy as permanent recourse to the originary simplicity of an act or a being, of a truism or of an intuition; in this sense, it seems that dialectic cannot be instituted except from instances al-ready constituted as such by a originary transcendental consciousness. Con-sequently, a dialectical philosophy has no right to proclaim itself a first phi-losophy. It is superposed on a phenomenology. It is quite clear that we need to do everything to go beyond a "worldly" dialectic. Hence, we shall have to reject the conclusions of Trân Duc Thao who, having, it seems, examined deeply and forcefully the movement of Husserlian thought[50] and having approached as closely as possible the transcendental purity of his dialectic, falls back into the difficulties posed by a "worldly" genesis and a materialist dialectic. In going beyond these conclusions, we will be faithful to the letter of Husserlianism. We do not claim to be so except in spirit, when we defend an explicitly dialectic conception in the face of his classical interpreters. Besides, we need to admit that there is an apparent philosophical and historical dishonesty in using dialectical solutions or descriptions; but it is part of the movement of a veritable dialectic to show forth its immediate dishonesty as more honest than immediate honesty, simple and monolithic as it is. Every unilinear conception of genesis seems to lead to an aporia, out of which dialectic emerges victorious since it determines this conception all the way to transforming it into its contrary, without altering its real content, which thus proves itself to be absent. But to say that the meaning of genesis is dialectic is to say that it is not "pure" meaning; it is to say that "for us" genesis cannot be presented with the absolute of its meaning. Thus, this is not to propose a "solution" to the problem; it is simply to affirm that in a dialectic known as such, the aporia "understands itself" as "real" aporia. So perhaps we shall meet up with philosophy.

It will also be found to be natural that our path toward philosophy, in its appearance of "method," is neither continuous nor unilinear. We have met many difficulties up to now, and have retained only one positive result from them: the feeling of the impossibility of a method that is pure and of a discourse that does not anticipate, does not turn back, does not oscillate, does not go beyond itself by itself and in itself, and so forth. The steps we make in this work will be awkward. We have alluded to the reasons why it is not consistent to follow the purely chronological thread of Husserl's work even if we do not have the right to keep to an order that is only logical and "essential." In exposing—à propos the problem of genesis—the movement of Husserl's thought according to a phenomenology of movement as it is given to us by an originary perception of movement, we will be faithful to the phenomenological intention. Every description of a movement (or of a genesis) which does not take on dialectic stumbles over the paradoxes of Zeno of Elea: on the one hand there would be an attempt to make movement as such totally intelligible and for that [attempt], it is reduced to the ideal unit of its "intention," of its sense, that is, that the ideal point of arrival is assimilated to the ideal point of departure; ideally, in fact, and from the point of view of the pure sense of a movement, no historical and real difference is possible: all the points and moments are analogous; their originality is contingent. But the effective temporality of movement, its existence, is suppressed: movement has become immobility. Conversely, it would be nice to restitute to movement all its effective, real, ontological consistency, by showing that it can be the sum only of full moments, of perfect instants, of finished totalities which are irreducible to some ideal meaning that might transcend them. And in fact, "objective" reality of movement could thus appear to be faithfully described. But it happens that this objective reality of movement is the opposite of movement, since it forces movement into immobility. Here one sees how one pretension of objectivist science is reduced to an absurdity because it has not been willing to recognize its rootedness in the ground of originary perception. For this latter, there is no movement which is absolute and in itself.[51]

Absolute movement in itself finds itself contradicted in its essence and prohibited in its appearance by a historicism or an absolute realism of point-like moments and [also] by an absolute idealism of total sense. Thus, it is in originary perception that the absolute alienates itself, divides itself, and finds itself again in dialectical moments. It can never be said whether it is the point or the sense that is absolutely first, whether it is the work or the idea. We shall have to give centers to the considerations that are going to follow, centers that are at the same time "themes" and "moments."

Introduction

The problem of genesis is at the same time the essential motivation of his thought and the locus of a dilemma that Husserl seems to have put off or dissimulated endlessly. The unity of this problem has never wavered; it is only differentiated in its development into several themes or loci that we will be content here to announce in schematic fashion.

Starting out from an intentional psychologism, Husserl had believed at the beginning of his career[1] that the objectivity of essences and the validity of any knowledge was founded on an empirical genesis—that is, here, a psychological one. It was from natural operations of a psychological subjectivity that the concepts and meanings of experience were engendered. As Brentano* had taught, the intentionality of consciousness was only a psychological "character" of thought. This intentionality was not yet a transcendental foundation of objectivity. The return to the becoming of perception, already sketched out, was going in the direction of an empiricism that was quite classical.

But to explain the genesis of number and elementary logical concepts, this psychologism already had recourse to the *a priori* idea of an "object in general," a condition of possibility for empirical genesis itself. More, into the themes from psychologist constructivism there was mixed the theme of an originary clear evidence, presupposed by every subjective operation. A new working out of intentionality seemed necessary.

Pure and *a priori* essences, the conditions of possibility for an objective

---

*Franz Brentano. *Trans.*

logic could not be produced starting from the operations of a natural subjectivity closed on itself. Intentionality could no longer be a psychological "trait" of thought; it had to be the first irreducible movement of a consciousness that was gaining immediate access in an originary evidence to the objectivity of logical essences.[2] These were not subject to any genetic production. From this moment, the absolute foundation of essences is dissociated from every genetic implication. Genesis belongs to the order of empirical facticity, put into brackets in phenomenology, which is a neutral and "unreal" domain of intentional lived experience. As such, genetic becoming is the concern of the natural and human sciences only, physics, biology, psycho-physiology, sociology, and history. These sciences are "vague" and *a posteriori* sciences. "Rigorous" science is possible only to the degree that an *a priori* was given in a concrete intuition to an intentional consciousness.

Now the intentionality and *a priori* intuition of essences could not consist in a simple meeting of atemporal logical meanings, which inhabited an intelligible heaven, without running the risk of becoming once more psychological and purely subjective accidents. These meanings had to be "founded" on a concrete "fulfilling" in an "originary donating intuition," where the real object gives itself "in person." The essences were thus not platonic ideas—in the conventional sense of the word; they had no sense nor any foundation "in itself" independent of intentional acts that aimed at them. Without that, one would be reduced to accepting a frozen logic of a scholastic type, for which development and becoming would be impossible. Now, Husserl already starts out from the possibility of an infinite transformation of logic. Thus, it was necessary to return to the concrete lived experience of a transcendental subjectivity, constituting source and foundation of essences.[3] These, being neither ideas "in themselves" nor constructed concepts in psychological operations, would allow us to go beyond the alternative of logicism and psychologism. But a serious problem of genesis was going to reappear at a deeper level.

Without recourse to an already constituted logic, how will the temporality and subjectivity of transcendental lived experience engender and found objective and universal eidetic structures? How will they be described themselves in terms of essence? The method of reduction, eidetic reduction and transcendental reduction, its scope made wider and wider, will have to allow us to attain the very act of temporal constitution by "suspending" and "neutralizing" facts and then the already constituted essences. But since [his] abandoning of psychologism, genesis, being in Husserl's eyes merged with a psychophysical causality, remains completely "neutralized," put "off-line" by the reduction. It is thus that the internal consciousness of time[4] will be described at its eidetic and noematic level. According to a procedure that Husserl will never abandon, the temporality which is effectively genetic will be replaced by its structure constituted as an "eidos" or as a "noema." Just by becoming a "theme" of a description, the constituting existence of time gives way to the known and constituted sense of time. This is why the constitution of different ontological regions, as it is described in *Ideas* I,[5] will be static and will take place at the level of a noetico-noematic correlation which Husserl will on occasions acknowledge is not absolutely constituting but produced by a more originary synthesis: that of the originary temporality of the transcendental "ego" itself. The absolute idealism of *Ideas* is thus in a certain sense a purely methodological one. To the degree that absolute subjectivity is itself produced in the temporality of an originary synthesis *(Ursynthese)*, genesis is reintroduced inside the neutral sphere that transcendental reduction had organized. The difficulties of the absolute reduction of existence and of time appear clearly and the constitution that is static must now be founded on a constitution that is genetic. Time was what in being, or what mixing with being, had resisted reduction; this reduction, condition of possibility for a phenomenology that Husserl is trying to deepen, must be enlarged and transformed.[6]

The theme of transcendental genesis, which from 1919[7] on takes a central place in Husserl's meditation, ought to lead us back to a moment that is before any eidetics and ought to bring us close to the sphere of antepredicative existence, of the "life-world" *(Lebenswelt)*, of primitive time, of transcendental intersubjectivity, all factors that as such are not originarily freighted with a sense arising from the activity of the "ego." That, it seems at least, is Husserl's argument. In fact, we will never leave a world of constituted essences. The ambiguity of constitutive analyses of the "life-world,"[8] of logic,[9] of the transcendental subject,[10] wavering once more between *a priori* ideas of an infinite totality, ideas that are not derived from any genesis and make possible the transcendental becoming, and a simply "worldly" genesis, succeeds in appearance in maintaining transcendental genesis (always opposed to worldly genesis) in eidetic structures that are *a priori* and universal. These, in fact, in spite of a pretension to originarity, are *always already* constituted and postgenetic. The genesis of sense is always *a priori* converted into a sense of genesis that supposes a whole philosophy of history.

Indeed, the theme of passive genesis gave rise to a serious feeling of discomfort. In spite of Husserl's attempts,[11] the passive synthesis resisted any reduction, and escaped through its very creativity, from the purely egological experience, from the active moment of intentionality, from the limits of absolute subjectivity which up till then took in all the real *(reell)* or possible moments of constitution. Now this passive genesis was presented by Husserl as the most originary moment of constitution, as the fundamental layer of any transcendental activity.

To be able to reintegrate the passive genesis into an eidetic and transcendental phenomenology, the reduction and the conception of intentionality had once more to be enlarged; *they had to be* extended beyond the purely egological lived experience right up to intersubjective experiences and right up to history. Once more it is an infinite idea[12] that, in the new and more precise shape of a "teleology," will give back an intentional sense—the only foundation of any eidetics—to passive genesis. This latter rooted the ego in history. The intentional teleology, of which one becomes conscious in a philosophy of history, hence had to found all the previous stages of phenomenology, which were then presented as superficial and given over to a "naive" or natural gaze, because it took as natural those structures that in the last analysis, it was perceived, were not primordial but produced by a historical finality.

But in our regression toward an originary synthesis, a new disappointment is awaiting us. To a historico-intentional analysis,[13] teleology too appears as a unity of sense that is *already* constituted. The sense of the genesis preceding historical genesis or being engendered by and for itself, the philosophy of history will be confused with a history of philosophy. Everything that in real history does not participate in the constituted unity of teleology is stripped of absolute sense and only presupposes a "worldly" genesis. The originary moment of genesis that constitutes sense will have to be at the same time prior to sense in order for the constitution to be effective, and posterior to sense in order for it to be given us in an *a priori* or originary self-evidence.

Such a complication could only be thematized if an originary and dialectical synthesis of being and time were the point of departure. The phenomenology of time had thrown light on the dialectical character of constituting temporality and constituted temporality. But to the extent that this phenomenology remained eidetic and retained the ontological thesis and the possibility of an originarily atemporal or eternal synthesis, its movement wore itself out in an indefinite phenomenological reduction; this latter, despite Husserl's intention, will remain a reduction and a dissimulation of effective genesis. Not having clarified its own ambiguity, Husserl's phenomenology will be reduced to being only a moment of the dialectic between phenomenology and ontology. Only the originary temporality could found the *a priori* synthesis of existence and essence. In spite of have ceaselessly referred to a deeper temporality which was indeed that of human existence being dialectically merged with its essence and resisting any reduction, Husserl nevertheless ends by reducing temporality to an eidetic structure that has already been constituted by an originarity that is atemporal, obeying in this way an intrinsic rationalism and idealism. Thus describing sometimes the synthesis, sometimes the *a priori* of genesis, Husserl refused to recognize that any point of departure for philosophy and for sense is an *a priori* synthesis whose absolute evidence refers to an indefinite that is irreducible; this was to refuse to cause philosophy to be born into an existence whose finitude was apparent to itself. In spite of the immense philosophical revolution that Husserl undertook, he remains the prisoner of a great classical tradition: the one that reduces human finitude to an accident of history, to an "essence of man"[14] that understands temporality against a background of possible or actual eternity in which it has or could have participated. Discovering the *a priori* synthesis of being and of time as foundation of any genesis and every meaning, Husserl, to save the rigor and purity of "phenomenological idealism," did not open up the transcendental reduction and did not adjust his method. To this extent, his philosophy cries out to be overtaken in a way that will only be a prolongation or, inversely, for a radical explicitation that will be a veritable conversion.

PART I

THE DILEMMAS OF PSYCHOLOGICAL
GENESIS: PSYCHOLOGISM AND LOGICISM

1

Meeting the Problem

When Husserl came to philosophy,[1] minds in Germany were already confronting each other over the problem of genesis. Must the relations between logic and psychology be posed in terms of genesis? Can logic be derived from a psychogenesis? Is the latter the ultimate foundation of every logical value? These questions are motivated by the incontestable progress of the natural and human sciences and, in particular, by the advent of scientific psychology, the horizon of which then seems infinite. Will not psychological science and its positivity put an end at last to the theoretical problems of knowledge?

The psychologist response is known: the knowledge of the "laws" of psychological becoming stands instead of a logical foundation and theory of knowledge for us. J. S. Mill in Great Britain, Wundt, Sigwart, and Lipps in Germany,* are the most advanced representatives of such a psychologism. In their eyes, in the same way that logic is a development or a prolongation, a translation or an explicitation of psychological processes, so a psychogenetic explanation of logic will be a reduction of it to the procedures of the natural subjectivity that produces it.

It is around Kantian themes that the debate between psychologists and antipsychologists is situated. Psychologism is accompanied at that moment by a decided reaction against Kant. Stumpf reproaches Kant with having cut his theory of knowledge off from psychology.[2] The theory of knowledge defines the theoretical conditions of possibility of the different types of universal knowledge. But the effective condition of possibility of these types of

---

*Wilhelm Wundt, Christoph Sigwart, and Thadeuz Lipps. *Trans.*

knowledge, their putting in action by a real historical subject, is that not the very object of a psychology? Does not any critical theory of knowledge start off implicitly from this psychology? Behind this objection one can hear the one that Husserl will continually address to Kant: If the transcendental is not merged originarily with its empirical content, if it is not presented as parallel to experience itself, this transcendental, being thematized outside experience, becomes logical and formal. It is no longer a constituting source but the constituted product of experience. It becomes psychological and "worldly." To go back to such a transcendental subject as to an absolute originarity, that is psychologism. This opposition to Kant gives us the key to the supposed pure psychologism by which Husserl is supposed to have started out on his philosophical itinerary. Husserl begins with a radical refusal of Kant's transcendental formalism. He will never go back on this. On the contrary, he will often show how a pure psychologist empiricism, such as that of Hume, for example, is closer to an authentic transcendental philosophy than the so-called transcendentalism of Kant.[3] So when Husserl definitively abandons the psychologism of his age, it will not be to go over to the opposed thesis, but in order to go beyond an alternative from which no one escaped at that time.

Hence Natorp, when he opposes the psychologism of Lipps, will have to adopt a Kantian position, somewhat against his will. Lipps saw in psychology the foundation of philosophy.[4] For example, he planned to pick out the psychological genesis of the principal of contradiction and of the conceptual approaches and the conceptual procedures belonging to knowledge in general. He claimed to find in such a study the origin and the guarantee, the driving force and the validity of any possible knowledge. The genetic constitution of the fundamental laws of knowledge starting from the primitive facts of psychological life was being mixed up with their epistemological validation. Natorp concedes to Lipps that mental facts have their importance in the laws of knowledge and that these facts, as such, belong to a psychological science. It is very obvious that, in a certain sense, all knowledge is an operation of the mind that comes about in the form of concepts and theories that are given *in* a psychological consciousness. The concepts and truths of geometry are in a certain sense mental facts. But nobody will dare to make laws of the psyche out of the axioms of Euclidean geometry. The truth of their "proof" does without psychological understanding. They do not need to be brought about by a real action of mind in order for them to accede to their objective value.[5] The discontinuity between logic or objective knowledge and psychology is thus one of essence. The foundations of objectivity are ruined if they are psychogenetic. Natorp separates logical consciousness from psychological consciousness. The first is independent of any empirical becoming. It escapes real time. That is the only condition for the principles of knowledge to be universal and autonomous in their foundations. Thus, the "psychology of knowledge" and the "critique" imply each other and condition each other to a certain degree. But the normative laws of knowledge are *a priori* and refer only to themselves.

Natorp also says that only one of two things can hold:[6] either there is no logic or else it must be entirely constructed on its own area, without borrowing its foundations from another science. To make logic into a branch of psychology[7] is to reduce it to being nothing more than an application of psychology. In this way the meaning[8] of logic which is given as autonomous and as a condition of possibility of every science is changed, but so is the meaning of the objective sciences in general, of psychology in particular.[9] The objective truth of knowledge cannot depend on a purely subjective experience. Logic is not born in an empirical subjectivity. The conquest of scientific objectivity supposes a victory *(Überwindung)*[10] over subjectivity.

A good many themes are announced here that were to be dear to Husserl: the idea of an absolute foundation of logic and of philosophy escaping in this way from any historical genesis, the distinction between a psychological consciousness and a logical consciousness (itself supposing a transcendental consciousness), these will be at the center of Husserl's thought. But already the essential difference makes itself felt and one can understand why Husserl's first writings, which are contemporary to Natorp's positions, keep a psychologist orientation. Indeed, Natorp stayed resolutely formalist in the theory of knowledge that he opposed to psychologism. When he opposed the idea of an objective validity of logic to the subjectivist explanation by genesis, he meant to point up an independence and an autonomy, a dissociation. But he lacked the concrete link, the continuity of a passage between the objectivity of logical meanings and a subject. For if the psychological subjectivity could not by itself produce objective laws, one can also ask how these laws, purely autonomous and in themselves, can give rise to operations and be known as such by a subject. Natorp said nothing about the constituting origin of logical objectivity. To which subjectivity was it accessible? From which subjectivity did it emanate? Following in this a Kantianism which he could not strip off from his thought and which, strangely, he reconciled with a Platonism, Natorp held that things in themselves were unknowable. Hence, empirical subjectivity being finite and closed on itself, the validity of logic supposed a formal subject. Correlatively, the foundations of knowledge will be objective formal units constituted before any empirical subjectivity. In the domain of mathematics, the substrates of what we know are not phenomena but formal categories that define the unity of determination for possible phenomena. The logical or formal consciousness supposed by these categories would later refer to a transcendental consciousness in Husserl's work, the concrete foundation of any formal logic. Natorp, who separates absolutely empirical subjectivity from the objectivity of the *a priori* laws of consciousness, would not allow himself to understand how knowledge could be *at the same time* a psychological act and a way of arriving at truth, an empirical production and a piece of originary evidence. Even if under a metaphysical hypothesis, one picks out by their substances a logical subject capable of universal truth and an empirical subject feeling its way in knowledge that is obscure and limited, one does not explain in this way why and how these two subjects occupy *one and the same piece of time.* The identity of this time appears absolute and indeed is the object of an originary intuition that nothing can reduce. This unique temporality, which gives itself at the same time as locus of a creative genesis and of a theoretical intuition, as locus of the empirical becoming enriching itself ceaselessly and of the logical truths [*évidences*] known *a priori,* finds itself taken apart by Natorp. On the one side there is an empirical time, fallen, degraded, hiding the possibility of a logical truth: it is the time of psychological genesis, of the conceptual operations that are really carried out in the life of the mind; on the other side, in opposition to this time that is opaque in itself, a pure atemporality, or, if it is preferred, an ideal or formal temporality, purely intelligible or transparent, a world of logical truths [*évidences*]. So, the psychological act, in its constructive aspect, in a way only accompanies the purely logical act, as a technical instrument or empirical mediation; their being together remains accidental and exterior. But the sense of their simultaneity or of their coexistence, recognized and underlined by Natorp, totally escapes us. And thus we are forced, as in every idealist perspective, to let the objectivity of knowledge rest on the formal conditions of possibility that escape the living in time and every genesis; the problem is then to base the incarnation and the application of formal *a priori* laws in the effective time of psychological subjectivity without having recourse to an ideality of time which would only push the problem one stage back.[11]

Thus, it is significant that Husserl, from the start, has not followed Natorp's logicism. The starting point for Husserl could not be formal or abstract. The psychologism of the young Husserl has to be seen as more than an aberration, and it must be understood in its continuity with the philosophy of genesis that will reappear later. The confidence that Husserl started by having in the psychogenetic viewpoint was accompanied by an explicit break from formal idealism. But though he quickly withdrew the confidence he had placed [in psychologism], that break remained definitive (in intention at least). The originary concrete lived experience is not yet described as it will be on the level of the phenomenological reduction, but it is already recognized as the source of philosophy.

Thus, Husserl is closer to the logician-psychologists, like Sigwart[12] than to such neo-Kantians or Platonists as Natorp. Sigwart in fact recognizes some essential differences between logic and psychology; a difference of intention: logic intends to define the conditions for any *true* thought in general and not the laws of any effective thought; a real difference: logic is only concerned with what in thought can constitute truth and not with the laws of movement of the mind in general. But logic, supposing an experience and a knowledge of the life of the mind in general, and not being able to be established except after the clear evidence of this life of the mind, will have to rely on a psychology. It is the inverse movement of the same vicious circle. It is certain that the life of the mind is a very muddled notion in Sigwart. It is not clear whether it is a question of originary lived experience and of intuitive evidence, or of constituted facts. In this sense, we are under and beneath every phenomenological psychology. However, the way in which Sigwart describes the genesis of judgment resembles in an odd way certain much later analyses of Husserl[13]— if what is presented in empirical terms is transcribed in transcendental terms. Thus, for example, the negative judgment is derived from a positive judgment that is always primitive. It is engendered from concrete experiences of failure and deception.[14] But these experiences, defined in terms of a subjectivist psychology, did not explain logical negation, whose possibility had to precede the constituted facts of experience. How, while safeguarding the originarity of lived experience, could we avoid psychologist empiricism and grasp the genesis of an objective logic when starting from concrete experiences? That is already the whole problem of transcendental genesis which is posed in advance for Husserl, at the point in time when, as a mathematician concerned with the deep meaning of his activity, Husserl is asking questions of philosophy.

If it was posed in Kantian terms, as it generally was at that time, the debate sank into immobility when faced with a dilemma. Either an appeal to the transcendental subject was made, one emerging out of every temporal lived experience and consisting in a system of *a priori* forms. That was to reject any genetic hypothesis and to risk making out of a formal subject, itself a stabilized product of a genetic constitution, something that could be claimed to be a constituting source. It was, in order to avoid a classical style of psychologism, to run the risk of the subtle psychologism of which Husserl would later accuse Kant:[15] any transcendental subject that it is claimed escapes from lived temporality is only a worldly or psychological subject, a form or a fact whose meaning is already constituted by a veritable transcendental subject. Or else, the other horn of the dilemma, a psychologistic empiricism is deliberately accepted but, by that [very accepting], is not to be founded absolutely. We stay prisoners of a subjectivist relativism, which Husserl shows very clearly in *Logical Investigations*[16] is a synonym of radical skepticism. Thus, there is only the choice between an empirical lived experience of a Kantian type, which, as such, gives no assurance of objectivity, and a logical formalism, which, closed to any genesis, not only appears inapplicable or unworkable but also runs the risk of being only the product of a dissimulated genesis, as Husserl will say later, a forgotten genesis.[17]

This alternative as such appears insurmountable. If the foundations of objectivity do not appear at the level of a lived proof, one that is concrete and temporal, they must be constructed, induced, deduced, or derived. In the products of such an operation, one will no longer be able to distinguish between the constituting moment and the constituted moment or between the *a priori* and the *a posteriori*. In fact it is only with already constituted objects that one will be concerned, some as facts of the consciousness, the others as logical forms. To make originary instances out of one or the other is the very essence of psychologism as Husserl will be led to define it. In both cases, in wishing to deduce the possibility of objectivity, that possibility will be supposed or anticipated. Either way, the originarity of lived experience is refused as the source of all objectivity. Lived experience is empirical, constructed by an I, one that is transcendental according to formal categories. It [lived experience] is thus not originary. In the same way, the originary transcendental I is not a piece of lived experience. Effective genesis is thus cut off from all transcendental originality. Effectively lived temporality is not constituting but constituted by a transcendental ideality of time that, in the last analysis, is the opposite of a genetic becoming. In a word, the transcendental conditions of genesis are not themselves temporal, and there is no transcendental genesis of objectivity. At the level where psychologism runs counter to Kantianism, it could be said that for the first there is a genesis without objectivity, and in the second an objectivity without genesis. Time and truth exclude each other *a priori*. Psychologism and Kantianism become identified, however, in that neither one nor the other explicitly sets out from an originary lived experience; both have recourse to a mediate definition of experience and of the world constituted in experience. What is lacking in both is the theme of an intentional consciousness.

Indeed, up to here, experience remained as a construction, whether it was made from a transcendental I and from formal categories or from exclusively psychological acts. Genesis, when it appeared, was only association or elaboration. The problems of origin were then insoluble. The elucidation of an originarily intentional consciousness should allow one to go beyond the debate in a radical fashion. An originarily objective consciousness, whose originary movement allows access to what is not it, ought to remove all the difficulties of genesis or at least modify considerably the appearance of the problem.

But at the moment when Husserl, under the influence of Brentano, takes on the idea of intentionality, he is still in debt to classical conceptions. Intentionality as defined by Brentano is anyway very different from the transcendental intentionality invoked later by Husserl. It is once more a psychological characteristic of consciousness. This consciousness, then, is not originarily intentional. It is not an attribute of thought that can immediately give it the keys to objectivity. Thus, the radical unveiling of intentionality will be very slow. As long as it is a question of an intentional structure of consciousness, the problem of genesis will remain posed in constructivist terms. Husserl's mission will be to make progressively explicit the theme of intentionality and, in doing this, to define a new set of problems. This could be started with the following question: If subjectivity is intentional and refers to its immediate perception of objects and meanings for its ultimate foundation, how can the genesis of logical meanings, of the objectivity of concepts and numbers be explained? But intentionality is still an empirical fact, and this set of problems is mixed up in a confused way with the classical set of problems. Husserl has to start by putting up a struggle in this confusion.

2

A First Recourse to Genesis: Intentional Psychologism

Genetic Implication and Absolute Foundation

The *Philosophy of Arithmetic*[1] is the book of a disappointed mathematician. The logicism that was then triumphant in the philosophy of mathematics was becoming one with the antipsychologism of Natorp. It is not well able to explain autonomous forms of mathematics and to situate them in the concrete life of consciousness. Prisoners of a psychological or logical conception of consciousness, the logicians of that time used to preserve the objectivity of mathematical meanings only by isolating them in their origin from any consciousness. But if one keeps to ideal mathematical forms, atemporal regulators of all the acts that aim at them, neither the progress of mathematics as a whole, nor the concrete possibility of any actual operation, of any synthesis, can be understood. For these cannot take place without an act of consciousness. This act, which Husserl still conceives as "psychological" and "real" *(real)*, refers to a constituting subject, temporal and intentional. Numbers are constituted by the act of counting multiplicities.[2] But if this synthesis is only done by a "real" subject, what can make us certain of its objectivity? What will guarantee us its a *priori* necessity? Will a multiplicity of acts of consciousness be enough to found the a *priori* unity of the sensible or intelligible object? It is the whole problem of a *priori* synthesis which is posed here in relation to every mathematical operation and the evolution of mathematics in general.

The problem of the genesis of mathematics is not yet treated as such by Husserl, but this is what is giving direction to his research. What is Husserl in fact setting out to do in his work? It is a question of "preparing with a series of psychological and logical inquiries the scientific foundations on which mathematics and philosophy could afterwards be based."[3] The idea of an absolute foundation, which will never leave Husserl, is in his eyes still accessible to a psychological science. The subjectivity that is alluded to is an empirical subjectivity. "I began work on the prevailing assumption that psychology was the science from which logic in general, and the logic of the deductive sciences, had to hope for philosophical clarification."[4] But at the same time, this empirical subjectivity is a source of absolute evidence. It is not a natural simple fact whose sense is already determined. From it alone, and not from the natural laws that govern it, from the intentional perception whose source it is, there will be an attempt to found mathematics and philosophy. Thus, the ambiguity of an intentional consciousness that is at the same time mental life and source of evidence leaves the problem open: Will the absolute foundation of mathematical objectivity be given in an originarily intentional clarity of evidence? And it is not known yet whether this latter is temporal and, if it is, what founds at the same time the *a priori* and the synthesis. Must the foundation of mathematics then coincide with its psychological genesis?

The revelation of this absolute foundation will be made by an intentional analysis, by descriptions and "patient analyses of detail."[5] The "implications"—here psychological ones—of essences and mathematical concepts will be revealed. In a regressive movement, the analysis of these implications will follow the genetic itinerary that leads to mathematical objectivities. At the end of his life, in the *Origin of Geometry,* Husserl will once more try to perform a "reactualizing" *(Reaktivierung)* of the originary sense of the mathematical operation or of the mathematical production *(Leistung).* This was also the object of *Experience and Judgment* and of *Formal and Transcendental Logic.* The point is ideally to dissolve the "sedimentations" that have been left after the genesis by a constituted becoming. But the "historico-intentional" analysis will have later to be maintained at a transcendental point of view. In the *Philosophy of Arithmetic,* the final implications of a genetic description have not yet appeared, but the demand for such a description is already present. The demand will never leave Husserl. Before being provisionally bracketed and then reappearing, in a more and more urgent way after *Ideas* I, such a description is still defined in 1894 as the only valid method, at the moment when Husserl begins to find his psychologism insufficient: "I think I may claim that no theory of judgment will be able to fit in with the facts if it is not based on a deep study of the descriptive and genetic relations of intuitions and representations."[6] So a unity of intention links the *Philosophy of Arithmetic* and the *Origin of Geometry* and makes its way through all the intermediary moments. Before arriving at the transcendental genesis, Husserl had, however, to start out from an empirical genesis. It is doubtful that this latter will allow us to attain the absolute bases of philosophy and of mathematics.

Abstraction and the Genesis of Concepts

What do genetic descriptions deliver to us here? In the first part of the work, Husserl applies himself to the analysis of the concepts of plurality, of number, and of unit. The point is to attain them not through the symbolic apparatus that refers to them, but in their concrete origin. Husserl quotes Weierstrass and accepts the idea that "pure arithmetic does not require any fundamental presupposition except the concept of number."[7] Cardinal number is the foundation of any numeration. But since it itself supposes the concept of plurality, it is this that Husserl begins by studying. What is the genesis of this concept? It is instituted by a psychological act of abstraction.[8] The concrete bases of this abstraction are the "totalities" *(Inbegriffe)* and the "pluralities" of specified objects. The objects on which the activity of abstraction is exercised are totalities of all sorts of objects: a group of trees, a feeling, an angel, and so forth.[9] The nature of the particular "contents" *(Inhalt)* is indifferent. Husserl rejects every theory that determines the origin of the concept of number by starting from such or such a type of content. It is thus that he considered the thesis of J. S. Mill, according to which number can designate only physical phenomena, inadequate. Psychological acts and states, Husserl tells us, can be counted as well as natural things.[10] Each time a synthetic unity is presented, each time there can be an abstraction starting from a given totality, number is possible.[11] The totality Husserl is speaking about is not something put together, something assembled, an *a posteriori* synthesis; it is given from the first moment of intentional perception.[12] It is an "*a priori* synthesis" that, already constituted, founds the possibility of abstraction. In this sense, abstraction is, as such, a superficial and secondary synthesis or genesis. It presupposes a more fundamental synthesis.

However, from these first considerations, Husserl's psychologism is quite distinct from the psychologism of his time. On the one hand, no doubt, in attributing the possibility of number—and, ultimately, of every concept—to a psychological act of abstraction, one lays oneself open to all the criticisms that Husserl himself will very soon be quick to make of all psychologisms. One single psychological operation cannot suffice to constitute the objectivity of arithmetical meanings and the unity of every object. Without an originary intentionality, no part of mental life [*aucune vie psychique*] can appear as constituting. Genesis is still conceived of on the psychological model, since abstraction, which is its principal driving force, produces general concepts of which it is not known whether they are founded on essences or not. Husserl himself tells us that what interests him is not defining the essence of the concept of plurality, but describing its genesis by a "*psychological characterisation* of phenomena, on which the abstraction of this concept is founded."[13]

But, on the other hand, this fundamental act of abstraction must already be harmonized with the intentional essence of consciousness. Certainly, Husserl stays with the definition of Brentano: intentionality is a psychological "structure" of consciousness. So he could miss an access that is originary to the signification of the object and could implicitly resort to a construction. This point of view is not yet clear. In any case, it is certain that the idea of a plurality constituted *a priori* as a totality and delivered as such to an originary perception, the idea of a genesis being developed from such a perception, seems to go beyond the limits of classical psychology. Consciousness is originarily consciousness of something. Perception is thus prime, objectivity has a foundation that is originarily lived; the synthesis that makes this objectivity possible is not a construction, an *a posteriori* association; it is more than the production of a unity starting from a multiplicity of subjective acts. Synthetic unity of the object (in the broad sense of that term) is *a priori* because it is the object *itself* that is immediately present to consciousness. Far from the unity of the totality being constructed by a genesis, it is this unity that makes the genesis possible: it is because the "*a priori* synthesis" is *already* constituted in the object that abstraction is possible. In going more deeply into the intentional sense of consciousness, it seems that the genetic viewpoint of Husserl is reversed. Thus, abstraction is no longer fundamental, because it presupposes a previous constitution of the object in its ontological unity by a transcendental consciousness. It is even on the basis of this already constituted unity that the multiplicity of psychological acts can appear or appear to themselves as such. One sees here why Husserl will endeavor[14] to show against Frege that number is not a concept in the usual sense of that term. Thus we are, it seems, here at the antipodes of a classical psychology. The foundation of possibility of number is immediately objective; number is constructed, in the last analysis, by an abstraction, but this abstraction takes place on the basis of an originary synthesis. In number, the concept is primordial, but it is founded on an originary essence. From this first chapter of the *Philosophy of Arithmetic,* the problem of genesis is posed in all its scope. The already constituted plurality and totality, from which conceptual unity and number were engendered, were not the product of an activity of the empirical subject; they were given *a priori* and made the activity of the subject itself possible. But insofar as it was a constituted plurality, that is to say, a synthesis, they implied duration and thus a genesis. The originary and transcendental act which it presupposes as its intentional correlative (of which Husserl is not yet speaking, but which already seems necessary), insofar as it is also originarily synthetic, takes place according to a time. Already one is referred back to the crucial problem, that of the time of transcendental constitution. According to which time does it take place? Is it a time itself constituted by an atemporal subject? Is the subject itself temporal? How does it appear to itself and does it constitute itself as an identical subject? Is the originary genesis ideal or actual? If it is ideal, what is originary will not be able ever to be lived. Every lived experience will be psychological and already constituted. This is the reproach Husserl will make to Kant. But if, conversely, the genesis is actual, it will not be able to take place without the real acts of a historical subject; will the lived experience not be still psychological? Thus, it is at the heart of lived experience that later, the distinction between the psychological and the phenomenological will have to be made, between "worldly" reality *(real)* and transcendental reality *(reell)*. This distinction will be possible only through the phenomenological reduction. For the moment, it escapes Husserl, and the time of the constitution of number remains a psychological time.

Psychological Time

Indeed, posing the question of the origin of the concept of totality, Husserl arrives at a psychological definition of the time of its constitution. Time is presented as a "necessary psychological factor."[15] Temporal succession is indispensable to explain the origin of the "aggregates" and the totalities of objects; in the same way, abstraction from these totalities and the constitution of numbers require the intervention of a time. The processes of collection and numeration suppose continuity and temporal succession. But here again, Husserl's thought oscillates strangely between an absolute psychological geneticism and a logicism. It is obvious that here the necessity of time is exclusively psychological in his eyes. Time intervenes only as a "factor" *(Momente)*, as an "element" in the production of number. Temporal succession must be possible for the acts of numeration and collection to be performed. But Husserl adds that the temporal succession and the logical order that links, for instance, the premises of a syllogism[16] to its conclusions must not be confused. The truth of the syllogism is, in some way, independent of the psychological temporality through which it is aimed at. Husserl quotes and approves

Herbart when he writes that "number has no more in common with time than a hundred other sorts of representation, whose production is always essentially gradual."[17] And, as the discussion develops, Husserl already distinguishes between the phenomenon as such and its "function" or its "sense" for us, that is, between the psychological description and the phenomenological description of an objective phenomenon. But from the fact that the phenomenological temporality of lived experience is still far from being explained, the sense of the logical object is founded in itself. Just like the order that links premises to conclusion, the objective sense is autonomous. The most ambitious psychologism coincides here with a logicism. And this meeting-up is not a matter of chance. The point was to construct the logical object by a psychological genesis soliciting divers factors such as time. Yet, in order to give a "unity of sense" to this genesis and to its objective product, it has to be supposed present, and autonomous, before the multiplicity of acts of consciousness. If time is an exclusively psychological condition, one will not be able to understand the becoming of objective essences; these latter will always have to be *already there,* in front of a passive consciousness whose presence remains accessory or accidental. The other way on, one can no longer understand the objective necessity of a psychological genesis without the help of a logical necessity that is itself also *always already* constituted. Psychologism and absolute genesis convert themselves into their opposite and become identified with it. Absolute becoming becomes, as it always does, eternity and negation of history. But this dialectic has not yet taken possession of its sense in the *Philosophy of Arithmetic.* It is still confusion. One can almost say the contrary to what is usually said of this work[18]: it is the simultaneous expression of a psychologism and of a logicism, because genesis, not being fully taken in to [the work], always appears on the foundation of autonomous logical essences. Statements are readily found that announce almost literally the leading themes of *Logical Investigations* (vol. 1), the work that we often call logicist. Thus, Husserl affirms that the concept of logical contents or of meaning must be distinguished from that of changing psychological contents that are actually experienced. When we represent to ourselves the totality ABCD,[19] we do not pay attention to temporal and psychological transformations in the acts of synthesis and analysis. From this, Husserl concludes that every effort to elucidate the concept of plurality and number through the idea of temporal succession is destined to fail beforehand. Time, in his eyes, is only a double psychological condition for the formation of these concepts: on the one hand, the synthesis of elements united in a totality implies a simultaneous "presentation" of this multiplicity of elements; on the other hand, syntheses producing totalities and pluralities produce themselves according to temporal processes.[20] But here the psychologism gives way in the face of a logicism: neither simultaneity nor succession are as such parts of the objective content of plurality and number. Notice is given of the dissociation between the effective genesis and the absoluteness of sense. It seems that it will only be accentuated all the way up to the problems of the transcendental reduction.

The "Primary" Relation and the "Psychic" Relation

The oscillation continues with the distinction between "primary" relation and "psychic" relation.[21] Husserl gave the name of "collective connections" (collective Verbindungen) to the relations that unified the plurality of objects into a totality. The question then arises whether these relations are psychological in origin (mental [psychiques] relations introduced by the subject) or of an objective origin (primary relations). There will thus be natural totalities that are constituted by primary relations, for example, the different parts of a rose;[22] on the contrary, there will be others that will be born from psychological relations: thus I can think the quality of red, the moon, and Napoleon as a multiplicity;[23] it is the intentional unity of a psychic act that makes a totality out of this plurality. But one is justified here in wondering whether it is the primary relation that founds the psychic relation or conversely. In one sense, it seems that the primary totality must in all necessity precede the psychic totality. Each object must be already constituted in its synthetic unity if I am to grasp it intentionally as such and associate it to other objects in an act of numeration. The psychological genesis would thus not be constituting. The passive and intuitive movement of intentionality refers us back to an already constituted ontology. But does that not come about because the intentionality envisaged here is psychological? Is not the very sense of the primary totality, as constituted before the *real* act through which I aim at it, a sense *for* a transcendental consciousness? The constitution of each object in its total unity refers back, as sense, to a synthesis that is carried out by a deeper subject than the psychological subject. The psychological genesis is not constituting, but an intentional synthesis is necessary for the unity of the object to have a "sense." Without this synthesis, the perception of the object, which has to be our starting point, would be dispersed in a dust cloud of elements that would not even be perceived as real multiplicity. Perception would be near to impossible. Once understood and made explicit, does not the subjective synthesis of the psychological genesis presuppose an originary synthesis of the subject and the object in a transcendental consciousness? Must not a distinction be made between natural genesis, which constitutes the real unity of the object by relations perceived as primary, and the genesis of the sense of the object, [that is,] a phenomenological genesis that intentionally constitutes an objective sense and that, to this degree, will be different from a psychological genesis as well? We will see later how this phenomenological genesis, which Husserl has not yet discovered, will in turn create serious problems.

Here, Husserl does not do more than oppose two types of relation, and he is interested exclusively in the genetic character of the psychological relation. The synthetic relation of one to the other, which pushes us up to another level of genesis, is not thematized,[24] so psychologism and logicism conflict or are merged without the reason for their dialectic being very clear. For, while describing the genesis of the concept as a process of abstraction, underpinned by the formal concept of "collective connection," Husserl shows that any abstract concept is only thinkable if it is accompanied in some way by a concrete intuition[25] of an object. It is not a question here of the problem of the possibility of an imageless thought but instead of a consequence of intentionality. Every concept is a concept of something: the possibility of a "something" in general *(etwas überhaupt)* founds the possibility of conceptual abstraction.[26] This "something" in general not being itself a concept, it escapes genesis. It is thus once again a nonpsychological and nongenetic element that founds empirical genesis. But this nongenetic element remains in a state of obscure implication.

The Polemic with Frege

Husserl does not pursue this and after having proceeded by the same methods to a psychological analysis of relations of degree, of more and of less,[27] and of equality,[28] he starts up a polemic with Frege and defends the value of a genetic explanation of arithmetic in general. Frege refused psychology any right of intervention in the domain of arithmetic.[29] A psychological analysis of the concept of number, he said, could not give us anything essential: "Number is no more an object of psychology or the product of mental operations than the North Sea."[30] The North Sea exists and can easily do without the intentional act that aims at it.[31] Husserl answers to this that only "composed" logical notions can be defined without referring to psychological genesis; these notions are mediate and hence insufficient. They are already constituted, and their originary sense escapes us. They suppose elementary concepts like "quality," "intensity," "place," "time," and so on, whose definition cannot, in Husserl's eyes, remain specifically logical. These concepts are correlative to the act of a subject. The concepts of equality, identity, of whole and of part, of plurality and of unity are not understood, in the last analysis, through terms of formal logic. If these concepts were *a priori* pure ideal forms, they would not lend themselves to any definition; every definition supposes in fact a concrete determination. This determination cannot be provided except by the act of actual constitution of this formal logic.[32]

Thus, we must turn toward concrete psychological life, toward perception, starting from which, abstraction and formalization take place. An already constituted logical "form" cannot be rigorously defined without unveiling the whole intentional history of its constitution. If such a history is not implied by all the logical concepts, these become unintelligible in themselves and unusable in concrete operations. Thus, Husserl maintains against Frege that one has no right to reproach a mathematician with describing the historical and psychological journey that leads to the concept of number.[33] One cannot "begin" with a logical definition of number. The very act of this definition and its possibility would be inexplicable. Thus, all that can be asked of a mathematician is to begin with a concrete description of the genesis of the notions they use and thus to bring to light the sense of these notions for a consciousness. Husserl thinks he has shown clearly that the concepts of plurality and unity are founded on originary perceptions. Since every number implies plurality and unity, its genetic description is possible. The logicist ambition of Frege is "chimerical." But the difficulty has not disappeared.

The Impossible Genesis of "Zero" and of the Unit*

If every logical form and every number refer to the intentional act of their production and to the perception of a plurality of objects, how then are the signification of "zero"[34] and of the number "one" to be explained genetically? The question is serious. It is posed by Frege, who rightly considers that everything in a theory of number that cannot be applied to zero or to the unit, has not got down to essentials.[35] Any genetic explanation must begin by the production of zero and of one. If it fails in this task, its whole principle is compromised by this. Now, the difficulty is huge; is not the essence of zero the absence of any concrete determination, or as Husserl will express it later, of

---

* In the following sections, the reader needs to remember that in French, as in German, the word for "unit" and "unity" is the same. *Trans.*

every "fulfillment" *(Erfüllung)* of categorial intuition and, correlatively, of every intentional act? This absence and this negation must be possible *a priori;* one does not get to zero through subtracting or abstracting from a concrete totality given in perception. On the contrary, zero must be possible from the outset in order for the operations of subtraction and abstraction to be performed. No psychological genesis can, by starting out from concrete totalities of perceptions and of acts founded by these perceptions, construct a logical objectivity whose essence is the very negation of these concrete totalities. A simple psychological abstraction will get indefinitely closer to zero without ever reaching it, so long as the sense of zero is not *a priori* possible, that is, before any genesis.

But, it will be objected, this impossibility is theoretical and formal. A "real" subtraction is, however, possible. With it, "zero" turns up. Probably, but that is because the unit was already constituted. But it is only constituted jointly with the possibility of the zero. The ultimate negation that leads to zero, and the sudden discontinuity that it supposes, are only possible if the unit is present. But with the unit we run up against the same problem.[36]

How can the unit be constituted in the movement of an empirico-psychological becoming? Is not the unit also a concept or an *a priori* essence that, far from being engendered, might be said to be there in order to found a subsequent genesis of arithmetic? A series of acts of perception, a series of abstractions, will never be able to attain an objective unity through a continuous movement. The indefinite of multiplicity will only join up with the unit/unity through a sudden jump, through a discontinuity that will interrupt genetic becoming or, at least, that will tear it away from psychological life. The sense of the unit/unity must be already present to start the genesis up and to steer it. To add or to subtract indefinitely from concrete objects that have not yet been constituted in arithmetical units will get us as close as possible to the unit, but it is not clear by what miracle the empirical juxtaposition of an element will transform into a totality a plurality that is not even aimed at as such. Such juxtaposition can do this only if the unity is already there, in the object, if the intentionality is not only psychological but also transcendental.

If synthesis is possible *a priori,* whether in the object[37] or in a logical *a priori* concept, psychological genesis, far from producing the synthesis, is simply derived from it. Its condition of possibility is not itself genetic. The description of the becoming of arithmetical meanings will only attach itself to secondary accidents, to elements that are accessory. Meanings are not constituted in an empirical becoming. So one is referred to a nongenetic *a priori.*

But even if it is intentional, this *a priori* must not be a formal concept; it must be synthetic. Now, there is no synthesis without genesis. So to which other genesis are we referred, and what is the response of Husserl here?

The Refusal of an Aporia

His reply is, in appearance, deliberately psychologist, that is, insufficient, but is, in fact, much more complex, containing virtually the whole of the subsequent sense of phenomenology. Applying himself to the ideas of equivalence and difference and to their relations with number, Frege had arrived at the following aporia:[38] If we look for the origin of number in an *a posteriori* system of concrete "different" objects, we obtain an "accumulation" and not a number. In this sense, it could be said that the constitutive unity of every number must be originarily given in order for the differences and the singularities of concrete objects to undergo an "abstraction"; the formal equivalence that will result from this will authorize number. But, conversely, if the possibility of this formal and theoretical equivalence is primary, if it *alone* is essential to the constitution of numbers, these will not be distinguished one from the other; none of them will have a content or a specific sense; arithmetical syntheses and operations will be impracticable, number will not appear. All the paradoxes of genesis are present here. Historical or psychological genesis of number does not suffice to explain the advent of arithmetical meaning. The pure concept of number has to be presupposed, as does Frege, before the psychological operation that "presents" it or "uses" it. But it is apparent that this concept, once defined in its purity, calls for an actual genesis to fulfill itself and take on sense. The accumulation of accidents can only produce a unity if the "equivalence" of accidents is presupposed. But if this equivalence is not determined by a concrete object or by a concrete essence (sensible object and essence of number), if, as concrete, it is not in some way synthetic or genetic, then it will never produce an arithmetic unity. For the equivalence that Frege invokes was an "*a priori* synthesis." Because it was *a priori,* it preceded any actual synthesis; because it was synthetic, it was already produced by a genesis. It was constituting only because it was *already* constituted. This originary synthesis refers to a genesis of essences that is concrete but not historico-psychological. It will give rise to a whole going-beyond by phenomenology of the logicism-psychologism debate in instituting a "neutral" domain of lived experience. Husserl's solution here prepares this going-beyond. Husserl opposes a description to Frege's conceptual antinomy.[39] He says that only singular and different things can be bound together in a totality, but in the totality as such, in its own meaning, there is no "difference" strictly speaking. Numeration supposes an "essential" distinction and not "real" difference. To grasp a number in a multiplicity, each of the singular objects is subsumed under the concept of "something in general." Numbers are born from an abstraction starting from "aggregates" whose elements are equal to one another "in some way." Collective association and the concept of "something in general" suffice to constitute number. Starting from concrete "aggregates," we ignore all the singular characters of objects, except the fact that they are "contents" *(Inhalt)*,[40] that is, an actually real "something." The intentionality of consciousness, as Husserl emphasizes, means this "something" to be concrete and irreducible to the formal equivalence that Frege speaks of. If we say that Jupiter, an angel, and a contradiction are "three," it is because they each have a concrete unity of an object, but that insofar as they are singular contents, they are each of them different. The equivalence is produced by an abstraction; it is not, as Frege wanted, presupposed by every abstraction. Frege has confused identity and equivalence. The latter is compatible with a difference in the concrete and singular determination of the object. Two numbers designating different objects can be equal. Thus, according to Husserl, the aporia that Frege formulated would be resolved. What has actually happened?

The "Something in General": Necessity of a Concrete "A Priori"

In one sense, Husserl has founded the value of the genetic viewpoint, since he has shown that the "collective association" and abstraction were real acts, indispensable for number to appear. Any essence of number refers to the act of its production by a concrete subject that is able to have a psychology and a history. The psychogenetics of arithmetic would thus be legitimated. But if the ultimate justification of the genesis of number is examined, then one perceives that it is this "something" in general that makes the arithmetical unit possible and, consequently, the abstraction that appears to give birth to it. Now, here, this possibility is *a priori;* if one wished to deduce or to construct the possibility of "something in general," one would already have to presuppose some other objectivity in general. The ultimate foundation of objectivity cannot be deduced empirically or psychologically. Is there a moment when a multiplicity of singular and empirical abstractions engenders generality? Is not the essence of that generality that founds every concept irreducible to a genesis? Is the moment when this generality appears to be produced by a logical or psychological "operation" a moment in history? Does it belong to empirical time in the usual sense of the term? The objectivity of the *a priori* concept and the essence of generality are irreducible to the empirical subjectivity that appears to produce them and only "reproduces" them. Once again, genesis appears accessory; it has only a complementary and quasi technical role in the birth and the operations of arithmetic. Apparently, genesis produces unity of sense; in fact, sense itself determines genesis *a priori*. How can Husserl, at the prephenomenological level that is still where he is at, come to terms with this contradiction between a psychologist doctrine and a logicist foundation?

It is surprising to see how Husserl, far from cutting down the complex sense of the debate, adapts his description to it with a meticulous suppleness: although produced by an abstraction, number is not a determination that is abstract and conceptual—Husserl refuses the nominalisms[41] of Mill, Helmholtz, and Kronecker,* according to whom numbers are supposed only to be "ciphers," that is, signs, names given to a multiplicity of practical objects; the "common" name of things which are two is "two." Number, Husserl answers, must not be an abstract sign, otherwise it is not clear how it would refer to concrete unities; it is not clear why each of the objects composing a multiplicity, three, for instance, would not be designated by the adjective "three." For it is not clear either how the number might be a simple predicate of real multiplicity, as Sigwart makes of it.

Thus, number is not a concept. Concluding thus, Husserl is in contradiction with the principle of psychological genesis, which can produce only concepts, but he is in agreement with a description that is already phenomenological, that respects the original signification of phenomena. His thought is distinguished from the narrow psychologism of Mill and Sigwart as well as from the antipsychologism of Frege; besides, psychologism and antipsychologism join together in the same unfaithfulness to the phenomenological meanings from which they start out, without acknowledging it. For Frege, the possibility of number was an *a priori* concept. As such, this concept was not, it goes without saying, "in experience." As in Kant, it referred to a formal and transcendental subject, starting from whom an empirico-psychological genesis became impossible or suspect. So much so that, finally, Frege ended up in aporias when he wanted to pass to a concrete determination of number—and he had to. Against his will, he was then reduced to making a predicate out

---

*J. S. Mill, Hermann von Helmholtz, and Leopold Kronecker. *Trans.*

of number and almost an exterior sign out of the thing. Thus, he came back to the empiricism from which he had tried so hard to separate himself. The law is already verified according to which, every time one refers, as Kant does, to a nonphenomenological *a priori*—that is to say, at the end for Kant, a nonempirical one—one is obliged to introduce the constituted into the transcendental consciousness, and one makes it impossible for oneself to understand the founding relation between the transcendental constituted and the psychological constituted. What Husserl will call later a transcendental psychologism is adopted.[42] The whole sense of the Husserlian attempt that is to come relies on the possibility of an empirical and phenomenological *a priori* (in the originary, non-Kantian, sense of the word). The *a priori* synthesis will then no longer be the object of a judgment but of an intuition.

But before the doctrine of the intuition of the *a priori* synthetic essences (since these are at the same time originarily distinct and absolutely indissociable from the facts), the use of an empirical *a priori* appears contradictory. If in the subsequent stages of his thought, Husserl will try to illuminate the sense of this contradiction itself, he maintains for the moment, as best he can, its two terms in association and juxtaposition. If he concedes to a logicist apriorism that numbers are not attached to objects as a qualification or characteristic, and if he takes into account here an original objectivity of essence (anticipating *Logical Investigations* and all the later themes), he maintains, however, that objects of perception are originarily bearers of number (and announces here the doctrine of the perceptual filling of eidetic intuition[43] and of the antepredicative sensible core as the ultimate substratum of sense[44]). If the existent is thus bearer and primitive foundation of essences, then the historical and psychological genesis of the acts aiming at the object according to one or the other mode is itself the support for the appearance of the arithmetic sense. The multiplicity of objects in themselves does not determine the totality and the unit. But the sense of the totality or the unit does not exist *a priori* outside objects or outside the "real" psychological act that poses it. When Husserl has realized that this psychological act, if it is real *(real)*, cannot produce the evidence of sense and remains constituted by another subject, when he has situated the act of the subject in a "neutral" sphere of lived experience, we will have attained the phenomenological level. For, just as he will do vigorously in *Ideas* I,[45] Husserl already does not allow himself to realize essences—here the arithmetical essences—separately and outside experience. The essence of number is *a priori*, but this *a priori* is concrete. It will then be able, when the doctrine of intentionality is more elaborate, to be given to an intuition. Thus, the possibility of an objective logical meaning and of a formal symbolism founded on "originary donor acts"[46] is already left open and legitimated. The primordiality of concrete operations and of genesis is safeguarded along with this abstraction starting from immediate perception.

But has it not been safeguarded in confusion? Husserl has not yet thrown light on all the presuppositions of his descriptions. It is evident that since he accepts implicitly the terms in which the problem has already been posed around him, and since he has operated neither a transcendental reduction nor an eidetic reduction, nor worked out any doctrine of the intuition of essences, then if his descriptions stay acceptable, his systematic "solution" and the doctrinal interpretation that he works out from them are highly fragile and contradictory. How can at the same time the conceptual *a priori* character of number be denied, "'numbers in themselves' *(Zahlen an sich)*"[47] be considered, and it be maintained that numbers are originarily "borne" both by concrete objects (of which it is not known whether they are already synthesized) and by those psychological acts of abstraction that produce numbers starting from objects? Where are these numbers "in themselves," where is the constituting source of arithmetical essences? Are these latter already constituted? Then genesis does not produce them. Does genesis produce number? This is only an empirical concept and needs an *a priori* formal concept whose originary constitution refers to a formal sign in order to have objective value. In both cases, recourse is had to an abstract form, either an eternal essence of number about which one wonders how a psychological act can attain it and use it, or a formal and intemporal subject, about which one will not be able to understand how it authorizes the psychological act of numeration. However, it does seem that Husserl's contradictory solution is the only one that respects and that restitutes the irreducible givens of the problem through a minute description: the simultaneous possibility of an objectivity and of an empirical genesis of number, of a "real" creation of sense and of its original "appearance" to consciousness.

Intentionality—An Insufficient Explicitation

After the *Philosophy of Arithmetic*, Husserl's whole effort will be to bring to light the postulates of a description, whose initial sense, at least, he will conserve, if not its content. Intentionality of consciousness, as it will be understood a little later, would have allowed the reconciliation of the act of the constituting subject and the objectivity of logical meaning. Without intentionality, a psychological genesis, a series of subjective acts constructing *a posteriori* the sense of the object, cannot have due regard to conceptual abstraction. Since the relations of consciousness and the world are always constructed, determining the absolute origin of this construction is the same thing as denying oneself the possibility of understanding its movement and making the passage from subject to object impossible. The value of a synthesis *which links a posteriori* the subjective act and the sense of the object is never assured. Sometimes the subjective act makes the objectivity of meaning doubtful. As Husserl shows in *Logical Investigations,* one winds up in a relativist skepticism. Sometimes, the logical and objective meaning being given *a priori,* the subjective operation that reconstructs it remains suspect and mysterious; perception and logical steps that are real seem to degrade the purity and the necessity of ideal forms.

On the other hand, if the intentionality is originary, consciousness is then immediately objectifying. It does not have to join up with an objective sense through a series of procedures and detours. It is intentionality that makes possible *a priori* a "something in general," which is not an abstract logical form bringing up the same problems as Frege's identity or equivalence. In a word, only intentionality founds the "*a priori* synthesis" and, through this, a genesis of number. Essence can then be simultaneously *a priori* and concrete: the act that apprehends it can be at the same time enriching and necessary.

But, for this, intentionality has to be described in its absolute originarity—something that Husserl does not do in the *Philosophy of Arithmetic.* He does talk of "intentional analysis," but the reason that these analyses seem so fragile to Frege and that Husserl abandons their principle himself later is that he was still caught up in a psychological intentionality whose idea was inherited too faithfully from Brentano: constituted intentionality, meaning or structure of consciousness, a character attributed to a substancelike subject. The problem remains insoluble: Through what *a priori* synthesis will this power of intentional objectivity be identified with mental life [*psychique*]?

The problem could not be resolved unless transcendental intentionality was turned into a theme. In a sense, Husserl, on the threshold of his career, asks the same question as Kant: How is an *a priori* synthetic judgment possible? But he is at the same time beyond and before Kant; he is before and below the critical problem, because he asks the question in psychological terms, that is, in empirical ones. But, in another sense, he has already gone beyond it, since the notion of intentionality—virtually developed—offers him the possibility of escaping from the formal constructivism of Kant. Paradoxically, it is because he is psychologistic at the level of the *Philosophy of Arithmetic* that he will later escape Kantian psychologism; this latter will consist in limiting the possibility of *a priori* synthesis to the nonempirical or mathematical realm and in cutting the empirical genesis off from *a priori* necessity. It [Kantian psychologism] will be constrained to this by the conception of a formal and nonintentional subject.

Going Beyond and Making Deeper

Around 1891, Husserl is still far from having examined in depth the theme of intentionality. The criticisms[48] that his book meets push him to abandon his psychologism. As Husserl will do later, Frege calls this psychologism "naive."[49] Further, and this is the essential point, he has nothing but sarcasm for this "something in general" that comes along, in contradiction to the empiricism of numeration, to save concrete perception or the abstraction of an infinite scattering through the series of subjective acts. And in fact, it is difficult to see, from inside a psychologism, what is the status of an "object in general" and of what Frege calls the "bloodless ghost." Is it constituting? Is it *a priori* or "abstract"? This essential ambiguity is reproduced afterward at every level in Husserl's analyses. It expresses already the irreducibly dialectical character of a genesis that is at the same time productive and revealing of a sense, preceding and constituting, that appears as necessarily already there. In the *Philosophy of Arithmetic* Husserl thematizes the effective genesis without setting out to examine its *a priori* conditions of possibility and the objective signification of what it has produced. But we have seen how research was slanted in this direction by the themes of intentionality and of "the something" in general. By deepening its examination of itself at every moment, psychologism put itself in question. Genesis referred back to an *a priori* foundation.

Husserl, as dissatisfied with his psychologism as he was with the mathematicians' logicism, gives up his researches on arithmetic. The second volume of the *Philosophy of Arithmetic* never appeared. Since the genesis of essences from psychological subjectivity has failed in part to give account of logical objectivity, it is the irreducibility of these last that he must now try to elucidate. "Logic left me in the lurch whenever I hoped it would give me definite answers to the definite questions I put to it, and I was eventually compelled to lay aside my philosophical-mathematical investigations, until I had succeeded in reaching a certain clearness on the basic questions of epistemology and in the critical understanding of logic as a science."[50] The method adopted had not allowed him to find out "how to reconcile the objectivity of mathematics and of all science in general, with a psychological foundation for logic."[51] Thus, in a certain sense, Husserl starts on the road of a pure and simple refusal of a psychological genesis of essences. We have seen how this refusal was contained in virtual fashion in the *Philosophy of Arithmetic*—the theme of intentionality that will preside over the analyses of *Logical Investigations* bears witness to [this] continuity and faithfulness. Objectivity of essences will once more refer to a constituting subject that will no longer be psychological but logical.[52] Like the psychological subject, this subject will reveal itself insufficient to constitute objectivity, or at least, the genesis and infinite becoming of logic.

3

The Dissociation
The Abandoning of Genesis and the
Logicist Temptation

Thus, after the publication of the *Philosophy of Arithmetic* and the discussions that followed, the insufficiency of a psychogenetic explanation appeared clearly to Husserl. Taking the opposite tack to that of his preceding researches, in *Logical Investigations* (vol. 1)[1] he proposes to show that logically objective entities cannot be reduced to psychological acts that aim at them or seem to produce them. In a series of articles,[2] Husserl is seen to move slowly toward the conception of a "pure" logic, to which *Logical Investigations* I is to serve as "Prolegomena." In his preface, Husserl retraces the reflection that led him to abandon his psychologism. In this way, he was led to undertake "general critical reflections on the essence of logic, and on the relationship, in particular, between the subjectivity of knowing *(die Subjektivität des Erkennens)** and the objectivity of the content known *(die Objectivität des Erkenntnisinhaltes)*."[3] Husserl had just tried to make a genetic passage from one to the other, but "once one had passed *(Übergang)* from the psychological connections of thinking *(des Denkens)*, to the logical unity of the thought-content (the unity of theory) no true continuity and unity could be established."[4] So, definitively giving up psychogeneticism, which he will now put himself to upset radically, he quotes Goethe: "There is nothing to which one is more severe than the errors that one has just abandoned."[5]

---

*All German inserted in quotations follows J. D.'s practice unless otherwise indicated. *Trans.*

The "A Priori" Unity of Logic

Wondering about the *a priori* possibility of a pure logic outside any conditioning and any historico-psychological production, Husserl begins by recognizing the insufficiency *(Unvollkommenheit)* of particular sciences considered in their multiplicity.[6] These latter refer to their foundation in a metaphysics or a theory of knowledge.[7] The theoretical unity of all sciences, the formal condition of possibility of science in general, must constitute a special science, a "theory of science" *(Wissenschaftslehre)*. This is logic. Logic must be normative. Its task is to determine what properly constitutes the idea of science.[8] But although it is normative, logic is not originarily a "practical art" *(Kunstlehre)*.[9] The practical norms are legitimated by theoretical propositions, ideal logical laws exist independently of every application to objects.

A difference can be perceived here, the difference between formal logic, which interests Husserl here, and transcendental logic, which he will try later to show is the origin and foundation of all logic. While formal logic is here considered in its origin as essentially independent of concrete experience and of any practical "application," transcendental logic will appear at the very heart of an originary experience.[10] It is only after the first volume of *Logical Investigations* that the objectivity of logical forms, held to be independent of the psychological act that aims at them, will appear insufficient and will reveal to us a constitution by a subject who is neither psychological nor logical, but transcendental. It can be said that, right up to the end of volume 1 of *Logical Investigations,* the problem remains posed in terms of psychologism and logicism; to go beyond one of these systems in absolute fashion is to go beyond the other. The neutralization of this alternative will be the phenomenological neutralization of lived experience [*vécu*], the idea of which appears for the first time in volume 2 of *Logical Investigations.* Without a concrete transcendental subject—described in its neutral lived experience—it is as futile to want to found the objectivity of meanings on a psychological subjectivity as to claim that they are accessible and usable by a logical consciousness that must be at the same time psychological and historical. Defining the propositions of a theoretical logic independently of any concrete application to objects presupposes a natural and psychological definition of the application. The latter is the action of a constituted subject on constituted objects; that also presupposes logical essences already constituted before the act of every consciousness; Husserl, bringing together in this way psychologism and logicism in the same condemnation, will show later that every subject, when it encounters in this way forms which have been constituted before it, is an empirical and "worldly" subject.

It can be suspected [from this] that the absolute opposition of logicism to psychologism, such as seems to be revealed in volume 1 of *Logical Investigations,* will be the motive for a radical going beyond [this position]; once again, this will not be a simple dismissal, but a progress in the description of concrete subjectivity and of objective meanings that an insufficient thematizing of intentionality places in opposition, like two poles closed in on themselves.

Defending Psychologism and Going Beyond It

Not having reached the level of transcendental constitution, Husserl must still ask himself[11] whether the "essential and theoretical foundations of normative logic depend on psychology." Reflecting about a complete logic that would be only self-referring, it is difficult to see how it can give rise to [logical] operations. Perhaps it is necessary that this logic at its origin be invented and inaugurated by a mind in a "mental life [*psychique*]." Concepts and judgments, deductions and inductions, classifications that the logician is concerned with, belong to mental life. Their sense is purified and formalized by real acts; affirmation or negation, error or true judgment which are necessary to the constitution of any formal logic are nothing outside the real [acts of] intervention, comprehended in a real historical becoming whose laws are given us by psychology. This is, at least, the psychologist thesis that Husserl exposes rigorously before refuting it. It is the thesis of Mill: "Logic is not a science separate from and coordinate with psychology. To the extent that it is a science at all, it is a part or branch of psychology, distinguished from it on the one hand as the part is from the whole, and on the other hand as the art is from the science. It owes all its theoretical foundations to psychology."[12] It is the thesis of Lipps, for whom logic is an "integral element" *(Bestandteil)* of psychology: "The fact that logic is a specific discipline *(Sonderdisziplin)* of psychology distinguishes them satisfactorily from one another."[13] To give psychologism all its force, Husserl emphasizes[14] that the classical arguments do not stand up to a coherent psychologism. So, following Kant,[15] there will be an attempt to distinguish logic by its normative character; logic is opposed to psychology as morals are opposed to life. In fact, Husserl answers, the "as it should be" is only a special case of being and it can be said, with Lipps, that the laws of thought do not allow this distinction; the rules of thought are "identical with the natural laws of thinking itself." "Logic is a physics of thinking or it is nothing at all."[16]

But does not the ambivalence of the term "law" or "rule" *(Gesetz)* authorize us to say of logic that it is not the physics of thought but its ethics?[17] On the one hand, laws would be said to define the necessity of intellectual operations, conceived as "real connections of mental events with one another."[18] The laws would be those of psychological genesis as such. On the other hand, the laws would determine the *a priori* possibility of the relation of this genesis to truth. The two domains of legality would be distinct and independent. But if it is considered, as it already has been, that the "must be" is a simple specification of being,[19] such a separation becomes purely methodological; now, it is the case that no psychologist has denied that the object of logic, considered as method, was different from the object of psychology. Only, logic is a "technology of knowledge."[20] Moreover, the modalities of a technique can be determined only by starting from the natural conditions of its exercise. Ideality is only a mediation by which a character of completed evidence is conferred on concrete operations, a character that is itself defined by a natural determinism. Any technique is founded on a physics; any possible formalization refers to this physics.

Husserl already refuses the "logicist" reaction to such a psychologism; this reaction leads to a vicious "circle"[21] (whose only solution would be a dialectic assuming the two contradictory theses and uncovering their foundations in a genesis understood differently. But at the level we are now at, this dialectic would not be able to escape confusion). The reply has indeed been made to the psychologists[22] that if logic had to appeal in the last resort to a psychology that is already systematic, the constitution of psychology itself as an empirico-deductive science already implied recourse to logical forms whose validity has been recognized; those concepts established *a posteriori* by a supposedly experimental science presuppose formal *a priori* concepts; the reply is thus Kantian: it is a formal *a priori* synthesis, whose purity is also found in mathematics, which makes possible any *a posteriori* synthesis and any *a priori* analysis. It is very significant that Husserl rejects this solution. The *a priori* synthesis from which he wants to start does not seem to be that of a judgment and of a formal concept, but indeed that of an experience that is originarily concrete. The whole future development of phenomenology is anticipated in this refusal. Intentionality and transcendental genesis will restore the debate between psychologism and logicism by resituating it at an originary level. Is it not in vain that both intentionality and transcendental genesis set up as opposites to themselves a psychology and a logic whose origin remains as obscure to the one as to the other? In the "worldly" perspective, that of an already completed science, immobilized in objective concepts and techniques, any solution is impossible. In the same way as psychology supposes an implicit logic, the experiencing *(erfahren)* of logic as science, that is to say, its human praxis, its explicitation by a subject, closes us into the same circle. It is natural experience that must sanction or found the "value" *(Triftigkeit)* of logical laws. Coming to a conclusion about the sense of this "circle," Husserl cites the example of the artist who "creates" without knowing anything about aesthetics[23] considered as a system of rules and values; may not the scientist construct and synthesize a discourse without appealing to Logic? In the same way, logical laws can exist without their explicit premises. The "moment" where logic and psychology are opposed is a constituted moment that is second. Husserl will later say that it is the long "sedimentation" and the structures superposed by tradition that forbid any exit from the problem and any access to an originary genesis. Probably the idea of penetrating the very opacity of traditional structures by a "historico-intentional" analysis is not yet ready. But Husserl already defines the necessity of a "regression" *(Rückfrage)* toward the originary "premises." The problem of genesis, he already senses, escapes from the antinomy of logic and psychology; the example of aesthetic creation *(Schaffen)* sketches out lightly the originary creation *(Leistung-Schöpfung)*[24] of sense that Husserl will later describe after a transcendental reduction. The authentic problem of genesis will not be able to be correctly posed except in the transcendental sphere. We already know, through having confronted psychologism with logicism, that we cannot content ourselves with either an empirical genesis (in the Kantian sense), understood by an empirico-deductive science, or with an ideal or transcendental genesis ("transcendental" in the Kantian sense), which would not give an account of an "experience" of logic that is originarily temporal. The genesis of sense must go beyond the antinomy of a formal *a priori* and a material *a posteriori*. Intentionality will again serve as "mediation" for such a going beyond. It is to this that any "appeal" will be made. But only an "appeal" will be made. It will not yet be the originary seat of a transcendental phenomenology, only the "structure" and the "sense" of a consciousness that is no longer psychological, but logical first and above all. This will encumber the debate with ambiguities somewhat similar to the preceding ones. Husserl seems to recognize it: "It seems to me that the greater weight of truth lies on the anti-psychologistic side, but that its key-thoughts have not been properly worked out, and are blemished by many mistakes."[25] It may be very original, but what comes to light in the first volume of *Logical Investigations* is nonetheless a very decided logicism. It will call up a return to lived subjectivity; this will be neither logical nor psychological but phenomenological and will totally renew the problem of genesis. How is this subjectivity required by an antipsychologism and the idea of a pure logic?

Psychogeneticism Is an Empiricism

Psychology is defined as the "science of psychic phenomena, of the facts *(Tat-sachen)* of consciousness, of the facts of internal experience *(innere Er-fahrung),* of experiences in their dependence on the experiencing individual."[26] Psychology is a "factual *(Tatsachenwissenschaft)* and therefore an empirical science."[27] Hence psychology is incapable of formulating "exact" laws. The laws that it enounces respond only to "vague" generalizations of experience, formulating the "approximate regularities of coexistence and succession."[28] If the natural sciences are vague, they are not empty. "Even natural science has vague 'laws' in many disciplines, particularly in such as are concrete. Meteorological laws, e.g., are vague yet very valuable."[29] Thus, for example, the laws of association of ideas, [the laws] to which it has been intended to give the place and sense of fundamental psychological laws, lose all their value of laws as soon as it is attempted to formulate them rigorously.[30]

How can a becoming that is purely psychological or "natural" produce or let rigorous essences appear if it presents only "vague" and approximative determinations, as such and in its content? The genesis of exactitude starting from the "vague" is impossible. Discontinuity is essential and insurmountable. Approximation as such will never reach its end if it is not an *a priori* approximation of something and if rigor is not a sort of originary and *a priori* horizon for it. It is because this horizon stays veiled for it that psychologism turns the movement of genesis into the only explanation, without accounting for an initial sense that is "already there." Genesis is enlightening because, as genesis, it requires a sense which it itself has put forward and [yet] which is eluding it.

Once again, vague synthesis or *a posteriori* synthesis appear against the background of an *a priori*. But if the *a priori* concept did not refer to a concrete essence, one accessible to an intuition, if the *a priori* was not given to a certain "experience," if the *a priori* synthesis was not constructed by a formal judgment, the procedure by which Husserl opposes "exactitude *(Exactheit)*" to the "vague" would once more resemble a Kantian critique.[31] And, in fact, the points of departure are close together. In the same way that Kant begins by refuting Hume, so Husserl begins by dismissing psychologism as empiricism.[32] This for three essential motives.

The Three Empiricist Motives

"The first is that only vague rules could be based on vague theoretical foundations."[33] Logical laws are often confused with vague empirical notions. But, in the strict sense of the term, "the laws which are pointedly called 'logical,' which as laws of proof make up *(ausmachen)* the real core *(Kern)* of all logic—the logical 'principles,' the laws of syllogism, the laws of many other kinds of inference, as e.g. equational inferences, the Bernouillian argument from *n* to *n* + 1, the principles of probability-inferences and so forth—are of absolute exactness."[34] "Plainly they are genuine laws, and not 'merely empirical,' i.e., approximate, laws."[35] A pure logic cannot be produced by an empirical genesis pure and simple.

So—this is the second motive—logical laws and laws of nature must be distinguished. "No natural laws can be known *a priori,* nor established by sheer insight, *einsichtig erkennbar.* The only way in which a natural law can be established and justified, is by induction from the singular facts of experience. [. . . The laws of 'pure logic'] are established and justified, not by induction, but by apodeictic inner evidence."[36] Thus, the law of gravitation, the fruit of "inductions and of verifications"[37] today is bereft of universal value. It is proved by making other factors intervene: yet these factors are in infinite number; "we know *a priori* that endlessly many laws could and must do the same work as the Newtonian law of gravitation."[38]

But it would be "foolish" ever to want to "remove" imprecision from natural "observations." It is essential to the sciences of facts; it is absolutely not essential in logic. "The justified possibility of the former becomes the open absurdity of the latter."[39] Logic gives us access, not to probability pure and simple, but to the truth of laws. "But if what follows from a demand for a psychological validation of logic is absurd, this validation is itself absurd."[40] Against that truth itself which we grasp by our intelligence, the most powerful psychologist line of argument cannot prevail. Psychological facts and accidents *(Umstände)* can produce nothing but empirical generalities. "Psychology certainly does not yield more, and cannot for this reason yield the apodeictically evident, and so metempirical *(überempirisch)* and absolutely exact laws which form the core of all logic."[41]

But there is something more important, deeper. If it is supposed that there is a genesis of rigorous logical essences out of the life of the psyche [*vie psychique*], must there then not be recourse to another genesis in order to distinguish between psychic life and logical activity inside the same subject? If a single and same type of genesis is envisaged, then the logical act can no longer

be made out against the background of psychic life nor especially can the logical "act" be distinguished from a logical "content."[42] If, conversely, there are
two geneses, then to save the unity of the subject, the one will have to precede the other in some way, and we come back to the same problem:[43] How
can the unity of genesis be reconciled with the *a priori* specificity of essences?
"Where," asks Husserl, "are the descriptive and genetic analyses which enti-
tle us to explain the phenomena of thought by two sorts of natural law,
one exclusively determining such causal sequences as allow logical thought
to emerge, whereas others help to determine *(mitbestimmend)* a-logical
thought?"[44] Husserl shows himself concerned to safeguard the sense of psychological genesis and the objective value of logical essences without spoiling
the unity of the subject. Does he succeed here?

It seems that in the first volume of *Logical Investigations* he does so by
having recourse to a logicist formalism that in principle he already rejects,
[but] that in fact he will only reject later. What can the unity of a nonpsychological subject be? If mental events as such, along with the totality of mental
life [*vie psychique*] pure and simple, are powerless to produce objective logical syntheses, we are obliged to have recourse on the one hand to a preconstituted logical form, which eludes any genesis, and thus obliged to have recourse to a formal logic, on the other hand, correlatively, [we are obliged to
turn] to a pure "I," a formal power of objectivity, also independent of any historical production. We fall back into a Kantianism; formal logic and the formal "I" that are already constituted outside time are held to be originary: it
is a transcendental psychologism. Because one wanted to free oneself from
every actual genesis, one lands in the least acceptable [type of] constructivism. The "genetic analyses" by which Husserl ironically asks the psychologists to describe the appearing of the unity of psychic and logical life, or the
passage from one to the other, are still impossible in his eyes; precisely because
there is no "real" genesis of logic out of the psychological, of the essence out
of the fact, of the idea out of the real, and so forth. Because the antithesis is
still between the real and the formal, the natural and the logical, and so on,
any genesis seems to spoil the sense or the reality of one or the other. It is because the struggle is still with constituted objects: logical essences are "canonized"[45] in a system of laws and principles; the mental facts are events
already freighted with a sense, classified, oriented, identified. Hence, no
mediation between essence and facts by genesis appears possible. Constitutive analyses situated this side of facts and constituted essences have not yet
allowed Husserl to throw a suitable light on their originary relations. The
possibility of a transcendental constitution in a phenomenological domain,

one that is "neutral" and "originary" in relation to the logical and the psychological, has not yet been brought out. The return to subjectivity, which will be sketched out in the second volume of *Logical Investigations,* will be the answer to the present difficulty. This constituting subjectivity will no longer be a psychological or logical subjectivity, but will be one that is already transcendental.[46] It is at its level that the problem of the "genetic analyses," which are here refused by Husserl, will reappear, and that obstacles will re-arise. The formal and the real, before a phenomenological elucidation, are at the same time irreducible to one another, hence the impossibility of any genesis [at all], and yet like each other because the two are either this side of or else beyond the lived time of an originary constitution. They are both secondary and derived. In the same way that a formal logic presupposes a transcendental logic, psychological subjectivity implies a transcendental "ego." In one sense, the logicism of the first volume of *Logical Investigations* has definitively gone beyond the psychologism of the *Philosophy of Arithmetic.* Husserl will never go back to it—at least in intention. But to the degree that the *a priori* that he opposes to it remains in many ways formal and constituted, to the extent that intentionality has a logical character and the intuition of concrete essences is still absent, logicism remains intimately at one with a psychologism. Both forbid the thematization of an authentic transcendental genesis, one because it gives everything to an empirical genesis, the other because it refuses everything to such a genesis. One makes of genesis a pure enriching, a creative synthesis, an *a posteriori* synthesis that inhibits the appearance of any necessary essence; the other makes of genesis a historico-empirical accident that not only does not produce logical meaning but is accessible only by a previous logical objectivity.

This difficulty is secretly behind the whole of the critique of psychologism. Presenting the third empirical motive of psychologism, Husserl writes: "Even the strict laws of the natural sciences are not without factual content. They do not merely concern facts, but also imply their existence."[47] It is for that reason that they are "vague." Exact laws in their normal formulation evidently have the character of pure laws; they do not hold any existential content in themselves.[48] Thus, exactness is formal. Now, it is not known how this exactness, envisaged in its objective aspect, can be the correlative of a subjective act, nor how the formal "I" to which recourse has to be made can have access to the existence of the object. Besides, this impossibility is the same in both cases. The *a priori* form cannot receive a necessary empirical determination. Its agreement with sensible intuition must be *a priori* determined as well. The problem is only put off. Only an intentionality that can be at the same time both sensible intuition and categorial intuition can throw light on this *a priori* determination. But it is still hidden. So the genetic or synthetic relation[49] that links form to an eventual content is still formal. A classic infinite regress seems inevitable. How does Husserl escape this? Through an appeal to a confused intentionality that always resembles the criticist "objectivation."

The Logicist Reply to the "Something" in General
The *Fundamentum in Re*

"All laws of fact in the exact sciences are accordingly genuine laws, but, epistemologically considered, no more than idealizing fictions with a *fundamentum in re*."[50] "Such systems as theoretical mechanics, theoretical acoustics, theoretical optics, theoretical astronomy and so on, really only hold as ideal possibilities with a *fundamentum in re*."[51] This *fundamentum in re* is very strange. What is the origin of the "real" determination and of the "real" foundation of ideal possibilities that have not been induced or produced by abstraction out of empirical facts? How is the *a priori* purity of these forms determined *a priori*? Why is Theoretical Mechanics a theory *of* Mechanics, Theoretical Astronomy a theory *of* Astronomy? No answer seems clear without recourse to an intuition of essences. So the *cum fundamento in re* is the substitute for a concrete intentional aiming at essences. *Mutatis mutandis*, it plays the role that the "object in general" played in the *Philosophy of Arithmetic*.

It is a sort of *a priori* category of objectivity in general. It intervenes suddenly to save thought from a psychological subjectivism, which would confuse its shortcomings with those of an idealist logicism. The one would be deprived of all "objectivity," the other of any "real" foundation. If theories are "pure," if they are not constructed by abstraction and generalization, then which is the *a priori* synthesis that accords them with natural experience, with the facts of which they are the essence? Neither the theories nor the synthesis that relates them to experience must be at the origin of the empirical activities, of the psychological acts of abstraction and subsumption; without a concrete intuition of essences—which are themselves as such *a priori* syntheses and which will later pose a similar problem—the ideal "fictions" always risk being the creations of an empirical genesis. It is conceivable, then, that they can give an account of the experience that has engendered them; the synthesis that links them with their factitious content is also *a priori* because the idealizations are "fictions" that, as such, are not distinguishable from an empirical content.[52] But idealities are then neither pure nor rigorous. The same aporias hold us prisoner. In the contrary hypothesis, ideal fictions can also be *a priori* concepts; pure and rigorous, they are prior to any empirical construction. But as a result of this, they are *a priori* abstract; at what moment and through what synthesis are ideal possibilities, intemporal and meta-empirical, going to be able to determine an empirical reality? What would be the foundation of this synthesis? Is it an ideal synthesis or a real synthesis? Ideality being already constituted, like reality, our logicism could just as well also be identified with a psychologism, its apparently irreducible opposite. In both cases, in asking about the *a priori* sense of genesis or the *a posteriori* genesis of sense, we end up in a dilemma. The three motifs, because of which psychologism appeared to be merged with an empiricism, are three motives for which logicism must also be merged with an empiricism, or be in danger of having no sense. An irreducible ambiguity remains present, although it is hidden throughout the vigorous polemic that Husserl conducts against psychologism.

Psychologism—Formalism—Finalism

Analyzing the psychologist interpretation of the fundamental principles of logic,[53] Husserl shows that it is incapable of giving account of the objectivity attached to such principles. It does not go further than vague non-apodictic propositions. Hence, for Mill[54] the principle of contradiction, an easy and primitive generalization of experience, "is taken [...] to be the fact that belief and disbelief are two different mental states which exclude one another." Husserl has no difficulty in denouncing the psychologist aberration that has led Mill to such a proposition: "all the gods seem to abandon Mill's otherwise keen intelligence."[55] As Husserl summarizes it, the real *(real)* incompatibility of acts of judgment *(Urteilsakte)* has been substituted for the impossible coexistence *(Nichtzusammenwahrsein)* of two truths.[56] Thus, the principle of contradiction cannot be the product of an act nor of a multiplicity of real acts of subjectivity; it is not created by an empirical induction. Is it *a priori*? But this objective *a priori* must not be formal. Husserl himself will not allow it.[57] Evoking Lange's efforts[58] to set up an original formal logic in the manner of the psychologists, Husserl brings them together with the Kantian project. At the limit, the "foundations of our intellectual organisation" to which Lange appeals are reduced to the "faculties of the soul" *(Seelenvermögen)* as a source of knowledge in the Kantian system. "For even transcendental psychology *also* is psychology."[59] All these theses come together at the end. Hume's or Mill's psychology, the anthropological relativism of Sigwart[60] and especially of Bergmann,[61] change the sense of truth as much as do the formalism of Kant or of Lange.

But it seems once again that Husserl refutes these two only by dint of an oscillation. All the psychologisms, he says, lead to skepticism because "the self-evident [*idéales*] conditions of possibility of a theory in general"[62] cannot be derived from experience. But the status of these ideal conditions that must be neither formal nor empirical is not yet worked out. The ideal conditions that are founded neither on a psychological genesis nor on a formalism nor on a transcendental psychologism imply a constitution of an original kind that is still absent. The thesis of Husserl remains critical. The prejudices of psychologism are denounced or dissipated[63] without any explanation being given as to the origin and the concrete situation of *a priori* possibilities. As in a Kantianism, the *a priori* seem to escape any constitution. Later, it will be precisely the concrete and transcendental constitution of these *a priori* that will interest Husserl. In this period, any idea of subjective constitution seems to be tainted with empiricist geneticism in his eyes. Before proposing a definition of pure logic, he puts aside the psychologism of Cornelius[64] and the teleological conception of the *Denkökonomik*[65] of Mach and Avenarius,* who wish to give an account of the principles and laws of science through the principle of least action or of economy of thought. Science is said to be a pragmatic adaptation by man to his milieu. Idealities are said to be signs, the laws of economical and fertile generalizations that start from empirical diversity. Husserl does not absolutely reject such a finalism. This latter is not without a certain explanatory value; it can probably throw some light on technical procedures and scientific methods.[66] But in no case is such an "interpretation" valid for the laws of pure logic. "The question is not how experience, whether naive or scientific, arises *(entsteht)*, but what must be its content if it is to have objective validity."[67] The genesis of which Husserl will speak will never be confused with a real *(real)* production and becoming. But for the moment, it is the thematization of *every* genesis that is inhibited. Any empiricism is already abandoned and "put in brackets," before that notion is invented:

> We must ask on what ideal elements and laws such objective validity of knowledge of the real is founded—more generally, on what any knowledge is founded—and how the performance *(Leistung)* involved in knowledge should be properly understood. We are, in other words, *not*

---

*Ernst Mach and Richard Avenarius. *Trans.*

interested in the origins *(Werden)* and changes *(Veränderung)*[68] of our world-presentation *(Weltvorstellung)*, but in the objective right *(Recht)* which the world-presentation of science claims as against any other world-presentation, which leads it to call *its* world the objectively true one. Psychology looks for perspicuous explanations of the formation of world-presentations. World-science *(Weltwissenschaft)* (the sum total of the different sciences of the real) wishes to know perspicuously what obtains in reality, what makes up the true, the actual world. Epistemology, however, wishes to grasp perspicuously, from an objectively ideal standpoint, in what the possibility of perspicuous knowledge of the real consists, the possibility of science and of knowledge in general.[69]

<h1 style="text-align:center">The Becoming of Logic
Prefiguration of a Teleology</h1>

There is a double resonance in this declaration. On the one hand, it presupposes a critical attitude and a concern to make clear the limits and the *a priori* conditions of possibility of any objective knowledge prior to any empirical determination. In fact, Husserl recognizes, in this sense, the relation of his plan with that of Kant. He feels himself, he says "more akin to Kant's conception of logic"[70] than to that of, say, Mill or of Sigwart. But Husserl reproaches Kant with having conceived pure logic as a set of immobile and definitively constituted forms, from a point of view that is not foreign to that of Aristotle and the scholastics.[71] Here Husserl wants to show what separates him once more from Kant. Logic is a pure infinite possibility.[72] Its becoming cannot be determined and delimited beforehand without danger of identifying logical laws with realities constituted in a time and in a space. This idea of an infinite horizon of logic, which prefigures the teleological idea of an "infinite task of philosophy," an idea that will appear only thirty years later, is the first appearance in Husserl's philosophy of an infinite (always synonymous with indefinite). It will always come in a rather mysterious way to put off a difficulty and to get over an aporia.[73] Here, it allowed Husserl to escape from a scholastic or Kantian formalism while still maintaining Kant's "critical" question. But we have a right here to ask ourselves how and where Husserl, who refuses to consider a genesis and a history of idealities, can situate the constituting source of a logic that is never completed. If in a Scholastic or Kantian perspective, invoking a closed, rigorous formal system, constituted for eternity, the putting in brackets of every historical genesis is authorized, this remains contestable in principle, but coherent. If, on the contrary, logic is a pure possibility, open to the infinite, then a concrete becoming of logic has, it seems, to be granted existence and credit. Because this becoming is not empirical, what is its status?[74] Because Husserl does not define it yet, it is impossible to say that he actually gets over the alternative between a formalism and a psychologism, which finish by meeting up. The neutral domain of phenomenology not being open, the domain between the ideality of time as Kant conceives it and the "real" temporality of the psychologists, between these two faces of one and the same "constituted" time, it is not clear yet to which constituting temporality Husserl is appealing. He accuses the theorists of the *Denkökonomik* of using a ὕστερον πρότερον;[75] but does he not doubly beg the question in criticizing the real genesis of the psychologists in the name of *a priori* formal possibilities and in rejecting a formal logic constituted in the name of a becoming of logic? But such a begging of the question is not a discursive sophism or a rhetorical error; nor is it an aberration of method or a logical confusion. Only, the phenomenological theme which, at the end of Husserl's life, would in some way be merged with the teleological theme, is still hidden. It is the only motif that could have given a unity to the Husserlian idea of logic at the level of *Logical Investigations* I.

The Idea of Pure Logic
The Necessary Return to a "Neutral Lived Experience"

When he tries to give a positive definition of the idea of a pure logic,[76] it is always through the same ambiguity that the phenomenological theme, which will at first take the form of a return to constituting subjectivity, is announced. The purity of which Husserl speaks is sometimes formal purity, sometimes concrete purity, sometimes conceptual, sometimes essential. Of the one, it can be affirmed that it escapes any empirical genesis, but Husserl does not appear satisfied by this. Of the other, it is impossible to say anything definitive before having brought to light a "neutral" temporality where the becoming of essences will not compromise their "rigor." Husserl takes up the idea of theoretical unity of Knowledge[77]: "we are not dealing with the proof of a factual, but of a *general* truth. . . . The proof of general laws necessarily leads to certain laws which in their essence, i.e., intrinsically, and not merely subjectively or anthropologically, are not further provable *(nicht mehr begründbare Gesetze)*. These are called *basic laws (Grundgesetze)*."[78] To define these fundamental laws outside any real genetic process, their generality necessarily must not be constructed. Some concrete, nonpsychological, intuition must determine them as laws of one or another ontological domain.[79] They must not be originarily conceptual, but only concepts founded on essences accessible to an experience that is still not perceived. If the experience is concrete, the purity of fundamental laws constituting the unity of theory must definitively escape from the formal abstraction of logicism and the empirical facticity of psychologism. Husserl evokes this going beyond only from afar. The whole "task" *(Die Aufgabe)* that he traces out for pure logic: the fixing of categories of meaning, of pure objective categories and of their "complications" in laws, the determination of laws and of the theories that are founded on these categories, the theory of possible forms of theories or the theory of pure multiplicity invites us implicitly—if one wants to escape the perils that are being denounced—to leave the level of classical philosophy. In keeping to simple psychology and to simple logic, one cannot know whether pure concepts were created by a real genesis or whether the real genesis presupposed pure *a priori* logical forms in order to be understood and to be organized in objective experience. It was not possible to choose between a genesis of sense and a sense of genesis.

The research is thus oriented toward the elucidation of these pure possibilities which must be possibilities of experience. For this, they must be constituted by the subject to whom they appear in their objectivity. They must be produced *in* a concrete becoming that appears to itself and must be *a priori* the sense of this becoming. This will be the proper theme of phenomenology. The radical autonomy and the absolute objectivity of logical meanings lose all validity if this objectivity does not have as an essential and originary correlative the act of a subject who, though it is not "empirical" (in the classical sense of the term), is nonetheless concrete. They no longer allow the determination of domains of research, the authorization of deduction and induction. They no longer "relate" to experience. The logical and scientific enrichment is impossible; it remains empirical and "vague." So it is not possible to avoid the rigidity of a scholastic logicism except by describing a genesis of meanings that might do something more than reconcile, that might weave richness and rigor the one with the other. Up till now it was only a question of a dilemma. There had to be a choice between becoming and essences. The former led to an empirical and factitious temporality; it was psychologism. What presupposed an ideality and an "emptiness" of time was logicism. In both cases, the origin and becoming of logic was missed, in a word, its genesis. It was only a matter of inert and opaque products. One found oneself confined in a world of mediations, of derived concepts, of secondary and constructed meanings. The dilemma was, above all, confusion. Husserl will not seek to cut the knot of the dilemma, but to throw light on the confusion. By assimilating and assuming the most legitimate, the most well-founded discourse of psychologism and logicism, he plans to bring to light a domain of constitution that is neutral and absolutely originary, where logic and psychology, both engendered and founded, resolve their opposition. Is then the serious problem of genesis, which up till now appeared insurmountable, going to disappear? Will not the same and irreducible paradox be found once more at the level of primordial constitution?

PART II

THE "NEUTRALIZATION" OF GENESIS

4

Noematic Temporality and Genetic Temporality

Access to Phenomenology, the Neutral "Lived Experience"

In spite of the return to lived experience and to constituting and temporal subjectivity, it seems that the difference that separates the two volumes of *Logical Investigations*[1] is less serious than has been implied. Doubtless, with *Logical Investigations* II the properly phenomenological level is reached. The great phenomenological themes are present: transcendental intentionality, the distinction between noesis and noema, intuition of essences, eidetic reduction. But all the problems that are studied from this moment on until 1919–20 still remain problems of "static" constitution, in spite of the great importance that the analyses of the consciousness of time acquire here. It is only after this date that the themes of genetic phenomenology will be unavoidable for Husserl.

But the appearance of genetic research was not a revolution in the thought of Husserl. It had been prepared, called forth by a long period when the genetic theme is "neutralized," kept absent from phenomenological description. In fact, it seems to us that it is the difficulty of this "neutralization" that animates the whole movement of Husserl's thought from 1901 to 1919–20.

We have seen that the constituting lived experience in its very temporality must be neither psychological nor logical. Hence, to the degree that any genesis is still envisaged by Husserl as a psycho-physiological causality belonging to the domain of an empirical science, the heart of the phenomenological reduction will be attained paradoxically only by a "reduction" of genesis. In this sense, the first volume of *Logical Investigations,* signifying the dismissal of psychologism and of historicism will be seen to be prolonged very late.[2] So the neutralization of genesis gives itself as the going-beyond of the irreducible dialectic between logicism and psychologism. How was this neutralization able in turn to be caught up in a new dialectic? Why was this future return to the genetic point of view inescapable right from the first moments of phenomenology? In what way did the refusal or the neutralization of the "worldly" genesis imply the unveiling of a transcendental genesis that, *mutatis mutandis,* will pose the same problems all over again? In a word, why is the radical distinction between "worldly" genesis and transcendental genesis, which gets underway from 1900 to 1920, already proving difficult? These are the questions that we are going to try to pose.

Constituted History and Constituting Temporality

History and psychology are then assimilated one to the other by Husserl. Both are sciences of facts, dealing with constituted events. Their limits merge. The rejecting of psychologism is simultaneously a rejecting of historicism. History cannot judge an idea, and when it does, this evaluating *(wertende)* history surreptitiously borrows from the ideal sphere those necessary connections that it claims to draw from facts.[3] How can Husserl at the same time conceive a history constituted in its very meaning, by something other than itself, and an originarily temporal lived experience such as is analyzed in the *Vorlesungen zur Phänomenologie des inneren Zeitbewußtseins?*[4] How can he reconcile the idea of a concrete and originarily temporal subjectivity with the idea of a secondary and constituted genetic history? How can genesis be "constituted" only if temporality is "constituting"? Is the "ideal sphere" from which a genetic interpretation must borrow its meanings temporal or atemporal? If it is atemporal and originary, subjectivity can no longer be simultaneously constituting and temporal: if it is temporal, then it is purely historical and psychological; if it is constituting, then it must be reduced to the ideality of a formal "I think." It seems that Husserl wishes to safeguard this double essence of the most radical subjectivity, insisting more on the transcendental originarity in *Logical Investigations* and in *Philosophy as a Rigorous Science,* more on the temporal character in the *Vorlesungen.* In these last, the alternative acquires all its sharpness: the search for the originary temporality ceaselessly contradicts the abandoning of genetic history.

The Reduction of Objective Time

"As soon as we make the attempt to account for time-consciousness, to put Objective time and subjective time-consciousness into the right relation and thus gain an understanding of how temporal Objectivity—therefore, individual Objectivity in general—can be constituted in subjective time-consciousness—indeed, as soon as we even make the attempt to undertake an analysis of pure subjective time-consciousness—the phenomenological content of lived experiences of time [*Zeiterlebnisse*]—we are involved in the most extraordinary difficulties, contradictions, and entanglements."[5] According to a now well-established method, Husserl causes his research to be preceded by a reduction and a "putting out of circulation" *(Ausschaltung)* of objective time, by the "complete exclusion of every assumption, stipulation, or conviction concerning objective time (of all transcendent presuppositions concerning existents, *aller transzendierenden Voraussetzungen von Existierendem*)."[6] "Just as a real thing or the real world is not a phenomenological datum, so also world-time *(Weltzeit),* real time, the time of nature in the sense of natural science including psychology as the natural science of the psychical, is not such a datum" . . . so "what we accept [...] is not the existence of a world-time, the existence of a concrete duration, and the like, but a time and duration appearing as such."[7] What remains after this putting out of circulation is thus phenomenological duration, immediate apperception of time that constitutes the only possible and valid beginning, the only originary certainty of a reflection on time; "The evidence that consciousness of a tonal process, a melody, exhibits a succession *(ein Nacheinander)* even as I hear it is such as to make every doubt or denial appear senseless."[8] This clear evidence is purely immanent to subjectivity. Before any existential thesis, the absolute evidence of phenomenological "sense" seems possible and necessary. However, in order that subjectivity not be purely psychological, closed in on itself, in order that it should not be a product constituted by a more originary temporality, intentionality must in this immanence be respected in its entirety and, with it, the immediate constitution of temporal objectivities such as the past, the future, and so on. For example, the past, as it is constituted in an immanent consciousness of time, will be a temporal objectivity that should be distinguished—this is the nub of the difficulty—from the "real" *(real)* temporal objectivity excluded through the reduction. "One cannot discover the least trace of Objective time through phenomenological analysis. The 'primordial temporal field' is by no means a part of Objective time; the lived and experienced [*erlebte*] now, taken in itself, is not a point of Objective time, and so on. Objective [*Objektiver*] space, Objective time, and with them the Objective world of real things and events—these are all transcendencies [*sic* for *Transzendenzen*]."[9] How will an intentional consciousness of time, producing itself and appearing to itself dialectically through retention and protention, and through a play between constituting and constituted, be accessible to a purely immanent apprehension? Will what is already constituted *in* the internal consciousness of time be given in an absolute phenomenological clarity of evidence and of the same type as the one just evoked? This temporal evidence is not immobile. Does not its essential movement consist in continuously escaping from itself toward the objectivity that it is constituting, starting from the objectivity that it has just constituted? What essential difference is there between the transcendence of moments constituted inside the pure flux of lived experience in relation to an originary "now" and the transcendence of "real" objectivities of time? "The nexuses of order which are to be found in lived experiences as pure immanences are not to be encountered in the empirical Objective order. They do not fit into this order."[10] The empirical order is the always already constituted order. Now, if it is recognized, as Husserl will, that the originary "now" appears only through a passive synthesis of time with itself and through an immediate retention of the past, that the present is constituting only because, in emerging from the radical newness of an immediately constituted past, it roots itself in it and appears to itself as present only against the background of its passive continuity with the former moment, then one has the right to pose the following question: What radical discontinuity is there between this already constituted past and objective time that imposes itself on me, constituted without any active intervention on my part? Husserl will not pose this fundamental question in the *Vorlesungen*. This is because he remains here with a noematic temporality, whose sense is *already* constituted and known.[11] Objective time is already known as such, and, its meaning being "thematic" already, it can be situated and put in brackets. In the same way, the time of lived immanence already has a sense *for me;* it is constituted by a deeper temporality that does not appear yet. Hence, the only essential difference between these two temporalities constituted as "noemata" is that one has already appeared to me as "mine," the other as objective. We are still at a superficial level, where the subject and the world are already constituted as such. Their genesis is completed. The inadequacy of all pregenetic constitutive analyses is already very apparent: a world and a constituted objectivity are "excluded," and instead of making an absolutely constituting origin appear, constituted products are still retained. It is even in the name of secondary meanings that the reduction is performed. The attitude that commands all the analyses of "static" constitution is hence "naive" and participates to a certain degree in psychologism and historicism as it itself defines and rejects them.

The Origin of Time

Indeed, Husserl claims to distinguish between a psychological and a phenomenological origin of time. The debate between "empiricism and innatism" is possible only by starting from a psychological question where "we are asking about the *primordial material of sensation out of which arises Objective intuition of space and time* in the human individual and even in the species. We are indifferent to the question of the empirical genesis [...] Psychological apperception, which views lived experiences as psychical states of empirical persons, i.e., psycho-physical *subjects,* and uncovers relationships between them, and follows their development, formation, and transformation according to *natural laws*—this psychological apperception is something wholly other than the *phenomenological.*"[12] What, then, is phenomenological apperception? Everything that Husserl puts aside under the name of "psychological" is real event, belonging to the transcendent world. These are the facts that have a situation in time. But as such, they teach us nothing about the pure laws of time. They are constituted for us starting from a lived time which originarily is not "part" of real time. If this were not the case, time would not appear as such to us. It is hard to see how starting from a simple natural and existential time, the consciousness of time would be possible. On the contrary, it is in this consciousness that the objectivity of time as sense for us is constituted. There is no doubt at all that temporal lived experience can, at one moment or another, be studied as constituted fact, as psychic event, as historical cause or effect. But it can only be studied as such against an originary foundation of phenomenological time. It is with the description of this time that we must begin: "We do not classify lived experiences according to any particular form of reality. We are concerned with reality only insofar as it is intended, represented, intuited, or conceptually thought. With reference to the problem of time, this implies that we are interested in *lived experiences* of time. That these lived experiences themselves are temporally determined in an Objective sense, *that they belong in the world of things and psychical subjects* and have their place therein, their *efficacy,* their empirical origin and their being—that does not concern us, of that we know nothing."[13] Even if we made a mistake about the situation, the role, the real determination of these temporal objectivities, even if in the final analysis they did not exist, the essence of time would be accessible to us. It is the idea of fiction and of imaginary variation, always part of the eidetic reduction. This reduction, which, excluding the factitious content of a meaning, brings out the purity of its "eidos," now has to be operated on temporal lived experience. "We try to clarify the *a priori* of time."[14]

The Psychologism of the "Originary Association"

Brentano had taken on the same problem.[15] But in trying to explain the origin and the formation of time through psychological laws established *a posteriori,* he had never succeeded in giving an account of the original production of time and of the irreducible differences of the diverse temporal lived experiences—past, present, and future (not to mention anything other than the principal specifications of temporal consciousness). No doubt, the analyses of Brentano mark a very decided progress in relation to preceding attempts; they describe, thanks to the idea of "originary association," the whole complexity of temporal processes. The "originary association" is "the genesis of the immediate presentations of memory [*Gedächtnisvorstellung*] which, according to a law that admits no exceptions, are joined to particular presentations of perception without mediation."[16] But this "double" which thus attaches itself automatically to every experience in order to detach itself afterward and to constitute the experience as a "past" cannot be absolutely originary. Two opposed movements are sketched out in it that cannot be grasped as such in an originary consciousness of time. "When, for example," says Husserl,

> a melody sounds, the individual notes do not completely disappear when the stimulus or the action of the nerve excited by them comes to an end. When the new note sounds, the one just preceding it does not disappear without a trace; otherwise we should be incapable of observing the relations between the notes which follow one another. We should have a note at every instant, and possibly in the interval between the sounding of the next and empty [*leere*] phase, but never the idea [*Vorstellung*] of a melody. On the other hand, it is not merely a matter of presentations of the tones simply persisting in consciousness. Were they to remain unmodified, then instead of a melody we should have a chord of simultaneous notes or rather a disharmonious jumble of sounds. . . .[17]

This dialectical life of temporal consciousness, uniting continuity and discontinuity, negation and promotion of self, going-beyond and conservation, appears as such, according to Husserl, only because of the impurity of an analysis that mixes empirical and originary. The difficulties it gives rise to derive from the fact that it is conducted from a genetic point of view, that is to say, psychologist (for Husserl, let us not forget, the two notions are still inseparable). It is genetic because it makes a real creation *ex nihilo* intervene in the constitution of time. From where can Brentano extract this double of experience which is thus "repelled" as past when the experience itself is no longer there? Does not Brentano introduce into experience a time exterior to it, one that comes to add itself to experience as a "character" or a "factor"? Such a genetic hypothesis ends in the idea of a creation of time through mental [*psychiques*] processes; these being already temporally constituted by definition, they cannot in turn engender or constitute time. And in fact, Brentano, as a decided psychologist, attributes the productive source of temporal representations to the faculty of the imagination. It is the imagination that holds the keys to the domain of absence in general and can conserve or retain a vanished experience to transform it into a "past," to anticipate an experience to come in order to produce the representation of the future. Husserl does not hold back from pointing out the lack of logic of such a hypothesis. On the one hand, it is not clear how an originarily atemporal experience, identical to itself in an absolute and flawless present,[18] can afterward receive a temporal determination from the outside. We would be in danger of making a mistake at every moment, as we localize one or other memory in the past; we would constantly mix together experiences and their images in the greatest confusion; the evidence of the past[19] and the essential possibility of a future would present no absolute guarantee, since they would be constructed by an activity of the imagination. Expectation and memory would be mixed together.[20] On the other hand, how could an imagination, an exclusively "reproductive" faculty, engender the absolute novelty of a present? The latter, an originary and clear evidence if ever there was one, cannot be constructed or reconstructed by a psychological faculty. Is not then the road open to make out of the past and the future "unreal" entities *(Nichtreellen)* with Brentano? "A supervenient psychical moment cannot make something non-real, or get rid of what presently exists"; time cannot thus be constructed from what is not time. Imagination is *a priori* temporal; it neither creates nor constitutes time. All the psychological moments that are "associated" to produce the formation and representation of time were already constituted in their temporality before any other possible constitution. The law of originary association is a "psychological law concerning the new formation of psychical lived experiences on the basis of given psychical lived experiences. These lived experiences are psychical, they are Objectified, they themselves have their time, and the point at issue is their generation and development. Such matters belong in the sphere of psychology and do not interest us here."[21] Any genetic explanation can thus be applied only to the domain of the "constituted." Genesis being only derived from constitution, this latter is static in its essence.

How can the constitution of lived time and temporal objectivities appear static if one does not limit oneself to an eidetic analysis of lived time in which the essence of time takes the place of time itself? It is time *as it appears* as "noema" or as a theme; it is the *a priori* law of temporal unfolding; in a word, it is the meaning of time that is static and that authorizes the whole of Husserl's analysis. But we know that any eidetics is constituted by a temporal subject, that any "noema" refers to a "noesis," that the meaning of time appears to a consciousness and against the background of a deeper temporality. If a separation between essence and fact appears possible in other ontological regions than that of consciousness, it seems that the eidetic reduction of lived time separates what is not separable in essence. The "eidos" of lived time is itself temporal, constituted in a temporality. It appears static only if it is uncoupled from the temporality where it is founded. This last is genetic in essence (but here essence has no need of an eidetic reduction in order to appear. It even excludes it *a priori*).

If certain flaws are removed from Brentano's theory, for example, the intervention of the faculty of imagination, it is still the case that in its most valid discourse, it tried to institute time starting from a dialectic of what constitutes and what is constituted, where the terms were at the same time distinct and yet stood together. Time appears as constituting phenomenological time only because it is constituted. Now Husserl, after having criticized Brentano, claims to keep exclusively to the constituting origin of time. Would he not be constrained, through a description that will also be dialectic (in the phenomenological sphere), to bring back the constituted into the constituting and to make of genesis a necessary moment inside the originary field? Phenomenology would no longer be quite mistress in her own house. Ontology would be *already* inside the fortress.

The problem of genesis, we said, was merged with that of a lived *a priori* synthesis, that of an enrichment and of a creation which were at the same time revelation or unveiling, that of an ontological productivity which was merged with a phenomenological transparency. Now, will not the analyses of lived time offer us the spectacle of a continual *a priori* synthesis where the temporal enriching and novelty are possible and appear as such only through a "retention" that assumes what has just been constituted in the preceding present? That this constituted phenomenological time is different from temporal objective facts is too obvious. I can reactualize immediately through memory the original sense of a constituted lived experience. But indeed, the eidetic reduction was applicable to material facts. In making this reduction on some piece of lived experience, are we not moving toward a twofold failure: on the one hand, if the eidetics of the region of "consciousness" is assimilated to that of the region "thing," every time a lived experience is constituted, it will become pure empirical facticity. And to the degree to which the unfolding of lived time presupposes necessarily the retention of a constituted moment, both in order to bring itself about and to appear to itself, the "fact" will be introduced into the internal consciousness of time. Conversely, if the irreducible originality of lived experience is taken into account, and if one refrains from assimilating constituted lived experience to the constituted world, the eidetic reduction becomes impossible. It no longer has any foundation, existence and essence not being separated from each other in the sphere of the consciousness. Are not the empirical or ontological geneses (which we do not identify with each other but which are both distinguished from phenomenological becoming) both essentially implied in the analyses of lived experience? Husserl does not think so.

The "Originary Impression"

Once the putting out of circulation of objective time has taken place, we are nevertheless still faced by purely temporal objects.

> It is indeed evident that the perception of a temporal Object itself has temporality, that perception of duration itself presupposes duration of perception, and that perception of any temporal configuration whatsoever itself has its temporal form. And, disregarding all transcendencies, the phenomenological temporality which belongs to the indispensable (*unaufhebaren*) essence of perception according to all its phenomenological constituents still remains. Since Objective temporality is always phenomenologically constituted and is present for us as Objectivity and moment of an Objectivity according to the mode of appearance (*erscheinungsmäßig*) only through this constitution, a phenomenological analysis of time cannot explain the constitution of time without reference to the constitution of the temporal Object. By *temporal Objects* in this *particular sense,* we mean Objects that not only are unities in time but also include temporal extension in themselves.[22]

Thus, for example, sound that resonates is a "temporal object." If the object's unity, insofar as it is constituted, serves as an intentional or transcendental "guide" (the expression that Husserl will utilize later) for a constitutive analysis, it is their temporal extension itself that is the final object of our description. The temporal object is constituted out of the "originary impression"[23] of the pure hyletic given; a retention and a protention unite the series of originary impressions in order to make an object out of them.[24] It would be the same for a melody, an objective totality of sounds. In order for a melody to be perceived, it is necessary that I retain the past sounds and anticipate the sounds to come. But what I retain or what I anticipate is not real;[25] otherwise we would not be able to disengage ourselves from a perpetual present. This is the essential difference between phenomenological lived experience and psychological lived experience or facticity in general. Because it "appears to itself" and through its essence, phenomenological "reality" *(reell)* is radically other than natural "reality." Retention does not define the persistence of a weakened impression but a "quasi" presence of the past.[26] What is true of a melody is true of a sound on its own; I cannot reduce an originary impression to the purity of a real point, and that is a matter of essence. The absolute point is still less perceptible in time than in space.[27] We cannot speak, as we can in psychology, of a threshold of sensation or perception. It is an *a priori* necessity of the perception of time and of the time of perception that an originary impression have some temporal density. As a result, absolute originarity is *already a synthesis* since it implies *a priori* a "retentional modification."[28] Husserl does not present the *a priori* necessity of this synthesis as ontological—and especially not as real—but as phenomenological. Which is to say that the originary impression is not sensation taken at the most elementary physiological level, but the originary impression in the immanent consciousness of time. But so that this originary impression may be intentional (which it has to be, of course, since retention and protention are described as intentional modifications by Husserl),[29] must it not as such "announce" a real object that is constituted in the same way since it is aimed at originarily? Does not the impression have to be originarily an impression *of* the melody or *of* the sound as *real,* even in the case of a hallucination? Is not the unreality of the "quasi" sound in retention constitutive of the phenomenological temporality because it is in its origin founded on the reality *(real)* of the sound already constituted? Is not the *a priori* phenomenological synthesis possible through an *a priori* synthesis that is ontological, fundamental, and more originary than the noematic lived experience? Not that the phenomenological synthesis is the simple "effect" or the simple "reflection" of a primordial synthesis; should this be the case, we would relapse into the difficulties discussed above. But, once again, can it not be said that phenomenological originarity maintains a dialectical relation with what is not it? In a certain sense, it is because there is a constituting consciousness of time that the "real" sound is constituted in an objective unity. This unity is in this way a production of con-

sciousness; but it is also because it appears as already constituted in its very being, prior to any noematic synthesis, that consciousness can experience originary constitution according to an attitude that could be called intuitive. Here,
the ambiguity of any intentional movement appears: production and receptivity, creation and intuition, activity and passivity. This ambiguity will stamp
all Husserl's thought with a dialectic mark. Here, the sensuous or hyletic datum of sound cannot be constituted by the subject's activity.[30] As soon as the
pure content of sensation is admitted as the correlate of an originarily intentional impression, is not passivity already about to be introduced into the primordial constitution? Is not the theme of passive genesis, taken up fifteen
years later by Husserl, already announced? When Husserl recognizes an "*a priori* necessity of the precedence of [...] impression over the corresponding retention"[31] and when, on the other hand, he maintains that retention presents
originarily a character of intentional evidence,[32] does not he reintroduce, in
the form of the "hyletic datum" passively received, the transcendent object
that he claimed to exclude from his analyses? This seems to be confirmed by
this text whose "exceptional" sense in the *Vorlesungen* seems to contradict all
the methodical idealism of its context. We will quote at length:

> In perception a complex of contents of sensation, which themselves
> are constituted unities in the primordial temporal flux, undergoes
> *(erfährt)* unity of apprehension. And the unitary apprehension is in
> its turn a constituted unity in the first sense. We are not conscious of
> immanent unities in their constitution in the same way that we are
> conscious of what appears in transcendent appearance or of what is
> perceived in transcendent perception. On the other hand, they must
> still have a community of essence. For an immanent impression is an
> act of presentation *(Gegenwärtigen)* just as perception is. In the one
> case we have an immanent presentation, in the other a transcendent
> presentation "through" *(durch)* appearances. Therefore, while tran-
> scendent appearances are unities constituted in internal conscious-
> ness, other unities, namely, *the appearing Objects,* must again be con-
> stituted "in" these unities.[33]

Thus, through the constituted appearings, it is the object itself, already synthesized, that appears; it is more than an appearing, it is the origin and foundation of every appearing. It is the being itself of time which is aimed at
through the temporal "noema." As Husserl will emphasize later, if there is an
originary reference from the "originary impression" to the object "given in

person,"[34] the ultimate foundation of intentional analyses, then the retention or "primary memory" implies in its synthesis the passive intuition of such an object. Now, it seems incautious to say, as for example does Ricœur,[35] that the activity and passivity of intentional consciousness do not resemble in any respect real activity and passivity in a system of natural causality. Husserl abides, no doubt, by this distinction, and to this degree Ricœur's commentary has to be accepted. Moreover, it is clear that intentional consciousness cannot be purely and simply introduced as an element into such a system.[36] But if the object of intentional consciousness, being always originarily a "real" substratum and not merely "noematic," if originary passivity—at the level of the *hylé*—is passivity in the face of "nature," then one wonders where the discontinuity between phenomenological passivity and natural passivity is to be situated. Here once again we need to opt for a dialectical description of the solidarity and essential distinction between these two "moments." For if passivity is placed inside a constituting sphere of activity, the problem is only pushed one stage back. This is a formalist temptation and Husserl will give in to it later. There is, for the moment, a continuous passage from perception to primary memory. "In an ideal sense, then, perception (impression) would be the phase of consciousness which constitutes the pure now, and memory every other phase of the continuity."[37] But just so, this is only an ideal limit, something abstract which cannot be anything in itself: "Moreover, it is also true that even this ideal now is not something *toto coelo* different from the not-now but continually accommodates itself thereto."[38] The originary and constituting present is thus absolute only in its continuity with a "non-present" that is at once constituted before it, through it, and in it. The originary synthesis is precisely one of constituted and constituting, of the present and the non-present, of originary temporality and objective temporality.[39] The temporality of immanent lived experience must be the absolute beginning of the appearance of time, but it appears to itself precisely as absolute beginning thanks to a "retention"; it inaugurates only in tradition; it creates only because it has a historical heritage. It seems then illegitimate to exclude right from the start of reflection any temporal transcendence and any constituted unity of time. The act of exclusion cannot be pure; it is originarily retentional.

Freedom and the Clear Evidence of Retention

The freedom of the reduction seems then limited *a priori* by the temporal necessity of retention. I cannot not make a temporal act out of an act of my freedom. To the degree that this act lasts, it must negotiate with the determinate temporality that it "retains," with the history that it assumes, in order to know itself as a free act. Its impurity is originary because it is *a priori* temporal. However, Husserl wishes to reconcile the subject's absolute freedom with its lived temporality. Here we see confirmed the idea we were putting forward earlier: Husserl is describing only a time constituted as a noema or as a theme in front of a subject whose genesis remains hidden.—This subject being itself constituted, it can appear atemporal and free in relation to a temporality that it "knows." "The presentification *(Vergegenwärtigung)* of a lived experience lies *a priori* within the sphere of my 'freedom.'"[40] Without this originary freedom, no clear evidence from memory would be possible as such; starting from empirical determinations, I can actualize only a past retained and reproduced in the form of habit; but I cannot escape from the absolute and perpetual present of experience to aim intentionally at a past as such. A radical freedom, that is to say, an absolute source of decision, is the *a priori* foundation of any phenomenological temporalization where becoming constitutes itself *as such.* But this freedom itself, though it may not be abstract and formal, must be itself temporal and made possible by a retention, in order to get back a concrete memory referring to an actual perception where the world has been given "in person." It must not be "pure" in the Kantian sense, that is to say, characterized in itself by the absence of any temporal (empirical) and actual determination. If it were thus abstracted from any concrete temporality, it would be the analogue of that imagination invoked by Brentano. It would become a separate faculty and be itself constituted as psychic fact. No *a priori* clear evidence of time and its concrete modifications would be possible starting out from there. Thus, this constituting freedom must be merged with time itself temporalizing "itself." Husserl will himself say that the constituting flux of time is absolute subjectivity.[41] But Husserl is still far from having brought out the absolute originary synthesis that unites absolute subjectivity and absolute temporality.[42] For the moment, he oscillates between the two poles of the synthesis. Freedom must not be a simple product of time[43] and a moment that is constituted in it. Under such a hypothesis, the diversity of the modifications of the temporal flux would not be able to appear. Once more, one would be submerged in a natural time, which is substantivized, cut off from its first source. Freedom and absolute subjectivity are thus neither *in* time nor *out* of time. The dialectical clash of opposites is absolutely "fundamental" and is situated at the origin of all meaning; thus, it must be reproduced at every level of transcendental activity and of the empirical activity founded thereon. Any authentic language, for example, must take on an *a priori* ambiguity.— Nothing can be designated or defined without immediately postulating an absolutely opposed discourse. Any philosophical discourse seems to have to be marked by this necessity. To cease to be "marked" by it and to assume it indefinitely, that is what seems to us to define the veritable "infinite task," the "practical idea" of philosophy.[44] In the *Vorlesungen*, Husserl is content to leave this domain of originary consciousness, which seems to escape from all eidetics and then from all "Logos," under a veil, like the ineffable; alluding in the shortest of his paragraphs to the identity of the constitutive flux of time and of subjectivity, he concludes: "For all this, names are lacking."[45] Whether time is included in subjectivity or comprehended by it, whether it envelops it, on the contrary, and determines it, it is still time constituted as atemporal "eidos" or as natural reality. Starting from it, no phenomenological time can appear as clarity and evidence. Hence, if it is said with Husserl that the pure flux of lived experience is absolute subjectivity, it cannot be a question of an immediate confusion, of a tautology or a formal identity. Subjectivity is not that attribute which is analytically linked to the being of time; nor is temporality the character or, at best, the essence of subjectivity. On the contrary, it is a question of an *a priori* synthesis that is ontological and at the same time dialectical. Subjectivity is time that itself is temporalizing *itself*. Time is subjectivity fulfilling *itself* as subjectivity. "Reflection" is not here secondary and mediate. It is not *a posteriori*, an empirical enriching or an ideal "becoming conscious."

The difficulties that Husserl will meet when he wants to reconcile this absolute subjectivity of dialectical time with the monadic "ego," which is also posited in *Ideen* I as an absolute subjectivity, can be guessed. How can this "ego" be considered as absolute unity of all the lived experiences if the unity of time and subjectivity is *already* synthetic and dialectic? Temporal dialectics constitutes alterity *a priori* in the absolute identity of the subject with itself. The subject appears to itself originarily as tension of the Same and the Other. The theme of a transcendental intersubjectivity setting up transcendence at the heart of the absolute immanence of the "ego" has already been called for. The last foundation of the objectivity of intentional consciousness is not the intimacy of the "I" to itself but [is] Time or the Other, those two forms of an existence that is irreducible to an essence [and] foreign to the theoretical subject, [two forms] always constituted before it, but at the same time, the only conditions of possibility of a constitution of self and of an appearance of self to self.

The Originary Impression and the "A Priori" Synthesis

But Husserl does not thematize and make explicit this dialectic as such any more than he ever does. The oscillation remains confused at the level of simple descriptions like those of the *Vorlesungen*. It is not clear where phenomenological time begins. Is it produced by a passive synthesis or by an active synthesis? Is it given to a atemporal subject? Constituted by it? Is it "lived" right from the hyletic moment or starting from the originary impression? And how does the passage from one to the other take place? Husserl does not answer this clearly. Sometimes the originary impression is the "absolute unaltered";[46] as such, it constitutes time and constitutes itself outside any retention and any protention; the subjectivity of pure time is anterior to any synthesis and any genesis. Dialectic is derived, constructed merely at the level of reproduction and secondary memory. But one no longer understands then how retentional and protentional modifications are still possible out of an originarity that is not modified. It is even harder to see where they will draw their phenomenological evidence from. Sometimes, on the contrary, each new Present is the content of a possible originary impression. But it does seem that this *a priori* possibility is empty and formal. No concrete lived experience corresponds to this but only a "boundary-point."[47] "It is evident that every temporal point has its before and after, and that the points and intervals coming before cannot be compressed in the manner of an approximation to a mathematical limit, as, let us say, the limit of intensity. If there were such a boundary-point, there would correspond to it a now* which nothing preceded, and this is obviously impossible. A now is always and essentially the edge-point *(Randpunkt)* of an interval of time."[48] Hence, in contradiction with the idea of an unmodified originary impression, the phenomenological Present is only pure and only appears to itself as such insofar as it is genetically composed.

The alternative is pursued. The absolute "subjectivity" of pure temporal flux is sometimes a transcendental consciousness, sometimes substantial temporality and "in itself," sometimes that activity from which the diverse temporal lived experiences are constituted, sometimes the substratum of all the phenomenological modifications of time. "It belongs to the *a priori* essence of the state of affairs *(Sachlage)* that sensation, apprehension, position-taking, all share in the *same* temporal flux and that Objectified absolute time is necessarily the same as the time which belongs to sensation and apprehension. Pre-Objectified time, which pertains to sensation, necessarily founds the

---

*Churchill's translation of *jetzt,* translated as "Present" in Derrida's commentary. *Trans.*

unique possibility of an Objectivation of temporal positions which corresponds to the modification of the sensation and the degree of this modification. . . . In the same way, the time of the perception and the time of the perceived are necessarily the same."[49] So what are the origin and status of this *a priori* necessity? It is neither exclusively objective, nor absolutely subjective; it brings together *a priori*, it seems, preobjective time, the pure being of time, and phenomenological time, the pure appearing of time. But it does so according to an identity that Husserl does not speak of and that anyway seems to have no analytical quality; between preobjective time and phenomenological time, which itself "appears" as source of objective temporal units [*unités*], there is nothing less than the constitution of these objectivities themselves through the processes of retention and protention. It is thanks to these that preobjective time, pure phenomenological time, and objective time "appear" as one and the same time. Now, if phenomenological time in its very essence implies preobjective time and objective time, how can it be "reduced" to its purity and, in that purity, "appear" to itself?

The Aporia—Necessity of an "Enlarged" Reduction

At certain moments Husserl presents the problem in the guise of a veritable aporia, which a deeper reflection could resolve. Thus, envisaging the flux of temporality in its absolute "unicity" *(Alleinheit)*, he recognizes that its objectivity cannot be exhausted by the immanent consciousness of time: the latter constitutes a time with which it does not identify itself totally. Escaping from time, this consciousness must not, however, be atemporal. How can a description give account of this ambiguity? Starting out from a constitutive consciousness of a time that is "given" to it, that it partakes of while still remaining foreign to it in some way, how can the formation of a single time be made intelligible? How will preobjective time recognize itself in objective time after its constitution in a phenomenological time? Husserl writes thus: "This prephenomenal, pre-immanent temporality is constituted intentionally as the form of temporally constitutive consciousness and in the latter itself. The flux of the immanent, temporally constitutive consciousness not only *is,* but is so remarkably and yet so intelligibly constituted that a self-appearance of the flux necessarily subsists in it, and hence the flux itself must necessarily be comprehensible in the flowing. The self-appearance of the flux *does not require a second flux,* but *qua* phenomenon it is constituted in itself. *The constituting and the constituted coincide, yet naturally they cannot coincide in every respect.*"[50] Thus, it is clear that the analysis of the internal consciousness of time gives us results here that give the lie to its very principles. At the beginning it was a question of excluding any genesis that was actually real, under the pretext that it showed itself in a domain already constituted in its temporal unity. Yet, precisely, at the end of the descriptions of the originarily immanent constitution of time, one recognizes that the constituting "recovers" the constituted. The "noema" of time refers to a noetic time where all the genetic problems will have to be posed again. The alleged exclusion of the constituted had only left a law or an "eidos" of time, themselves both constituted. The eidetic reduction then seems insufficient to escape the contradictions of genesis, [that is,] this continuity of infinite becoming and absolute beginning, of continuity and discontinuity, of tradition and creation, of passivity and activity, and so forth. The originary absolute escapes us to the degree that its sense is probed. In order for the immanent consciousness of time not to be a subjectivist illusion, in order for the essence of time not to be a concept, for them both to be consciousness and essence of *an* actual time, they must be linked by an originary synthesis to time and to being constituted *a priori*. Intentionality will then find all its sense again. Is it not indeed contradictory to place transcendences "off-line" and to claim to grasp the pure immanence of lived experience while still maintaining the intentionality of consciousness? In lived immanence, intentionality could reappear only if the real was conserved as a "noema" aimed at intentionally by a noetic act. Then genesis could be reduced to its "sense." But this "sense" itself being constituted by the originary and temporal act of a subject, it must itself be "reduced" to allow the constitutive analysis to be deepened. Transcendental intentionality must once again be the object of a wider explicitation. To attain its originarity, the method of the reduction must be amplified and modified. Then, as this latter no longer defines itself as an exclusion or a putting "off-line," the being of the transcendent world and of what is constituted in general will be "suspended" without being suppressed; genesis will be placed in brackets without being negated or put aside. Perhaps then we will understand the veritable sense of a phenomenological "neutralization" of genesis.

5

The Radical Ἐποχή and the Irreducibility of Genesis

From 1905, the date of *The Phenomenology of Internal Time Consciousness* [*Vorlesungen zur Phänomenologie des inneren Zeitbewußtseins*, also cited as *Lectures*], all Husserl's efforts are directed to the same end: to define the sphere of originary and concrete transcendental constitution. The efforts are based on one and the same possibility, which is at the same time a first necessity of method: that of a phenomenological reduction whose sense Husserl will never stop making deeper and more precise. It is this necessity, in particular, which seems to direct the evolution of phenomenology in a way that is more and more urgent and to determine the decisive moment when Husserl moves from a constitution that is static to a genetic constitution. So, rather than studying directly the complex content of "static" descriptions, we are concentrating on their ultimate condition of possibility.

Access to the immanent consciousness of time was possible only through putting transcendences "off-line." It appeared that the "privative" character of this reduction left us with no way out. Without the passive constitution of the hyletic temporal datum in the "originary impression," it was impossible to understand how the absolute subjectivity of temporal flux—which then remained [only] formal—was identical with the phenomenological lived experience and the temporal objectivities that constitute themselves in it. In a certain sense, one still remained at a prephenomenological stage. The theme of intentionality was hidden, the phenomenological subject remained constituted, whether as subject or formal freedom, or as temporal moment. Either every concrete becoming, every genesis had to be denied, or else the constituting subject had to be plunged into them, like an empirical object. A more radical explicitation was necessary. The idea of reduction had to be reformed. Now, the whole history of the theme of reduction[1] shows quite clearly that the more Husserl approaches a radicalism of reduction and gives it control over wide and diverse domains (natural thesis, natural sciences, sciences of the mind, transcendence of God, transcendence of eidetics, pure logic, etc.) the more he distinguishes it from an abstraction, from a "subtraction" that would purely and simply cross out its object so as to leave only an individual and formal residue. More and more, he insists on the difference that separates neutralization from pure and simple negation. Reduction is not skeptical doubt or ascetic retreat into immanence as lived experience. It conserves what it suspends. It maintains the "sense" of the object whose existence it "neutralizes."

So if it is now agreed that every "suppression" of genesis as empirical fact is insufficient from the point of view of transcendental phenomenology itself, we must ask ourselves the following question: Is the simple "neutralization" of genesis, as Husserl understands this after a slow elaboration,[2] enough to found the description of static constitution? Or rather (since we cannot pretend to ignore either that Husserl himself did not remain satisfied with this and saw it necessary to go on to a genetic constitution) how and why has the best form of the ἐποχή as reduction of genesis come to reveal itself to Husserl as insufficient?[3]

THE REDUCTION AND THE IDEALIST EXCLUSION OF GENESIS

The search for the originary constitution[4] still excludes, it goes without saying, any idea of historico-psychological genesis. "We are not talking here in terms of history. In this reference to originality, there need not be, and should not be, any thought of genesis along the lines either of psychological causality or of evolutionary history. What other meaning is intended will become clear only in the sequel and in the light of scientific reflexion. But everyone feels at once that the priority of empirically concrete knowledge of facts to all other knowledge, to all knowledge on ideal mathematical lines, for instance, must not be taken in any temporal sense, though intelligible in non-temporal-terms."[5]

From Eidetic Reduction to Transcendental Reduction

This historic genesis was first excluded by an eidetic reduction; this latter, thanks to the technique of "imaginary variation," allowed the passage from fact to essence, from real singularity to eidetic generality. This latter had to be a concrete *a priori*.[6] Since it was not constructed but seized in an intuition, it posed a new genetic problem left in the shadow by Husserl: How could what is concrete in essence escape a constitutive synthesis that supposed some temporality, however originary it might be? Either this *a priori* was formal, and Husserl denies this energetically, or else its concrete determination, although it might not be purely empirical, had to refer to a transcendental genesis. Yet Husserl does not spend time on this difficulty. He remarks simply that essence is constituted—statically—by the act of a transcendental consciousness that a reduction will now reveal to us, a reduction that is no longer eidetic but phenomenological. The difficulty will be carried over into this reduction.

The "thesis" of the natural attitude is that of history lived spontaneously: in it "I am aware of a world, spread out in space endlessly, and in time becoming and become without end."⁷ Which is to say that the temporality lived in this attitude is objective; I partake of it, I take account of it, but not having any originary or creative consciousness, it can be said that I am there at its development, and although I know something of it, its first sense escapes me. Husserl had already said in *The Phenomenology of Internal Time Consciousness,* "Naturally, we all know what time is; it is that which is most familiar."⁸ Far from appearing as it is, that is, more originary than space, it is indistinctly mixed into our spatial world, and everything said about the latter, "the world in its ordered being as a spatial present—the aspect I have so far been considering—[can be said about] the world in respect to *its ordered being in the succession of time.* This world now present to me, and in every waking 'now' obviously so, has its temporal horizon, infinite in both directions, its known and unknown, its intimately alive and its unalive past and future."⁹ The spatio-temporal world is a total world; it is never a question of distinguishing it "really" from a transcendental sphere or from a formal *a priori.* It is the whole of being in its infinity and its incompletion. "It is continually 'present' for me, and I myself am a member of it. Therefore this world is not there for me as a mere *world of facts and affairs (Sachen)* but, with the same immediacy, as a *world of values,* a *world of goods,* a *practical world.*"¹⁰ It defines my natural environment, the "ideal"¹¹ environments, and the environment that is of an intersubjective type.¹² In the couple of pages that follow the description of the natural attitude, evoking the possibility of a radical altering of this attitude by its being put "off-line" or "in brackets" *(die Ausschaltung, die Einklammerung),* Husserl distinguishes it very clearly from Cartesian doubt, which it resembles in many ways. "A procedure of this sort, *possible at any time,* is, for instance, *the attempt to doubt everything* which *Descartes,* with an entirely different end in view, with the purpose of setting up an absolutely indubitable sphere of Being, undertook to carry through."¹³ It is thus clear that at the beginning Husserl's intention is not to "subtract" from the natural world a "region" that cannot be doubted. What interests Husserl is not doubt itself but the "attempt" to doubt.[14] "It is likewise clear that the *attempt* to doubt any object of awareness in respect of its *being actually there necessarily conditions a certain suspension (Aufhebung) of the thesis;* and it is precisely this that interests us. It is not a transformation of the thesis into its antithesis, of positive into negative; it is also not a transformation into presumption, suggestion, indecision, doubt (in one or other sense of the word); such shifting indeed is not at our free pleasure [in the power of our free will]."[15] All these acts, these modalities of belief, like the free will Husserl alludes to, are understood in the "worldly" sense of psychological reality; what would a freedom of action on "real" events mean? Would it be "real" in turn? It would then lose its essence of freedom through this. Unreal, then, by simple opposition to reality *(Realität)*, it could not operate or actualize itself. In fact, the opposition between reality and unreality is neutralized by the reduction. What remains of our relation to the world after the reduction is a neutralized belief beyond or below the opposition between belief and unbelief. When Husserl affirms that *this conversion of values depends on our entire freedom,*[16] it is no longer a question of real freedom but, once again, of a transcendental freedom that is not included in the "worldly" conflict between determinism and free will. The reduction is distinguished from Descartes's methodical doubt; it is even less a sophistical negation or a skeptical doubt about the existence of the world.

> *Rather it is something quite unique. We do not abandon the thesis we have adopted, we make no change in our conviction,* which remains in itself what it is so long as we do not introduce new motives of judgment, which we precisely refrain from doing. And yet the thesis undergoes a modification—whilst remaining in itself what it is, *we set it as it were "out of action," we "disconnect it," "bracket it."* It still remains there like the bracketed in the bracket, like the disconnected outside the connexional system. We can also say: The thesis is experience as lived *(Erlebnis), but we make "no use" of it,* and by that, of course, we do not indicate privation [...] rather [...] it transvalues it [the original thesis] in a quite peculiar way.[17]

So it seems that the privative character of the reduction, which made the supposed neutralization oscillate between a psychologism and a formalism, has disappeared, in spite of the "worldly"[18] images of the disconnecting and of the bracketing. This radical altering of the thesis has taken nothing away from it, precisely because it is absolute altering. It would be interesting to verify in detail this dialectic of altering: it is because there is absolute altering that nothing has changed—the absolute of the Other is the Same.[19]

However, Husserl has not yet tested the fertility or the sterility of the reductive method by many analyses. The sense of the reduction is still ambiguous for him After all the precautions that we have just mentioned, the pure or transcendental consciousness that he thematizes, is understood as a phenomenological residue.[20] Thus, we are not at the originary source of transcendental constitution. Husserl poses here a question that marks a clear regression from the initial methodological considerations.

Consciousness, Eidetic Region and Phenomenological "Residue"

"For what can remain over when the whole world is bracketed, including ourselves and all our thinking [cogitare]?"[21] This implies that after the reduction there *remains* intact an ontological domain, and not, as Husserl said above, a sphere where the totality of being is neutralized. We proceed thus only to the determination of a regional eidetics whose constitution and becoming will pose the problems already met with. Genesis is not neutralized but excluded as a domain of empirical facticity. We fall back to before the phenomenological posing of the question. The present intention of Husserl, although it may contradict his initial statements, is nonetheless explicit, it is indeed a question of *"the winning of a new region of Being, the distinctive character of which has not yet been defined,* a region of *individual* Being, like every genuine region."*[22] To this degree, it is seen, phenomenology has not yet gone radically beyond the debate between classical philosophies, between empiricism and criticism. Either consciousness, as an ontological region, is constituted in the same way as the other regions to which it is opposed according to the relations of absolute alterity. We are still in a psychologist empiricism. The alterity of the region "consciousness," as absolute immanence in relation to the region "nature," is contrary to transcendental intentionality. Whatever he may say about this, Husserl cannot maintain intentionality here except on a psychological footing. Phenomenology is not yet beyond an intentional psychology. Or else, as pure consciousness whose correlate is the world, the pure "I," "distinguishing" itself from the world as from a different region from its own, is neither concrete nor temporal. As such, it is no longer "lived" as constituting origin.[23] One is then prisoner of a formal "I think"; "in the words of Kant, *the 'I think' must be able to accompany all my presentations."*[24] But this atemporal "I think" cannot be at the origin of the becoming of my represen-

tations. It is thus, like them, *already* constituted. The sphere of originary constitution is not yet unveiled.

This oscillation between an intentional psychology conjugated with a formalism and a genuine transcendental phenomenology is pursued throughout all the methodological considerations on reduction, right down to its results. Indeed, on the one hand, this narrow transcendental reduction that determines consciousness as ontological region (thematized in a regional "eidetics") is often presented as a methodological or rhetorical mediation toward a more radical reduction that would cause this region to appear as originary *(Ur-Region)* and constituting in relation to the other regions. "[The phenomenological reduction had delivered to us the empire of transcendental consciousness; it was]* in a certain definite sense, a realm of 'absolute' Being. It is the original category of Being generally (or, as we would put it, the original region), in which all other regions of Being have their root, to which they are *essentially* related, on which they are therefore one and all dependent."[25] The definition of consciousness as pure essence thus was only preparing the reader for a properly transcendental comprehension of consciousness as originary region. "Important motives which have their ground in epistemological requirements justify us in referring to 'pure' consciousness, of which much is yet to be said, also as *transcendental consciousness,* and the operation through which it is acquired as *transcendental* ἐποχη. On grounds of method, this operation will split up into different steps of 'disconnexion' or 'bracketing,' and thus our method will assume the character of a graded reduction. For this reason we propose to speak, and even preponderatingly, of *phenomenological reductions* [...]"[26] (in the plural!).

All the paradoxes of the phenomenological reduction are lodged in this necessity, in appearance rhetorical or pedagogical. Why must we always start from what is natural, constituted, derived, and so forth in order to discover pure originarity only *at the end*? It is the whole problem of genesis which will not cease to worry Husserl implicitly or explicitly. It was necessary to start out from the psychologist description in order to discover an *a priori* purity of formal logic. It was necessary to ask oneself about these formal *a priori*s in order that they might appear in their infinite becoming as constituted by a transcendental subjectivity. One had to start out from objective time to go back to lived time, and so forth. One must now begin with the description of the

---

* The English translation differs substantially from Ricœur's here; my translation from the latter is substituted in the square brackets. *Trans.*

natural attitude in order to define the possibility of the reduction; but this latter, still "worldly," leaves behind it only a "consciousness" region whose description must later refer us to a purely originary consciousness. Thus, the more reflection probes the sense of originarity, the more numerous are the mediations it must cross. This itinerary, which is followed in the opposite direction from phenomenological becoming and from phenomenological constitution, has its own temporality, its actual sense. If its necessity is inescapable, it is valid *a priori*. It is essential. What relation does it have with phenomenological temporality? It must not be related to it in external fashion. Why is it always at a certain moment of historical becoming (reproduced here and specified in Husserl's account of reductive method) that transcendental reduction is possible? This is not yet given to us to know. If we are *always* constrained to begin "really" or "formally"[27] with an already constituted moment that we must greet and accept passively, if that is an essential and *a priori* law, then we need to ask ourselves whether this necessity is not linked to the very movement of transcendental constitution and transcendental becoming. Husserl does not ask himself about a necessity that remains and must remain accidental for him. He is content to announce here and there the necessary fulfillment of the reduction by the discovery of a concrete nonformal consciousness: "*pure consciousness in its own absolute Being* [...] remains over as the 'phenomenological residuum' we were in quest of: although we have 'Suspended' the whole world with all things, living creatures, men, ourselves included. We have literally lost nothing, but have won the whole of Absolute Being, which, properly understood, conceals itself in all transcendences, 'constituting' them within itself."[28] To speak in images, what is put in brackets, says Husserl, is not effaced from the phenomenological picture; it is precisely only put into brackets and in that way given a certain index.[29] As Ricœur notes: "This important phrase marks the turning point away from the reduction which leaves a 'residue' toward the constitution which retains '*in*' *itself* what it seems to exclude '*from*' *itself*. The reduction remained limited while it 'separated consciousness'; in bringing 'reality' back to it, it became indiscernible from the transcendental constitution which discovers the sense of the world."[30]

But statements like that remain rather rare, and do not fit in well with the content of the analyses alongside them. Husserl thinks that if the sphere of consciousness is not "isolated" at the beginning, as an eidetic region clearly distinct from the "real" which it aims at, then transcendental becoming will have to be merged with empirical becoming in a perspective that will of necessity be psychologist. The distinction between transcendental genesis and empirical genesis is not yet ready. Thus, at the price of staying below the phenomenological level which his analyses are aiming at, Husserl must keep to the formalism of a pure "residual" consciousness which will be opposed to the transcendent world as the indubitable to the doubtful, the pure to the impure, the originary to the constituted, the absolute to the relative. This theme brings together the most important statements of *Ideas* I. "*Consciousness in itself has a being of its own which in its absolute uniqueness of nature remains unaffected by the phenomenological disconnexion*. It therefore remains over as a '*phenomenological residuum*,' as a region of Being which is in principle unique, and can become in fact the field of a new science—the science of Phenomenology."[31] As is said a little farther on, "The essence of Consciousness" is taken as a "theme of enquiry."[32] It is clear how such eidetic analyses forbid any research into a properly originary constitution. On the one hand, an eidetic region cannot, as such, constitute another. On the other, its becoming is in itself inexplicable. It belongs to the temporal order of transcendent "temporal objects" which Husserl will ask himself about in vain in *Phenomenology of Internal Time Consciousness*. It is not clear how the becoming of this "consciousness" region can "appear to itself." Even less, how it can appear to itself as the same as that of the other regions. There is thus no answer given to the problem of time [as] posed in *Phenomenology of Internal Time Consciousness:* How to explain the fact that constituting and constituted coincide? A region which has itself been constituted, even if it were the region of "consciousness," will not teach us that.

In the end, we stay at the level of the first volume of *Logical Investigations*, which, keeping to a world of essences that are constituted and atemporal, calls for a return to [a] constituting subjectivity. No doubt consciousness is here "essentially" temporal. But it is a question of a temporality that is thematized in its a *priori* and itself "atemporal" essence. The insufficiency of a logicism has not been made up for. The origin and the movement of transcendental becoming are described at the eidetic level of a static constitution. The phenomenological neutralization of genesis is spoiled by a logicist dissociation.[33] On one side there is the world of immanent lived experience, the realm of "adequate" perception[34] and of absolute indubitability, on the other there is the world of exterior perception, subject to doubt.[35] "Every immanent perception necessarily guarantees the existence [*Existenz*] of its object. If reflective apprehension is directed to my experience, I apprehend an absolute Self whose existence *(Dasein)* is, in principle, undeniable [...] it would be nonsense to maintain the possibility of an experience *given in such a way not* truly existing."[36] We know the essential difference between "immanent perception" and "transcendent perception." The first is adequate, it immediately grasps the totality of its object since it merges with it.[37] On the contrary, there is an *a priori* necessity for the transcendent thing only ever to give itself in sketches, profiles *(Abschattungen);* by definition, it cannot be exhausted by the act that apprehends it. "It is [...] an essential feature of the thing-world that no perception, however perfect it may be, gives us anything absolute within its domain; and with this the following is essentially connected, namely, that every experience *(Erfahrung*),* however far it extends, leaves open the possibility that what is given, despite the persistent consciousness of its bodily self-presence, does *not* exist. It is an essentially valid law that *existence (Existenz) in the form of a thing is never demanded as necessary by virtue of its givenness,* but in a certain way is always *contingent*"[38]; in that, the sphere of the transcendent world is removed *a priori* from the absolute and immanent sphere in which "opposition, illusion and being-otherwise have no place" and which remains "a sphere of the absolutely established [*absoluter Position**]."[39] Certainly, no critique can be addressed to these analyses as such and in their own eidetic content. It seems that there is no reason to go back on them and, indeed, Husserl will never touch the question again.[40] But to the extent that they are only eidetic analyses, they need a more extended explanation. What is the "founding" relation of these two eidetic regions? How are the "transcendences" announced *in* immanent lived experience? How will lived experience be, and indeed what lived experience will it be, in accordance with its intentional essence, experience lived *by* what is not it? How can what is doubtful present itself in the sphere of the indubitable, or the "relative" in the "absolute"? In a word, how can immanent lived experience be reconciled with the transcendent world in one and the same time? How, starting from a pure flux of lived experience, can temporal objectivities be constituted? "The stream of experience which is mine, that, namely, of the one who is thinking, may be to ever so great an extent uncomprehended, unknown in its past and future reaches, yet as soon as I glance towards the flowing life and into the real present it flows through, and in so doing grasp myself as the pure subject of this life [...] I say forthwith and because I must: *I am,* this life is, I live: *cogito.* To every stream of experience, and to every Ego as such, there belongs, in principle, the possibility of securing this self-evidence."[41] But this absolute, immanent to itself and immediately evident "for itself" offers us no

---

* This insertion of German is Boyce Gibson's, *Ideas* I. *Trans.*

guarantee as to the temporal objectivities that are founded in it. Either these transcend the flux as constituted realities: the intentionality that originarily founds the evidence of their "given," in order to complete its movement, must escape from the immanence of the pure flux of the lived experience. The latter will be originarily correlative to the objective flux. Or else—and this, it seems, is the case in *Ideas* I—the temporal objectivity is originarily part of the pure flux of consciousness as noematic meaning. The noetico-noematic correlation is situated in the area of absolute subjectivity. But intentionality as originary attaining of the given object "in person" has not been developed as it should have been. In fact—and this is the primary cause of all the difficulties in *Ideas* I—the world is not considered in its "reality" during these analyses, but in its noematic value. Husserl never envisages in *Ideas* the relation of real substrate with its noematic sense which will define the problem of a genesis of sense. Since the real world can be reduced to its *sense,* which is *originary for* consciousness, one can imagine the nonexistence of the real world and of real objectivities without suppressing the intentionality of consciousness. This latter—not being defined here as an originary access to the being of the "real" object, an indeterminate *X,* the pole and ideal of an infinite noematic determination,[42] but as an originary access to its noematic sense—can be preserved, according to Husserl, independently of the "real" existence of the object. The noematic objectivity replaces real objectivity. In the same way, the time of the world, which is harmonized with immanent time through the intermediary of "temporal objectivities," is not real time but noematic time originarily in correlation with a noetic time.

The Foundation of Absolute Idealism: An "Already Constituted" Structure

All the difficulties and obscurities of *Ideas* I, everything which allows one to affirm that Husserl has not moved beyond an idealism,[43] depend on remaining enclosed in the "structures" of the noetic-noematic correlation. With the natural world "being only" the intentional "correlate" of consciousness,[44] it was inevitable that the outcome should be the project of an absolute idealism, such as appears in the famous § 49, where absolute consciousness is presented as the "residuum after the nullifying of the world."[45] "What we have said does not imply, on the other hand, that there *must* be a world or thing of some sort. The existence of a world is the correlate of certain experience-patterns marked out by certain essential formations. But it is *not* at all clear that actual experiences can run their course *only* when they show these patterns [...] *the Being of consciousness,* of every stream of experience generally, *though it would indeed be inevitably modified by a nullifying of the thing-world, would not be affected thereby in its own proper existence.*"[46] As Paul Ricœur stresses: "the nullifying of the world is not absence of intentionality, but the destruction of every intentional truth by internal conflict, the generalized 'simulacrum.'"[47] "In the ruin of the world, I would still be intentional consciousness, but aiming at the chaos."[48]

But the problem only moves one stage back, and intentionality is not yet explicited radically as originary attaining of the antepredicative being of the object.[49] This is why, while still recognizing the originality of his, one can define the philosophy of *Ideas* as a subjectivist and formal idealism. Husserl explains this better than any commentary would:

We thus see that consciousness (inward experience*) and real *(reales)* Being are in no sense co-ordinate forms of Being, living as friendly neighbors, and occasionally entering into "relation" or some reciprocal "connexion." Only that which is essentially related to an other, each related element having its own proper essence, and on the same lines as the other, can in a true sense be said to form a connexion with that other or build up a whole with it. Both immanent or absolute being and transcendent Being are indeed "being" *(seiende)*, and "object" *(Gegenstand)*, and each has, moreover, its objective determining content; but it is evident that what then on either side goes by the name of object and objective determination bears the same name only when we speak in terms of the empty logical categories. Between the meanings of consciousness and reality yawns a veritable abyss. Here a Being which manifests itself perspectively, never giving itself absolutely, merely contingent and relative; there a necessary and absolute Being, fundamentally incapable of being given through appearance and perspective-patterns.

It is thus clear that in spite of all talk—well-grounded no doubt in the meaning intended—of a real *(realen)* Being of the *human Ego,* and its conscious experiences *in* the world and of all that belongs thereto in any way in respect of "psychophysical connexions"—that in spite of all this, Consciousness, considered in its *"purity,"* must be reckoned as *a self-contained system of Being (für sich geschlossener Seinzusammenhang),* as a system of Absolute Being, into which nothing can penetrate, and

---

*In Ricœur, *le vécu. Trans.*

from which nothing can escape; which has no spatio-temporal exterior, and can be inside no spatio-temporal system; which cannot experience causality from anything nor exert causality upon anything, it being presupposed that causality bears the normal sense of natural causality as a relation of dependence between realities.

On the other side, the whole *spatio-temporal world,* to which man and the human Ego claim to belong as subordinate singular realities, is *according to its own meaning mere intentional Being,* a Being, therefore, which has the merely secondary, relative sense of a Being *for* a consciousness. It is a Being which consciousness in its own experiences [*Erfahrungen*]* posits, and is, in principle, intuitable and determinable only as the element common to the [harmoniously] motivated appearance-manifolds, but *over and beyond* this, is just nothing at all.[50]

At first, the absolute and systematic idealism that is defined here seems to present no weakness. Thanks to the safeguarding of intentionality, it escapes the reproaches commonly leveled against Berkeleyan idealism. Thanks to the lived experience which is here described as the ultimate source of evidence, it is distinguished from the constructions of a post-Kantian type of metaphysical idealism. Existence is integrated as a noema; alterity (or intersubjectivity) not being given originarily here as such, it too remains an eidetic configuration, a noematic composition; finally and especially, time is nothing other than an intentional lived experience. Thus, antepredicative existence as such, that of the material substrate of the object, of the primitive flux of time, of personal alterity, has, according to the point of view chosen, either been definitively expelled out of lived experience or been integrated into lived experience as a noematic correlate. We said above that there it was a question of an insufficient unveiling of intentionality. We still think so, but it seems that here this truth is negotiating with its opposite. For it can be said conversely: the deep intuition that legitimates this whole approach is the most daring elucidation of intentionality. Indeed, if, in developing the whole scope of intentionality, this was made into a direct and originary grasping of "real" *(real)* existence,[51] then this grasping would itself have to be "real." The intentional act would be a "real" act, a "fact." The whole of phenomenology would thus be made to collapse. Nothing would allow us to distinguish between lived experience and natural

---

*Boyce Gibson's insertion of German. *Trans.*

facticity any longer. No "evidence" would be possible. We would be caught up in a science of nature whose sense and condition of possibility would escape us. No access to objectivity could be originarily defined.

Husserlian idealism is thus not in this sense a reduction or a psychologistic or subjectivist narrowing of intentionality; on the contrary, it restores all its noetic power to intentionality. But such a coherence is disquieting. In giving account of the absolute validity of knowledge in such minute depth, has anything more been done than to "replace" existence by the essence *of* existence, time by experience of time, alterity by its eidetic configuration? Instead of describing the genesis of essence starting from antepredicative existence, has anything more been done than to allude to the *a priori* sense of genesis which presides over the genesis of sense? Has not a movement been followed which is the inverse of real movement, being thus certain to make what has "become" *a priori* intelligible for itself? It is doubtless necessary that intentionality be not a "real" act, for in that regard, as a fundamental element of a lived experience which is not "real" in essence, it would be a deceiving power, a constituted facticity. Our feeling of originary evidence would also be a pure phantasm. But, to the degree that it is founded by an "originary donating act,"[52] in which the object comes and gives itself "in person," does this evidence not necessarily imply a fundamental passivity, anterior to noetic activity and to the formation of noematic sense?[53] Intentionality is at the same time active and passive; to the degree it is passive, is not the object that it "receives" at the origin necessarily "real" and prenoematic? Without being a real act, must it not be consciousness of the "real" object as such? Does not perception, the originary donating act, break up this world of pure lived experience? If passivity is introduced into the noetico-noematic structures, which are only reconcilable with the constitutive activity of intentional consciousness, is not the whole system ready to oscillate or to vacillate? Is not this reduction, which leaves only the closed world of intentional consciousness, a reduction of what is not primitively constituted by consciousness? Cannot intentionality be deepened in the direction of activity and passivity, of the generation of sense and of the originary "seeing"? Why do we still find the two sorts of reduction between which Husserl is oscillating? And in *Ideas,* why does Husserl finish by choosing the reduction which is privative, which does not safeguard intentional activity except by shutting it up in the subjective sphere of noetico-noematic correlation? Because the theory of reduction is of a piece with an insufficient description of perception, where the relation between an activity and a passivity that are simultaneously originary still remains unbalanced. It is this relation that we must now examine. It will show us that it is indeed the difficulty about genesis that Husserl is eluding by all these procedures.

GENESIS OF PERCEPTION: HYLÉ AND MORPHÉ*

The Pure "I" and the Actual "I"

Let us still stay inside this noetico-noematic circle. It seemed that up till now all the declarations of Husserl were universally valid for a "consciousness in general." The concrete individuality of the perceived was individuality that was "aimed at," hence endowed with a noematic sense and, as such, assimilated to lived experience. Individuality not being "real" in the way known in the eidetic configuration, it was straightaway universalized as perceived individuality or as perceiving individuality. On the other hand, what remained after the reduction was only a pure "I."

> After carrying this reduction through, we shall never stumble across the pure Ego as an experience among others within the flux of manifold experiences which survives as transcendental residuum; nor shall we meet it as a constitutive bit of experience appearing with the experience of which it is an integral part and again disappearing. The Ego [...] belongs to every experience that comes and streams past, its "glance" goes "through" every actual *cogito,* and towards the object. This visual ray *(Blickstrahl)* changes with every *cogito,* shooting forth afresh with each new one as it comes, and disappearing with it. But the Ego remains self-identical. [...] as that which remains absolutely self-identical in all real and possible changes of experience, it can *in no sense* be reckoned *as a real (reell)* part *or phase* of the experiences themselves. [...] In the words of Kant, "The *I think must be able to accompany all my presentations.*"[54]

Thus defined, however, this "pure I" which guarantees the "unreal" character of intentional activity seems purely formal; to this degree, it is hard to see how its harmony or coincidence with the multiplicity of concrete lived experiences can be carried out. Nor can it be imagined how it can be "at the same time" pure Ego and a concrete person and especially how it can be itself and as such intentional, since intentionality ought to cause it to escape originarily from the purity of its immanence to itself and of its analytic identity with

---

*There being no settled convention for transliteration of these words, I have used the acute accent to mark the pronunciation of the last letter. *Trans.*

itself. Husserl, aware of those risks and not wanting this "I" to be a pure and formal condition of possibility, specifies that "a *quite peculiar* [*original*] transcendence simultaneously presents itself—a non-constituted transcendence—*a transcendence in immanence.*"[55] But what does he do here, other than describe the difficulty? A difficulty of reconciling and unifying a transcendental thing purely lived, which would risk being nothing more than the totality of lived experiences and thus forcing us into an "empiricism," with a transcendental source which is not lived, which—while causing us to escape from a pure and simple empiricism, as cut off from lived evidence—would run the risk of being only an empty and formal product, an objective unity, a constituted transcendence? This contradiction is permanent. The constituting origin of lived experience is in the lived experience and outside the lived experience, in time and outside time, and so on, and one cannot exclusively determine absolute originarity in one sense or the other. Now this dialectic would be possible in a genetic perspective where, since the becoming constitutes *itself* originarily and the "I" temporalizes itself in originary fashion, it would constantly come out of itself while still remaining immanent to itself; this in the continuity of the originary "now" at the same time constituting and constituted by protention and retention of itself. But genetic becoming has not yet any originarity in Husserl's eyes; always constituted, it refers to a static primitive constitution.

This latter, in its *logical and systematic coherence,* can then only "suffer" from a contradiction that would, on the contrary, be the very motor of a genetic constitution. Indeed, this absolute consciousness must be at the same time "actual" consciousness: "*Immanent Being is therefore without doubt absolute in this sense, that in principle* 'nulla re indiget ad existendum.' *On the other hand, the world of the transcendent 'res' is related unreservedly to consciousness, not indeed to logical conceptions, but to what is actual.*"[56] What is it here that causes consciousness to be "actual," that is to say, on the one hand concretely "present," on the other, conscious *of* something? It cannot be, originarily at least, this pure "I" which crosses through "all" the moments of lived experience and of the "gaze of consciousness." Must one then say that the actuality of the pure "I" is conferred on it by something other than itself? Is that not to make of it a consciousness that is essentially logical and that becomes concrete and actual only through exterior intervention, through an object that is imposed on it, through a time that is affixed to it? Conversely, if one wanted to attribute to the pure "I," in spite of its "atemporality" or its "omnitemporality,"[57] the faculty of giving actuality "to itself," then—and this is no doubt the deep tendency of *Ideas* I—it would be made into a *purely and exclusively active* intentionality; that is, a mutilated intentionality. Pushed far enough, it can even be said that *pure* intentional activity is the opposite of intentionality. For it would no longer be clear why noetic activity still requires a noematic correlate nor why this correlate would be able to be founded on an object given "in person" in perception. A purely active perception ought not to have any sense for Husserl. In it, intuition must originarily "see" and "receive" the concrete presence of the object which gives itself to any construction, to any derivation, and refers us to this originary donating act. Whether perception is perception of time or of a spatial object, it seems—as Husserl will later recognize—that a primitive passivity constitutes the actuality of a consciousness.

The Matter and Form of Intentionality

But does not this passivity introduce a mixture into the interior of this "I," pure constituent of itself? In this closed world of noetico-noematic structures and of "unreal" intentional lived experience, will the *originary* passivity where the real object "itself" gives itself, be integrated without making a mystery of it?

Without being altered in its essence, could it lend itself to an *originary* noetic activity that, animating it, "activating" it, will make of it a noema assimilated to the unreal lived experience in the structured totality of intentional experience? This veritable genesis of the noema starting from the "real" object, passively received, is not clear in Husserl. Pure passivity, like pure activity, suspends the exercise of intentionality. A dialectical genesis, taking account of the double movement of intentionality and merging it with the pure genesis of time itself in its auto-constitution, could assume this contradiction that Husserl wants to suppress by throwing a veil over the mysterious relations between the sensuous "hylé," real *(reell)* and nonintentional element of lived experience, the intentional and noetic "morphé" which comes to animate it, and the non-*"reell"* intentional noema[58] which constitutes itself from them.

The passages relating to the "hylé," not very numerous in *Ideas* I, are among the most difficult and the most obscure in this work. "Under *experiences* in the *widest sense,*" says Husserl, "we understand whatever is to be found in the stream of experience, not only therefore intentional experiences, *cogitationes* actual and potential taken in their full concreteness, but all the real *(reellen)* phases to be found in this stream and in its concrete sections."[59] Difficulties start to show themselves. What is going to be the status of the moments of lived experience which are "real" *(reell)* but not intentional? Where, when, and through what will they be constituted? Since they are not as such and originarily constituted as noemata through an intentionality, will they not be the constituting motor itself? But could what is a nonintentional constituting constitute intentionality secondarily? Would intentionality be only a product? That's impossible, and in contradiction with the fundamental principles of phenomenology. So what is it then? Should one not pass into a more primordial sphere of constitution to grasp again at another level the passive originarity as constituting intentionality?

The question is serious, since these pieces of "lived experience," are "real" *(reell)* but not intentional and are constitutive of all perception. They are the sensations themselves: "*not every real phase* of the concrete unity of an intentional experience has itself the *basic character of intentionality,* the property of being a 'consciousness of something.' This is the case, for instance, with all *sensory data,* which play so great a part in the perceptive intuitions of things."[60] We must take care, the *sense-data* as lived experience are not the very materiality of sensation in its transcendent "reality" *(reall)*. The matter (hylé) of sensations is immanent to the "cogitatio" through opposition to the perceived object which transcends it. As Paul Ricœur notes so aptly, "the German word *reel* is always reserved for this negotiation of the cogitatio and the word *data* for this matter 'animated' by intentionality."[61] In other words, the sensuous hylé, as such and in its purity, that is to say, *before* being animated by intentionality, would *already* be a piece of lived experience. Without which, it would be impossible for an "unreal" intentionality to animate a "reality" *(real)*. It is thus as a nonintentional piece of lived experience that the hylé is animated by intentional form. But what evidence permits us to decide in this way? How can it be affirmed of a reality *(reell* or *real)* that it is lived *before* being intentional if absolute evidence is made into an intentional act? One has the right to determine the hylé as lived *only from* that moment when an intentional morphé has come to animate it, but we are told that as such and in its purity, the hylé is not intentional. Is this not then to recognize that it is only starting from the moment when the hylé is animated that it can be identified as lived? In consequence, cannot the hylé, as such and before being endowed with an intentional sense, be a worldly reality just as well as a phenomenological reality? Husserl opposes nothing very precise to this danger. "As the content which presents the whiteness of the paper as it appears to us, it [the sense datum] is the *bearer of* an intentionality, but not itself a consciousness of something."[62] A very obscure pronouncement: it is not clear if this "bearer" of intentionality precedes intentionality or is constituted *as a bearer* by the intentional act. If it precedes it, what is intentionality's originary autonomy? Does it not consist only in the revealing through a "gaze" that which constituted itself without it? If on the contrary, it is intentionality alone that constitutes hylé as hylé, as an *a priori* substrate of intentional sense, then all the original reality *(reell)* of the hylé is lost sight of. It is no longer clear what distinguishes it from the noema, which is included in lived experience as nonreal *(reell)*.[63] *If the hylé is, as nonintentional, a real* (reell) element, animated with a sense by a noetic intentionality, is it not necessarily identical to a "noema"? The whole reality *(reell)* of lived experience would then be reduced to its constituted meaning.

Husserl's descriptions do not throw much light on the question. Hyletic matter not being the transcendent matter of the perceived thing nor the matter of the perceiving body, its "animation" through intentionality would proceed from hyletic variations about which one could ask how they can still refer to a transcendent object, if they are not, as such, already intentional. "We must keep this point clearly before our eyes," writes Husserl,

> that the sensory data which exercise the function of presenting color, smoothness, shape, and so forth perspectivally (the function of "exhibiting") differ wholly and in principle from color, smoothness, shape *simpliciter*, in short, from all the generic aspects which *a thing* can show. *The perspective variation (the Abschattung), though verbally similar to the perspected variable (the "Abgeschattetes"), differs from it generically and in principle*. The perspective variation is an experience. But experience is possible only as experiences, and not as something spatial. The perspected variable, however, is in principle possible only as spatial (it is indeed spatial in its essence) but not possible as [lived] experience.[64]

This seems very clear, but we are still left in ignorance about what a representation or a variation* of something could be, which as such and in its proper moment, is neither the thing which is varying itself, nor an intentional aiming of the thing. What is then this mediation between the transcendent real *(real)* and intentionality? Must not this latter in its essence do without mediation? The hyletic lived experience as such does not give itself through a variation[65]; it is the place or the moment where the perceived thing is varying itself. But since the relation between the hyletic lived experience and the

---

Abschattung, which Ricœur translates as "sketch," is translated by Boyce Gibson as "perspective variation." *Trans.*

thing is not intentional, it is only the morphé which makes us "recognize" in the hylé the figuration of one thing and not another. Is the hyletic matter then absolutely indeterminate in itself? That seems inconceivable, for since the intentional form is also as such and *a priori* absolutely indeterminate (if it were not, it would do without the hylé), every perception would be impossible. Is it only a synthesis of matter and form that makes perception possible? Beyond the fact that then one would not know on which of its moments to found the synthesis, this would suppose that the intentional form is only a constituent part [of synthesis] and not the act of synthesis itself. One would then be referred to a more originary intentional form or matter which would make the synthesis itself possible *a priori*. The level of noetico-noematic constitution is then left behind, revealed thus as superficial, in order to go down to the level of this "primordial constitution" *(Urkonstitution)* which Husserl tried to analyze only in texts that are still unpublished.[66] Not going more deeply into the sense and foundation of this primordial synthesis, Husserl confesses that "as regards the possibilities left open above, they might also be entitled *formless materials* and *immaterial forms.*"[67] Which clearly indicates that at this level he remains a prisoner of an *already constituted* noetico-noematic correlation; without elucidating the originary constitution of the sensible givens, he remains this side of an authentic transcendental phenomenology, including a "transcendental aesthetics," a concern for which is present only in the unpublished material. Nothing is said to us, in fact, about the constitutive processes that allow one to distinguish between the noesis and the hylé, both defined, unlike the noema, as "real" *(reell)* elements of lived experience. To know whether one is more originary than the other, the eventuality of a form without matter and of matter without form must in fact indeed be envisaged. We do not know if it is the hylé that begins by calling for the attention of the "informing" intentionality or if it is the latent and potential intentionality that animates the matter encountered. "Whether such sensile experiences in the stream of experience are of necessity everywhere the subjects of some kind of 'animating synthesis' which informs them (including whatever features this in its turn demands and renders possible), or, as we also say, whether they ever take their part in *intentional functions,* does not here call for decision. On the other hand, let us also leave undecided in the first instance whether the characters that enter essentially into the setting up of intentionality can find concrete embodiment apart from any sensile foundation."[68] Husserl thus asks with the greatest rigor a question to which he does not reply; and he continues, contenting himself with bringing the contradiction to light: "At all events, in the whole phenomenological domain (in the whole, that is, within the stage of constituted temporality, as must always be born in mind)[69] this remarkable duality and unity of *sensile* ὕλη and *intentional* μορφή plays a dominant part."[70] On his own admission, Husserl does not then look to elucidate the constitution of sense from the duality or the unity between noesis and hylé; he accepts as such the ambiguity of a unified duality or a plural unity at the level of an already completed constitution. The genetic synthesis is accomplished at the moment when the analysis begins. Husserl does not try to find out whether the unity is the foundation of the duality or conversely. Above all, he does not make explicit what is originary in the duality, what is *a priori* in the synthesis, the non-intentional hylé or the intentional morphé. Husserl probably supposes, and it seems rightly so, that to attribute to one or the other an absolute and exclusive originarity is to disallow oneself the intelligibility of any constitutive process. In one case, deriving form from matter, intentionality from hylé, the intentionality of lived experience is transformed into constituted passivity. Intentionality becomes a merely eidetic character of lived experience. We do not get out of the ruts of intentional psychology. In the other case, if the hylé has no originary autonomy in relation to the intentional morphé, if it is not sensual lived matter constituted *before being animated*, if it does not suffice for itself, if it does not carry "in itself," so to say, the conditions of the variation of *such or such object,* it seems impossible that intentionality should aim through this at an individual object, a real transcendence. The paradox here is the following: If only intentionality is absolutely originary, it must stay closed into the interior of the subject. We end up again in a subjectivist idealism, which is not essentially distinguishable from an intentional psychologism.

The "duality" must then be originarily constituting in order to escape this danger; it must constitute the noema after having constituted itself as [a] correlation; in a word, it must constitute this unity while presupposing it. That is what is called dialectic.

Everywhere, duality as such can only be already constituted—this is a law of essence. Originarity and duality exclude one another on principle. This is something obvious that is not even a subject to be talked about, because it is originarity itself. To make an origin out of a correlation, a synthesis, a totality, is that not to stay at a level where everything is already given? To make the point of departure for a piece of reflection out of the noetico-hyletic ensemble is to stay the prisoner of a science of nature or a psychology, of a metaphysics or a transcendental psychologism. That is to stay this side of transcendental phenomenology.

This dilemma, this mishap, cannot be avoided each time originarity is thematized in terms of static constitution: that is what Husserl does, who is still afraid of giving a temporal sense to the theme of originarity. In a constitutive sphere where genetic becoming is absent, duality can no more engender unity than unity can duality. It is because Husserl does not yet place originary temporality at the core of his descriptions that the dialectic of unity and multiplicity fails and with it the whole transcendental project. In spite of the frequent allusions to the flux of lived experience, at no time does time intervene in a decisive fashion in the analysis of noetico-noematic structures. The temporality that is evoked is always a temporal object, a constituted noema, a meaning of time more than the time of meaning. It is never a question of the temporal hylé,[71] which, more than the sensible and spatial hylé, might be a source of difficulties for a static analysis. This hylé which would be the most originary existential "core" of constitution and the one most irreducible to an ἐποχή remains hidden from description. In general, hylé occupies only a secondary place in the static constitution. "Naturally *pure hyletics* finds its proper place in subordination to the phenomenology of the transcendental consciousness. [...] it wins significance from the fact that it furnishes a woof that can enter into the intentional tissue, material that can enter into intentional formations."[72] This subordination is possible only through an exclusion of originary temporality; an exclusion that delivers us a completed synthesis, a constituted lived experience. This is what we must now verify to see confirmed the insufficiency of a static phenomenology and to watch the starting up of the thematization of a "transcendental genesis."

NOETIC TEMPORALITY
INSUFFICIENCY OF A STATIC CONSTITUTION

The Methodological Reticences

All the difficulties raised by the reduction and by the relations of hylé and morphé were finally dependent on an insufficient clarification of the "I" as a constituting source; this latter was sometimes a pure me transcending the flux of lived experience, sometimes an immanent element of this flux. In both cases the temporality of the "I" was [a] constituted temporality; whether it was a form or an object, atemporal or omnitemporal, the "I" could not by definition be confused with an originary temporality. Thus, since the reduction had not attained its absolute scope and [was] such that, "suspending" all constituted transcendence, it could conserve its constituting sense, [the reduction] always had to sink to a superficial level where the exclusion of a "worldly" facticity always left behind it an eidetic region, consciousness, which was as such *already* invested with a sense. Its intentionality was a synthesis that had already been brought about. Likewise, with temporality being introduced only as a factor, a moment in the relations of the active intentional form and the passive sensual matter, we ended up in an aporia; everything antecedent and absolutely original about the one inhibited the apparition or the production of the other. In fact, a reduction of the originary temporality was worked without seeing that it was this temporality itself which made the act of reduction possible. This act takes time. It is already synthetic. In supposing the reduction to be already effected and always possible, Husserl stayed at the superficial and prephenomenological level of a constituted time.

Besides, Husserl freely acknowledges that here he places himself at the level of a constituted temporality. But it is, he thinks, evoking the necessities which are in some way exterior here, that he "must begin" in this way. On two occasions he is concerned to underline this: "at the level of discussion to which we have so far been limited, which stops short of descending into the obscure depths of the ultimate consciousness which constitutes the whole scheme of temporal experience, and accepts experiences rather as they present themselves in immanent reflexion as unitary temporal processes."[73] From the point of view of a reflection which is regressive, this consciousness is final. It is, in fact, originary. Is it only through a "psychological" or "historical" accident that the originary always appears as the final moment of philosophy? Is it not precisely the problem of genesis to know how what is *a priori* present in history cannot be revealed except at the end of historical synthesis and how history can be the creator of what appears as "already there"? This, without it being possible to assert that the act of production absolutely precedes sense or inversely. How can essences be revealed by a genesis if they are essences in the full and absolute sense of the term? Why do they need a genesis in order to appear? If, on the contrary, genesis is not any longer revealing of essences but is creative of them, by virtue of which preliminary sense of genesis will these essences appear to us as absolute and necessary? Husserl is not bothered about this yet. It is to be remembered that, speaking of the ensemble of the phenomenological domain, he was content to add: "that is to say, inside the level of constituted temporality which must be constantly conserved." So the eidetic regions of temporality having *already* been endowed with a sense, the problem of genesis, that is to say, of the originary sense of temporality or of the originary temporality of sense, has *already* been resolved, or has not *yet* been posed, but certainly it is not posed at the moment of these *Ideas* which provide "a general introduction to pure phenomenology."

It is because of this that in *Ideas* I, all the analyses of temporal lived experience reproduce exactly the difficulties met with before. Reiterating the definitions of *Phenomenology of Internal Time Consciousness*, Husserl invites us to "note carefully the difference between this *phenomenological time*, this unitary form of all experiences within a *single* stream of experience (that of *one* pure Ego) and *'objective,'* i.e., *'cosmic'* time."⁷⁴ This latter [time] is "measurable" and entertains the same relations with lived time that the transcendent material object entertains with the hyletic variations. "Just as it would be absurd to bring under the same generic essence a sensory phase such as color or spread, and the phase of the thing proper which manifests itself perspectively through it, such as the color and extension which belong to it as a thing, so is it also in respect of the phenomenologically and the cosmically temporal."⁷⁵ But the meaning of this variation was already obscure when it was a question of spatial perception; it is even more so when the perception of time is envisaged. What is brought out by variation, or figured, by the temporal hylé? If this latter has a specificity and is to be originarily distinguished from the spatial hylé, if it is not derived from this latter, it cannot "figure" cosmic time as the spatial measure of time. Husserl recognizes that under a "community of nature"⁷⁶ there exists an important difference between the temporal hylé and the spatial hylé. But he does not insist on this, and especially he does not ask himself whether every spatial hylé does not presuppose and is not founded on a temporal hylé. To recognize this founding relation would have been to make the inadequacy of the analyses of a static constitution blatantly obvious, a constitution in which the hyletic variation plays a fundamental role. The truth is that, at the interior of the spatial hylé taken in itself, the problem of the constituting becoming is still being posed; for if the sensuous datum is a nonintentional real *(reell)* lived experience, its determination cannot take place except by a passive constitution. Being a variation of an individual reality *(real)*, it must as such precede the animating intentionality. Now, a passive constitution cannot be a real element of nonintentional lived experience except by participating in the same time. For the same reasons, this unity of time must include an originary passive moment in its constitution. It can be constituted in this way only in or through an "originary temporality" of consciousness,⁷⁷ which seems deeper than intentionality itself. This latter seems yet to authorize only an active constitution that remains static, according to a paradox whose necessity has made itself felt. The idea of genetic constitution and the difference between passive genesis and active genesis does not seem ready yet for Husserl. It is especially the idea of passivity that resists analysis. Now, as we will see, it is because there is passive synthesis that one will have to thematize genesis in general, the idea of a purely active genesis reconciling itself very well with a static constitution.

After having compared the spatial extension and the temporal extension of hylé, Husserl reduces his whole analysis to a series of suggestions and reservations: "Time is the name for a completely *self-contained sphere of problems* and one of exceptional difficulty. It will be seen that in a certain sense our previous exposition has been silent, and necessarily so, concerning a whole dimension so as to maintain free of confusion what first becomes transparent from the phenomenological standpoint alone," and he adds, summing up the whole insufficiency of static phenomenology whose epoch is in the process of being closed: "The transcendental 'Absolute' which we have laid bare through the reductions is in truth not ultimate; it is something *(etwas)* which in a certain profound and wholly unique sense constitutes itself, and has its primeval source *(Urquelle)* in what is ultimately and truly absolute."[78] So all these reductions have been possible only because a subject whose form is still not known (individual ego, originary temporality, history understood in the teleological sense, intersubjective community, etc.) has engendered and is engendering itself. The very act of reduction temporalizes itself according to the *a priori* laws of time, which themselves refer to an originary and passive synthesis of time. If there is reduction of a certain time, there is also a certain time of reduction. It is this that must be probed. The subject "for whom" phenomenology is possible is a temporal subject. Now, on the one hand, an active constitution of time through something other than itself is thus impossible. Since everything which is in itself foreign to time constitutes itself in time, it is really the autoconstitution of this latter that serves as last foundation for every other structure. On the other hand, it belongs to the essence of time not to constitute itself according to a purely active mode; retention of the constituted past implies a synthesis or a passive genesis of the new "now." No transcendental activity can "retain" the already constituted past as such in consciousness. If the constitution and retention of the past were active, they would, like any pure activity, shut themselves up in the actuality of an originary "now," or in the project or the protention of a future; the past would never be retained and recognized as such.

The thematization of passive genesis, so called, ought to upset already all the results of the phenomenological results acquired by this date. Must not the pure "ego" be replaced by a subject producing itself in a history which, passively received by the subject in its intentional moment, can no longer be individual and monadic? If passive genesis constrains us to grant a constituting role to what has already been constituted in a continuous becoming, must not the relationships between phenomenology and the constituted sciences in general (history, psychology, biology, sociology, etc.) between transcendental lived experience and empirical facts, be profoundly modified in the direction of a dialectic "composition"?

Husserl does not yet anticipate such an enlarging of the future theme. Especially, he does not see its "necessity." "Fortunately we can leave the enigmas of the time-consciousness in our preliminary analyses without imperiling their rigor."[79] But this eidetic "rigor" is perhaps only validly opposed to the conceptual "exactness" of natural sciences, to the degree that essences are explicated in their transcendental origin. Before the profound analysis of their constitution, nothing allows the distinction of essence from concept, of constituting rigor from constituted exactness. To the degree that the themes of *Ideas* I are given structures and already constituted, the rigor of their description does not offer in itself more of a guarantee than does the rigor of a psychological description. However, confident in a method whose foundation remains, one has to say, pretty obscure here, Husserl thinks that an eidetic description of time can precede in an exposé a properly transcendental description which it never ceases to involve and imply; the idea of "transcendental guide," of "guiding thread," to which Husserl so often makes allusion, must be evoked here. Thus, an eidetic region, the "thing" region for example, can serve as "transcendental clue"[80] for phenomenological research. Here the eidetics of temporality must bring us slowly toward the originary constitution of time-consciousness. "The essential [eidetic] property which the term 'temporality' expresses in relation to experiences generally indicates not only something that belongs in a general way to every single experience, but *a necessary form binding experiences with experiences.* Every real experience (we ratify this as self-evident on the ground of the clear intuition of an experiential reality) is necessarily one that endures; [...] It belongs to *one* [unique] endless 'stream of experience.'"[81] Do we thus go beyond a pure and simple eidetic description uncovering the "essential character" of every piece of lived experience for us?

Originarity of "Now" and the Idea in a Kantian Sense

It is probably too clear that this "necessary form which links lived experiences to lived experiences" has nothing in common with an ideality of time of Kantian type, a condition of formal possibility of a succession and of a causality or an *a priori* form of sensibility. Not being a "character which possesses in general way every piece of lived experience" it must itself be a concrete piece of lived experience. What then distinguishes it from any piece of lived experience in particular? How then to reconcile the multiplicity of temporal experiences and the homogeneous unity of time? Not being abstract, this unity is immediately a unity *of* this concrete multiplicity. But if it is only a unity *of* this multiplicity of lived experience, it is hard to see how every piece of lived experience as such and in its immanence, can be originarily conscious of belonging to the infinity of time. Indeed, Husserl writes: "Every single experience can begin and end and therewith bring its duration to an end—for instance, an experience of joy. But the stream of experience cannot begin and end."[82] What does this flux of lived experience mean, taken in its infinite totality and nevertheless distinct from every piece of lived experience in particular? It cannot be lived as infinite. On the other hand, its infinity cannot be constituted from finite lived experience as such. Its transcendence in relation to the finite cannot on the other hand, Husserl makes clear, be transcendence in the mode of the transcendent thing. It is still transcendence in immanence. The one and infinite flux is thus, like the pure ego, a transcendence that is not constituted in immanence, a lived experience that does not mingle itself with lived experiences and remains distinct from ideality. This text is unintelligible if one does not modify, in the light of a genetic description, on the one hand, the idea of pure ego and of lived experience, on the other hand, the relations of the constituting and the constituted in the interpretation of history in general.

If in effect lived experience understands itself as lived without coming out of this noetico-noematic circle such as was defined in § 49, it is impossible that the infinite flux of lived experience should appear to it. Time, which indefinitely passes by, must be neither the spatialized time of a cosmic conception nor this "noematic" time which is constituted by each piece of lived experience and which fades away with it. It must thus involve a pure time; this latter, totally antepredicative, can, for example, take the form of an absolutely undetermined future; now, such a future is absolutely inaccessible, as such and originarily, to an intentionality that attains only noematic structures which are already integrated into lived immanence. With it is sketched out a new transcendence that takes us out of the framework defined in *Ideas* 1. *Mutatis mutandis,* the same thing can be said of the past. The intentionality thus deepened in the double sense of its activity and of its passivity must link the pure ego, as concrete totality of lived experience, to antepredicative time constituting itself passively. Lived experience can no longer be defined by a pure immanence, however intentional it may be.

The consequence of this is the following: the I, transcendence in lived immanence, can no longer appear to a purely monadic "ego." The theme of transcendental intersubjectivity is in the background of these analyses. The I, being neither in time nor out of time, nor analytically merged with time, must be time itself, producing itself dialectically through protention and retention, in its infinite future and past, as noesis and noema; as activity and passivity, and so on. Dialectic being here originary, the constituted constitutes the constituting and inversely; the absolute monad originarily welcomes "the other"; whether that "other" be the antepredicative existence of the sensuous thing, of time or of an "alter ego," it must be granted a transcendental sense, however strange that appears. So the pure "I" must constitute itself temporally, in a dialectical genesis composing passivity and activity.

With passive genesis, a constituting value must be granted to everything that up to now has appeared as constituted: the natural attitude and everything that answered it or made up the object of natural and human sciences; all that participates in one and the same history from which the notion of lived experience is thus reformed and enlarged. The immediacy and the obviousness of lived experience are synthetic *a prioris*, since they are originarily temporal. They cannot not thus be described except in terms of contradiction. And this is indeed what Husserl implicitly does in *Ideas* I, that is, several years before having brought the genetic theme to light, when wanting to describe this at the same time pure and temporal "ego," he identifies it *at the same time*—and obscurely—with an absolute Present and with an Idea in the Kantian sense. "The Ego *is able* to direct its glance upon *the way in which* the temporal factor is being *given,* and to know self-evidently [...] that no enduring experience is possible unless it is constituted within a continuous flow of modes of givenness as the unitary factor in the process, or the duration."[83] But this unity, not being a formal concept exterior to duration itself, is in turn a piece of lived experience "although of a different kind." It is this new "kind" that Husserl does not define in a sufficient way. On the one hand, indeed, in order that this form might be the form of all the pieces of lived experience, it has to appear or appear to itself as a present piece of lived experience whose actuality never flags. But this actuality must not be merged with the successive one, of the multiple pieces of lived experience. Turning to these latter "I can also pay attention [...] to the modus of the actual 'Now,' and to this feature also that with this very 'now,' and in principle with every 'now,' a new and continuously new 'now' links up in necessary continuity, and that in concert with this every actual now passes into a just *(Soeben)* vanished, the just vanished once again and continuously so into ever-new just vanishings of the just vanished, and so forth."[84] It is inside this lived experience that one must distinguish between the pieces of lived experience themselves in their changing multiplicity and this pure form of temporal lived experience which is at the same time immanent in them and transcendent to them. This originary tension between immanence and transcendence remains mysterious. "The actual *now* is necessarily something punctual and remains so, *a form that persists through continuous change of content.*"[85] If this punctual limit is never really lived as such, it is an *a priori* concept that informs lived experience; it is a constituted and atemporal ideality. If, on the contrary, it is lived, it cannot be punctual. Pure punctuality is the negation of continuity and hence of the very self-evidence of temporal lived experience. However, without this pure punctuality of lived experience as such, the evidence of continuity is also impossible. This latter lasts across one single present that continues, always punctual and always new. Without the rigorous pointlike form of each present, the diverse phenomenological modifications of time, present, past, future, would be cut off from their self-evidence and from their originary distinction. "*Every* present moment of experience, even if it be that of the initial phase of an experience freshly developing, has necessarily *a before as a limit.* But on grounds of principle this can be no empty previousness, a mere form without content, mere nonsense. It has necessarily the meaning of a past now which in this form contains a past something, a past *experience.*"[86] The pointlike form of the "now" thus implies, as such, an anteriority; it brings with it a retention, then a retention of retention, and so forth. It has a continuous density. It is concrete. The pure form or the pure ego are thus impossible without a genetic history where the creation of "nows" that are always new is continued by an incessant and necessary retention. The purity of the temporal form or of the ego being manifested in a pointlike actuality is "essentially" and *a priori* born by a past and oriented by a future. Its very sense, that is to say, the originarity and the originality of its "now" is founded on the possibility of this double movement. Its absolute consists in being taken in a lived "relation"; its purity reveals itself and is enriched in what is not itself.

It would also be possible—and Husserl still tries to do this here—to conceive the formal purity of time as the lived totality of real and possible "nows." Since the punctual "now" is impure and complicated, one can hope to find once more the pure unity of the ego and of the temporal form in the form of a "totality." But Husserl admits, "In principle this *whole* connection [*totalité de cet enchaînement*] is *never* one that is or can be given through a single pure glance."[87] Is one not then forced to have resort to a conceptual construction and a formal extension of a restricted cycle of connection in order to take in an infinite totality of possible "nows"? Husserl believes in an "intuition" of this possible infinity of connections. "Notwithstanding, even it is in a *certain,* though in an intrinsically different, way intuitively graspable, namely, along the line of *'limitlessness in the progressive development' (Grenzenlosigkeit im Fortgang) of immanent intuitions.*"[88] In introducing here a supposed intuition of an infinite totality, Husserl tries, in vain it seems, to safeguard the immanent and monadic purity of the temporal ego. He pretends to probe this temporality only in order to make it escape from its dialectical essence: there is no actual intuition of the infinite totality of chains of connections, but an intuition of the very indefiniteness of this totality of the chains of connections.[89] It is its essential incompletion that would be apprehended at each moment through a concrete intuition; this latter is the very movement that constitutes the pure present. "Advancing continuously from one apprehension to another, we apprehend in a certain way, I remarked, *the stream of experience as a unity also.* We do not apprehend it like a single experience, but after the fashion of an *Idea in the Kantian sense.*"[90] And a little farther on, Husserl speaks of an "intuition of this idea in the Kantian sense." If one thinks that the idea in the Kantian sense is, first of all, and for Kant himself, what cannot be filled by an intuition, the revolution projected by Husserl in regard to criticism and Kantian formalism takes on all its meaning. At the level of *Ideas* I, which is that of a constituted temporality, this revolution, however, does not seem founded. How is an intuition of what is not yet there possible? How can nonbeing and absence be immediately and concretely apprehended? That appears all the more difficult because, with Husserl, the origin and the foundation of any act and any intentional aim are in a positive thesis of being. Must not the transformation of the infinite into the indefinite, introducing negation into originary lived experience, force us to use conceptual mediations or other kinds of mediations to attain a totality that is not "given" to us? This totality remains formal and the intuition that claims to aim at it cannot be "fulfilled" by an originary presence.

This is because this intuition remains an eidetic intuition of time; time is here a concrete noematic essence which, for all that, does not become mixed with the concrete temporality of the noetic subject. It is only a concrete eidetic necessity that time should appear in an indefinite continuity of originary "nows." But on the other hand it is known that essences, although perceived in a feeling of absolute self-evidence, are constituted as such through the act of a transcendental subjectivity. If in considering atemporal essences as such, we could already be surprised that consciousness as simple eidetic region were able to produce and apprehend εἴδη, that is all the more so if it is a question of the essence of time. It is a transcendental consciousness which should thus constitute time in its essence. But this consciousness as pure Me is also the concrete form of time. It constitutes the essence of time only because it is *already* temporal. In it, the synthesis of matter and form, of lived experience and the "now," of its concrete actuality and its indefinite possibility is always *already* made.[91] While for other eidetic domains we could try to describe lived experience according to the constituted structures of the noetico-noematic correlation, without perverting the sense of the analyses, the essence of time resists such discourse. The noetic act is already temporal, already constituted through an originary synthesis. The pure form is essentially *already* material. In terms of hylé and morphé, before the explicit intervention of the morphé, the temporal hylé is already "passively informed" and to this degree the morphé meets a matter that it can "animate" only because the temporal synthesis has been carried out passively the moment before. This time, at the level of a lived experience which is at least passive,[92] the genesis of the transcendental "I" itself cannot be contested. With it we begin to make explicit this absolutely originary pre-noetico-noematic time, which is proposed to us as the ultimate transcendental source. And if it is true, as Husserl writes, that "*One* pure Ego, *one* Stream of experience filled with content along all three dimensions, and in such filling holding essentially together *(zusammenhängender)* and progressing *(sich fordernder)* through its continuity of content: these are necessary correlates,"[93] it remains that this correlation is neither balanced nor static since, on the one hand, this unique pure Me is already constituted in temporality and, on the other, the flux of lived experience is already unified in its relation to a subject; and thus inside each of these terms one finds again a constituting synthesis that needs both poles of the correlation at the same time. This correlation is thus superficial and refers us to a more originary synthesis. At the limits of purity we will always encounter the synthesis or the genesis of time constituting itself as subject. This genetic synthesis is so originary and *a priori* that we can in no wise determine whether time precedes pure subjectivity or inversely—the dialectic is infinite because constituting subjectivity is synthetically mixed with time, because existence is a finitude "for itself."

The "Primordial Synthesis"
The Necessity of a Genetic Constitution

If Husserl does not speak yet of transcendental genesis, he nevertheless refers to a new domain which remains to be explored: that of a "primordial synthesis" *(Ursynthese)* of the original consciousness of time itself (which is not to be conceived as an active and discrete synthesis) and which has "expressly excluded this primary synthesis of the original time-consciousness [...] with the forms of inquiry which belong to it."[94] This is how the whole foundation of the phenomenological analyses pursued up to now is hidden out of purely methodological necessity. This foundation is a genesis.

Thus, at the end of this "General Introduction to Pure Phenomenology," we see a reversal: the whole initial intention of phenomenology seemed to motivate a refusal or a taking "off-line" of genesis. Thus having been led to a transformation of temporality into an atemporal "eidos," we needed to come back to the actual temporality of the pure subject. The whole reduction of genetic temporality was deepened down to the temporal genesis of reduction itself. Since at this moment of subjectivity, the synthesis between the fact and the essence of time, between the existence and the intentional consciousness of the temporal subject, are absolutely originary, the whole distinction between fact and essence, the validity of the eidetic reduction and of the transcendental reduction are put in question again. The passive synthesis of the temporal hylé and, through this, of every hylé in general seems to bring us to reconsider the distinction between the real *(real)* and the lived *(reell)*. We thus get to a point such that not only does it seem necessary to thematize a transcendental genesis, but even, and just through doing that, to look for a new foundation for the distinction between transcendental genesis and real *(real)* genesis. The empirical and the transcendental seem to resist any rigorous dissociation. A new phenomenological effort must try to find this again, far away and in depth. This is the price to be paid for philosophy.

PART III

THE PHENOMENOLOGICAL THEME OF
GENESIS: TRANSCENDENTAL GENESIS AND
"WORLDLY" GENESIS

6

Birth and Becoming of Judgment

The whole movement of Husserl's thought toward a genetic phenomenology was, we saw, oriented from the beginning. However, it was not unilinear. Hence it is impossible to decide whether the apparition of the genetic theme from 1915 to 1920, after *Ideen* I, constitutes a completion of or a revolution in the preceding philosophy. For that it would be necessary to give to Husserl's philosophy the "systematic" character of a "syllogistics": conclusions not verifying their premises would destroy a whole [style of] philosophical coherence. Besides the fact that this kind of view would contradict the deep sense of Husserl's thought, a glance at the complication of themes in the manuscripts, at the tangled nature of their chronology, is enough for one no longer to believe in the idea of a brusque turn or in a rupture. The idea of "theme" on which Husserl insists more and more after *Ideas* I, accords with the very intention of phenomenology: the unveiling or the elucidation of meanings adds nothing to a construction. These meanings no more create or invent than they devalue or destroy what preceded them.

This is true for all the Husserlian themes in general. But if one were to open a long parenthesis, it would be, precisely and for once, to ask whether the idea of theme is compatible with the idea of a genesis of essences. Is not treating genesis like a theme the same as reducing it to its noematic sense and to that degree to a becoming that has been "canonized," to an essence already present on which an atemporal consciousness need do no more than project the light of its gaze? Is not the appearance of the theme of genesis at the same time a creation and a revelation, as every genesis [is]? Let us not meet this problem head on; it would distance us from our argument.[1]

It is enough for us to indicate that important and explicit allusions to

the possibility of a genetic phenomenology appear a few years after *Ideen*
I.[2] In 1919–1920, Husserl's lectures deal with a genetic logic. These lectures will be the fundamental texts from which L. Landgrebe will put together and edit *Experience and Judgment*.[3] From the moment of these lectures right to the end of his life, Husserl made the problem of genesis the
center of his reflection.

There is doubtless nothing in common between this genesis and an empirical genesis that Husserl claims to exclude or to "neutralize" as he did before. Husserl's faithfulness to a transcendental search will never lapse. The
thematization of genesis, of the "life-world" of historicity, has often been
presented as the abandonment of the initial claims to a transcendental phenomenology. It was never a question of this, at least not for Husserl. This hypothesis once put aside, it can nevertheless be asked to what degree the situation which the genetic theme now occupies does not make more urgent
the danger of a confusion between the "real" *(real)* and the intentional
lived experience, the worldly and the transcendental, constituted historicity and originary temporality. The project of a rigorous split between these
"moments" had not been sustained by a static phenomenology. Will it be
from the point of view of a genesis which, by confusing becoming with the
constitution of meanings themselves, will make the continuity or the dialectic solidarity that links these diverse factors even more irreducible? With genetic becoming no longer being constituted in its meaning by the activity
of a transcendental subject, but constituting the "ego" itself, the sphere of
phenomenology is no longer defined by the lived immanence of noetico-
noematic structures; it is no longer immediately transparent to a theoretic
spectator of essences. Phenomenology must in a certain sense finish up with
a genetic becoming. It is there that it must be fulfilled, but it must do so in
becoming an ontology or in entertaining fundamental relations with ontology. The transcendental subject which engenders itself is no longer a theoretical consciousness, but an existence. Husserl does not speak of a passage
to an original ontology. He thinks that phenomenology has already defined
the relationships that linked it to ontology.[4] Hence, he believes that the new
progress of his reflection in the genetic domain must continue all its preceding moments.

But this serenity is no answer: can the transcendental "I," absolute
source of constitution, be engendered in a history while maintaining itself
in a pure "phenomenologising"[5] attitude? If it is itself a temporal "existence," what would be the value and objective purity of the essences that it
constitutes?

Antepredicative Evidence and the Foundation of Genesis

Right from the beginning of *Experience and Judgment,* which is presented as a "genealogy of logic," we have already left the level of *Ideas* I behind. The frontiers of the originary world have been opened. Husserl approaches the problem of the originary evidence of the existent as such. Knowledge strives toward the existent. "But, if the striving for knowledge is directed toward the existent, if it is the effort to formulate in a judgment what and how the existent is, then the existent must already have been given beforehand."[6] It is starting from this existent, given in its antepredicative evidence, that the genesis of judgment and the predicative evidence must be described. "Cognition, with its 'logical' procedures, has always already done its work whenever we reflect logically (or [when we become] 'logically' conscious, that is to say, when logic 'appears': *wenn wir uns logisch besinnen*); we have already passed judgments, formed concepts, drawn conclusions, which henceforth form part of our store of knowledge and as such are at our disposal [they are pre-given us as such]."*[7] All of which implies that before logical reflection, we are instructed about the difference between true judgment and judgment that only gives itself as such. But if the logician is orientated toward a logic in the serious sense of the word, his interest goes to the laws of formation of judgments (principles and rules of formal logic) not as simple rules of the game, but as rules which the formation of judgments must satisfy to the very degree to which it is thanks to them that knowledge in general is possible.[8] Now if "attention is thus directed to the act of judgment as an achievement *(Leistung)* of consciousness,"[9] the gaze encounters a traditional problem of logic, one always left to genetic psychology. The problems of origin not being posed at the simple level of a formal logic, they were referred to psychology as the science of real and natural formation of concepts and judgments. Now the project of a genetic psychology[10] of judgment is fundamentally distinct from the project of a genetic phenomenology of judgment; the first, in fact, has never taken seriously the problems of clear self-evidence which yet are the only point of departure for all subjective regression when it is a question of logical forms. One believed that one knew in advance what evidence was

---

*The translations in square brackets [ ] are of a phrase from Derrida's own French translation of the German in his text. The phrase in parentheses is Derrida's commentary on the quotation. *Trans.*

because knowledge was realized somewhere, something which allowed the measuring of all empirical knowledge. It is thus not in its genetic claim that Husserl contests the value of psychology; on the contrary, psychology is insufficient because its genetic claim is timid, because it supposes that the sense of originary evidence is known already from the outset, because it has not thrown light on its first implications. Genetic phenomenology, on the contrary, far from being a "psychological technology of precise thinking" proposes to retrace the absolute itinerary that leads from antepredicative evidence to predicative evidence. In that, it supposes that the broader transcendental reduction has been carried out, which no longer leaves us facing eidetic structures, even were they those of consciousness, but facing the purity of experience itself. It is from this source that the genesis of evidence starts off. It seems that the movement of intentionality is fully respected. It places us *a priori* in contact with the existent as such. But it is not yet known how the immediacy of this experience is going to engender complicated predicative acts. How will it be possible to escape a precritical empiricism in order to found a logic in general? The giving up of every formal *a priori* is now total and complete. The transcendental "I," pure, concrete, and temporal accedes directly to the existent as such. Will the genesis that will follow this access be active or passive from the point of view of the "I"? Will the activity be a modified moment of passivity or inversely? On the other hand, if every logic and every "theory" in general refers to a perception of the existent where this latter is presented "in person," will not phenomenology be referred to a yet more originary domain where perception is elaborated in a preobjective attitude? Another hypothesis—will not phenomenology exhaust itself in a sensualism[11] in which any objectivation, whether predicative or antepredicative, will appear mediated and suspect? Does not the idea of a transcendental genesis lead to an empiricism? It does so through a limitless pretension to originarity and through the will to undo tirelessly the sedimentations of predicates and formal systems.

The existent, aim of knowledge, must always be "pregiven."[12] But it must not be given in any old fashion. It must be given in the evidence of the "self-givenness" [given in person] *(Selbstgegebenheit)* and not in a simple "presentification" *(Vergegenwärtigung)*[13] of imagination or of memory. The self-evidence that founds apodicity is not confused with it; apodicity belongs, in effect, to the order of predication starting from evident substrates. Thus, there are two degrees to the set of problems: that of the evidence of objects pregiven in themselves and that of predicative acts completing themselves on the foundation of the evidence of these objects. There is thus a genesis of predication from out of the world of antepredicative evidence. This genesis is not studied either through a formal logic, or through psychology, both of which keep themselves at the upper, superficial level of the set of problems.[14] "But for the phenomenological elucidation of the genesis of the act of judgment, this regressive inquiry is necessary."[15] If we look for the phenomenological genesis of judgments in the originarity of their production, it then becomes apparent that *"mere judging is an intentional modification of cognitive judgment (daß blosses Urteilen eine intentionale Modifikation von erkennendem Urteilen ist)."*[16] It is clear how far we have come from the neutralization of any genesis as causal and psychological genesis. The genetic point of view is now the only one to lead a search for foundations. Since the origin is in the real substrates given over to perception, we have come a long way, we are out of lived immanence and the world of noetico-noematic meanings. Every noema is a predicative structuration of the substrate; every noesis is founded on the evidence of the "given in person." But more than ever, psychophysiological or historical genesis is put aside; the concrete purity of the transcendental is safeguarded. "We see, already here, in what sense we shall be dealing with questions of genesis. Our concern is not a first genesis (of a history in general, or of an individual history) or a genesis of knowledge in *every* sense; rather, we shall be dealing with that mode of production through which judgment and also knowledge in their original form, that of self-givenness, arise."[17]

It might seem here that, psychologism and historicism being definitively left behind, we also go beyond the whole idealism of *Ideas* I, through the thematization of a primordial genesis. In fact, judgment is not a psychological act, that is to say, not "immanent in a real or individual sense," but rather an "unreal"[18] immanent, in the sense that it was said of the noema that it was an immanent and unreal lived experience. But the problem is once again posed about how an unreal lived experience of evidence is founded on the reality of the existent. In one sense, it is necessary that evidence be an unreal lived experience; without that, it would once again be confused with constituted reality; truth would be impossible. But if the genesis took place inside an unreal lived experience, it would be separated from the existent as such and deprived of its foundation. We would be once again prisoner of the idealism of *Ideas*. If, on the contrary, as Husserl seems to wish, genesis does not start off from a sense, from an essence, from a predicate, but in fact from the antepredicative reality of the existent itself, then we would have to admit that knowledge has made a jump, passing from evidence of the given to the categorial judgment. In order for the product of judgment to be indefinitely valid, as Husserl[19] wants, in order for it always to give the same knowledge (which is a criterion of universal truth) the judgment must be an "unreal immanent" and "supratemporal" *(Überzeitliches)*.[20] There is thus a genesis of the "supratemporal." We always run up against one and the same irreducible paradox, at all the levels of constitution. The supratemporal, once admitted and described in its specificity, is detached from its genesis. It seems then impossible to attribute to it a temporal situation in transcendental becoming and to make of it the "product." As a logical form or supratemporal category, it will just as well then be *a priori* in relation to a genesis that it makes possible. This genesis would be again accidental and psychological. This would be the whole sense of the Kantian attempt. Inversely, one could—this would be closer to the intention of Husserl—consider this supratemporality as an omnitemporality: the product of the genesis would thus at the same time be rooted in transcendental and autonomous temporality in relation to psychological temporality. But that is to make of this supratemporality a modification of temporality in general. The autonomy that it seems to have acquired is only a modality of its dependence. It is in this sense doubtless that Husserl intends it, and this thesis will see itself confirmed by Husserl in the *Origin of Geometry*. But indeed, to make of supratemporality or omnitemporality a simple specification of time, time needs to be envisaged not only in its antepredicative moment, but also outside the lived and unreal immanence of a transcendental ego. Without which, one would not understand that it agrees with the temporality of the existent as such and that it is the place of infinite predicative sedimentations such as the supraindividual tradition of logic delivers to us. Originary time is a more fundamental time than that of lived immanence. It must be what makes possible phenomenological time. At the limit, it is merged with the infinite temporality of historical sedimentations; if it was not thus, we would run the risk of turning antepredicative time into substance or perceptions of the senses, forbidding every predicative objectivation and every constitution of supratemporal logical forms. But this infinite totality of sedimentations is an idea: the idea of an absolute and completed history or of a teleology constituting all the moments of history. The absolute of the antepredicative is thus at the same time the most concrete and the most formal, the most determinate in itself and the most empty. If the genesis is absolutely and exclusively informed by a teleology, then it appears "useless" in itself; if it always alludes only to the antepredicative moment of first perception, it appears "impossible." If it is the idea of a total history of logic that animates genesis *a priori*, one wonders why this latter must embody it in a time which is strange to it, and which runs the danger of perverting and alienating it. If, on the other hand, the antepredicative moment is really pure, it is not known how it can engender and found a sense that becomes progressively complicated and that gains autonomy while remaining dependent on its origin. Only an originary and thus infinite dialectic allows one to assume this phenomenological paradox. Whatever Husserl's conclusion on this point may be, the dual necessity, of a transcendental intersubjectivity and of a teleology, can already be seen. But Husserl does not yet[21] present them and is wondering about the relations of this genesis of logic to transcendental activity.

The Ambiguous Sense of the "World"

If the "world is the universal ground of belief," and if, from this fact, it is "already passively pregiven in its totality in certainty,"[22] what is the sense of transcendental activity? If this activity is exercised on a pregiven substrate, one already constituted as such, that is to say, with its meaning of "pregiven," will it do more than idealize or formalize an antepredicative sense immanent to the substrate and passively taken on board? Is not judgment added as a simple modalization of what is pregiven in sensuous experience? The genesis of apodicity from out of antepredicative evidence often appears in *Experience and Judgment* as a genesis which produces only what is already there, which makes what is in the object "appear," that is to say, a genesis that itself took evidence for granted and could easily be assimilated to a simple empirical genesis. The predicate, being purely and simply determined by the antepredicative being that founds it, is not originarily constituted by a transcendental activity; or, more exactly, the latter is consumed in a passivity that originarily defines it. "The being of the world in totality is that [which is absolutely obvious *(die Selbstverständlichkeit)*, which can never be put in doubt] which is not first the result of an activity of judgment but forms the presupposition *(die Voraussetzung)* of all judgment."[23] If then we need to return to this world, to found logic in its transcendental constitution, it is nevertheless evident that the notions of activity and passivity must be understood in their transcendental sense. The "life-world" *(Lebenswelt)*, locus of all the antepredicative pieces of clear evidence, is not, as it is often presented, an already constituted world, preceding or determining in the strict sense of the word a supposed transcendental activity of the subject. The world is defined by Husserl not as an actually real world of which the knowing subject would be prisoner, but as "the horizon of all possible substrates of judgments."[24] It is a possibility open to the infinity of pieces of evidence founded in it.

Foundation of any "worldliness" of traditional and formal logic, it is not it-self "worldly."

We run up here against a serious ambiguity in the concept of "world."[25] On the one hand, the world is the antepredicative in its actual "reality." Al-ways already there, in its primitive ontological structure, it is the preconsti-tuted substrate of all meaning. But on the other hand, it is the idea of an in-finite totality of possible foundations of every judgment. In it are opposed the actuality of existence as substrate and the infinite possibility of transcenden-tal experiences.[26] Which makes the problem of genesis take a new turn. The world as infinite horizon of possible experiences cannot itself be a predicate or a modalization of the "real" antepredicative world. It is originarily an infi-nite horizon of the possible, as a great many texts indicate.

Here the possible is not a predicate of the actual and it is not engendered out of a concrete antepredicative evidence. It is in itself neither an existent nor a set of actual existents. It is thus a formal *a priori* possibility, irreducible to a transcendental genesis. I cannot, starting from an antepredicative moment of the existent or of an actual, that is to say, "finite," totality of existents, get to the idea of an infinite horizon of predication. The antepredicative thus takes on a dual aspect.

Sometimes, [as] indefinite determinability, it is the opening or the "open-ness" of being to consciousness; it is the infinite totality of what can be man-ifested. Its being "already there" signifies what is waiting for the act of a con-sciousness to reveal its sense. Its character as preconstituted, passively taken on by consciousness, is a pure and simple absence of phenomenological meaning before the transcendental activity of a subject. Far from being op-posed to this, transcendental passivity will be the formal condition of tran-scendental activity. But we do not any longer see then what is the concrete foundation of constitution. If the concrete antepredicative existent has no sense in itself before transcendental activity, no determination that is intelli-gible in itself, it is not clear how consciousness could give it one or, in the last resort, recognize it intentionally as such or such. If what the transcendental ego receives passively is only an indeterminate substrate, the sense that it will "lend" to it will be able to be confused with a subjective construction, an in-vention or a pragmatic fabrication of sense. Idealizations will be conceptual mediations. No essence inherent to the substrate will be able to found them, but only a relation or a subjective, psychological, anthropological, and so on situation in relation to the object. We would have there a subjectivist, an-thropologist deviation from intentionality. The immediate access to the sense of the object passively perceived would be only a "factitious"[27] producing of essences. Not being inherent in the substrate, these latter would remain concepts. A fundamental intention of phenomenology would be perverted.

Now this is not only a hypothesis or a prolongation of Husserl's texts. The idealizations of predicative logic are defined in several places as the products of an artificial genesis. Engendered out of an antepredicative existence, they figure a cultural sedimentation that theoretically one can and must always undo. It is because this sedimentation is superstructural that the "reactualization" of the originary sense is always possible. All the regressions at the origin of the antepredicative world are possible because the logical sedimentations are in some way superadded to a pregiven world, by necessities of method and of practice. The paradox is thus the following: It is because the world is formally pregiven to transcendental passivity that the idealizations produced by transcendental activity remain conceptual and invite us to find again the pregiven reality as their foundation. "The retrogression to the world of experience is a *retrogression to the 'life-world*,' i.e., to the world in which we are always already living."[28] The world in which we live, from which emanates everything that affects us as substrate of possible judgments, is always already pregiven us as the sedimentary structure of logical productions. The sense of this pregiven being is determined through us, who are "adults of our epoch" thanks to all the discoveries of modern sciences[29]; even if we are not interested in the sciences, the world is pregiven us as in principle determinable through science:

> In this way, the world of our experience is from the beginning interpreted by recourse to an 'idealization'—but it is no longer seen that this idealization [...] is itself the result of a function of cognitive methods, a result based on the data of our immediate experience. This experience in its immediacy knows neither exact space nor objective time and causality. And even if it is true that all theoretical scientific determination of existents ultimately refers back to experience and its data, nevertheless experience does not give its objects directly in such a way that the thinking that operates on these objects as it itself experiences them is able to lead by itself—by its explication, colligating, disjoining, relating, concept-forming, by its deductions and inductions—immediately to objects in the sense of true theory, i.e., to objects of science.[30]

And it is here the phrase is encountered that some, for diverse motives, judge to be scandalous: "And it is always overlooked that this universe of determinations in themselves, in which exact science apprehends the universe of existents, is nothing more than a garb of ideas *(ein Kleid von Ideen)* thrown over the world of immediate intuition and experience, the life world; [...] it is through the garb of ideas that we take for true Being what is actually a method."[31]

This grave declaration, which seems to be in contradiction with the doctrine of categorial intuition, thus defines the whole life of ideas in pragmatic and conceptual terms. Every predicate is a conceptual formalization, a tool of scientific intelligence; the supposedly transcendental genesis of logic would only be the putting-together of tricks that hide the nakedness of antepredicative existence—a disappointing conclusion which rigorously follows the definition of the antepredicative world as absolute and unique foundation of predication. In all good logic, the absolute antepredicative must not receive any determination; absolutely concrete, it becomes, at the end and because it is absolute, an empty and formal totality. The determinations it "received," not having by definition any validity by themselves and referring to a pregiven with which they have only external relations, are then perforce conventional. The genesis of logic is a practical necessity, a total degradation of pregiven purity. Becoming is decline. Temporality is thus not originarity since it defines only itself and appears only in relation to an intemporal which it spoils. The originary and absolute pole of genesis was thought to have been found, but once again the absolute of genesis is only negation and devalorization of genesis. Through its very indetermination, the absolute has been converted into its opposite. The absolute of time is intemporality. But if genesis is made out to be lived experience and the originary, then as soon as this intemporality is thematized as such, it appears engendered and accidental. It will be mystification. One does not escape from dialectic.

On the contrary, Husserl sometimes presents the antepredicative world no longer as indefinite and formal possibility, but as the always present actuality of the given. But he seems to end in the same aporia. All the "genealogy" of the predicative judgment presupposes, in fact, the distinction between simple *(schlicht)* experiences and "founded" experiences. The regression toward simple experiences will bring us back to the originary world. "Though we have already acquired a concept of experience as objective self-evidence of individual objects, such experience is still multiform in itself, even if all the idealizations which overlie its originality have been dismantled."[32] The "life-world" which then appears is not only the world of logical operations, the domain of objects pregiven as possible substrates, but also the world of experience, in the most concrete and most everyday sense of the word; the everyday sense, Husserl adds, is not linked purely to an activity of knowledge, but also to a "habituality" *(Habitualität)* which gives some security to life's decisions and actions. So it refers to practical and "appreciative" *(wertende)* behavior rather than to theoretical behavior. In going back from predicative judgments, we have thus got to a domain of passive belief, to a "consciousness of the pregivenness of the substrates of judgment *(Bewußtsein der Vorgegebenheit der Urteilssubstrate)*,[33] which has revealed itself to be the domain of the world. Thus, this passive "doxa" is not only the foundation of theoretical operations of knowledge but also the foundation of singular evaluations and of "praxis." In it "The world, as it is always already pregiven entire in passive *doxa*, furnishing the ground of belief *(Glaubensboden)* for all particular acts of judgment, is at bottom given in simple experience as a world of substrates apprehensible simply by sense *(schlicht sinnlich erfaßbarer Substrate)*. Every sensuous experience [...] is *sensuous* experience."[34]

This ultimate reference to the sensible which is given to the passive "doxa" defines the antepredicative world quite well as a pure actuality, closed in on itself. Starting off from an originarily passive belief, it seems then impossible to constitute or to see the world appear as infinite possibility of predication. There is here an idea or a concept of the world that must either precede *a priori* passive belief or else, as a genetic product and a complication of "simple" experience, be nothing more than a methodical idealization, a useful formalization.

Under the first hypothesis, we allow ourselves to be misled by a formalism; this *a priori*, preceding the originary "doxa," is abstract; it is not founded on the antepredicative clear evidence of the sensible. It is a pregenetic ideality that makes any genesis possible; this latter is then "worldly," empirical, *a posteriori*. We are still close to a Kantianism.

Under the second hypothesis, the world itself as infinite horizon, as indetermination or determinability *(Bestimmbarkeit)*, must necessarily be founded on simple evidence, at once sensible and actual. It itself becomes predicative complication, formal generalization, a veil over ideas. The infinite of the world thus constructed and engendered is also an empirical *a posteriori*. It is a false infinite, produced through a conceptual negation of the sensible finite which precedes it in being and in time. It no more partakes of the negativity of the indefinite than of the actuality of the infinite. Instrument of a formal logic, it is not rich in any originarity. The genesis which has awakened the idea of it is itself only superadded to primitive existence.

In both cases, the genesis and the absolute originarity are mutually excluded; on the one hand, the world is the *a priori* place of any possible genetic experience. In this sense, it is not distinguished from an idea in the Kantian sense and cannot be grasped in a lived intuition. On the other hand, according to Husserl, it is in fact perceived in an intuition. This intuition can be that of a sensible originary world. So it seems impossible to define the necessity according to which a genetic process can carry out the passage from the individual sensibility to the infinite totality of a horizon. According to a hypothesis even less acceptable, the world is a predicate which is added to the given of the passive doxa. In this sense, it is engendered and carried by something other than itself. The possibility of the horizon and of the infinite totality is no longer originary.

This irreducible alternative, whose two movements are contrary to the very vocation of genetic phenomenology, reappears at the center of the main analyses of *Experience and Judgment,* and most notably each time that it is a question of the "world." The world is different from the individual and sensible substrates that are seized originarily; it founds them and envelops them: "Every finite substrate has determinability as being-in-something *(als In-etwas-sein),* and this is true *in infinitum.* But in the following respect the world is absolute substrate, namely, everything is in it, and it itself is not an in-something; it is no longer a relative unity within a more comprehensive plurality [...] *everything* [*worldly*], whether a real unity or a real plurality, is *ultimately dependent (unselbständig); only the world is independent, only it is absolute substrate in the strict sense of absolute independence.*"[35] The idea of this world is thus not constituted from individual substrates; nor is it the object of a simple *(schlicht)* clear evidence; its unity is neither the totality of its parts[36] nor the individual unity of a single existent. It is thus neither passively received by an originary "doxa" nor constructed by a logical activity. What then is the origin of this unity? Husserl does not say. And it is not known whether the regression that has to be effected to return to antepredicative existence has to end in a sensuous reality or in an absolute indetermination. The ultimate reference is sometimes the absolutely determinate unity of the sensuous world (the genesis of the predicates is thus a superstructure), sometimes a pure determinability: the logical genesis lacks real foundation. It is confused with the progress of a technology of knowledge. In both cases, it does not arrange for any access to the *truth of the world.* The two worlds, real world and possible world—beyond the fact that one could never produce the other— appear in the end to answer, whatever Husserl says about this, to the definition given of "worldliness." This latter is synonymous with "constituted" and thus applies just as well to transcendental sensible realities as to logical forms. The two depend on a transcendental constitution.

Here, as before in relation to the hylé, by making out of passivity the first moment of transcendental activity,[37] a rigorous distinction between tran-

scendental originarity and constituted worldliness is disallowed. The transcendental cannot then be the activity of an "I" as formal totality of pure activity and passivity, but the genetic becoming and production of activity starting from passivity, of the world as absolute substrate and infinite possibility of
experience, starting from sensuous and individual substrates.[38] This is what
Husserl seems to glimpse when, wanting to distinguish the "originary" world
from the constituted world of psychology and inviting us to a regression toward the absolute substrate,[39] he wrote these astonishing phrases which seem
to contradict the whole doctrine of sensuous antepredicative self-evidence
where this *object here* comes to present itself: "such regressive inquiry does
not involve seeking the factual, historical origin of these sedimentations of
sense in a determinate historical subjectivity [...] Rather, this world which is
ours is only an example through which we must study the *structure and the
origin of a possible world in general* from subjective sources."[40] While facticity
was described in general as the ultimate substrate of predicative sedimentations, now it becomes a sort of contingency, an example with which the sense
of a "possible world in general" is studied as the locus of the unveiling of the
truth through transcendental subjectivity. It is that on which the activity of
the subject is exercised. So genesis is in itself stripped of any facticity. Only the
transcendental sense of becoming interests Husserl. It is the idea of a teleology of history that is already prefigured, which will not be at all easy to square
with the empirical reality of history. The sense of genesis is a permanent element in becoming; it is not produced by any genesis. The radicalness of sense
and the radicalness of becoming can only exclude each other or negotiate
with each other dialectically. At the level of *Experience and Judgment,* they get
mixed up in confusion. In no analysis does one see what is prime or fundamental: the real or the possible, passivity or activity, individuality or totality,
and so forth.

The Origin of Negation

After having described the "passive doxa" and the "life-world" in their originarity, Husserl must pass to the modalizations of this primitive certitude and
try to elucidate the origin of negation.[41] This latter would only be pure and
simple modification of a thetic or doxic attitude that always precedes it. In the
act of negation, "the interest taken in the perceived object can persist. The
object continues to be examined; it continues to be given in such a way that
it can be further examined. However, instead of the fulfillment of the intentions of anticipation, a *disappointment* enters in."[42] There follows a long and

remarkable description of the phenomenon of negation.[43] It could have been thought after this description that negation, simple modification of an origi-nary certainty, was situated in a critical sphere. Negation might have been a judgment, negativity an attribute of the absent object which remains present as an antepredicative "center of interest." Since the doxic positivity or the un-modified certainty are originary, negation might have appeared as the logical product of a genesis and thus might be assimilated to other types of predica-tive judgments. It would thus be comprehended at the level of constituted formal logic constituted by a transcendental logic. But such a hypothesis would present grave dangers; first of all, a negative predicate could not be linked necessarily with a positive substrate. The genesis of negation starting from unmodified certainty is seen to be stripped of any essential necessity. It runs the danger of being the product of strokes of psychological chance. What, in fact, would be the status of this disappointment? In making of it a purely psychological attitude, the originary constitution of negation would be missed and we would end up in a psychological solution of a Bergsonian type. So negativity must not answer to a predicative activity. Husserl under-stands it indeed thus: "negation is not first the business of the act of predica-tive judgment but in its original form it already appears in the prepredicative sphere or receptive experience."[44] In spite of avoiding the dangers indicated, this interpretation is no less paradoxical. It is in the sphere of doxic passivity and of originary certainty that negation is constituted. Not being produced by a logical certainty, negation is thus born of a transcendental activity: "Negation is a modification of consciousness."[45] But this activity is originar-ily, Husserl also tells us, a receptivity or a passivity and takes the form of an ir-reducible belief in the world. So that in spite of its belonging to the ante-predicative sphere, negation is seen to be refused any originarity; it is at the same time epiphenomenal and precritical modalization of a fundamental cer-tainty. "It is always a partial cancellation on the basis of a certitude of belief which is thereby maintained, ultimately, on the basis of the universal belief in the world."[46]

The interest of this analysis is that it seems to force Husserl to define an intermediary moment between the two poles of genesis which he describes ceaselessly, that is, between "antepredicative receptivity" and "logical activ-ity," transcendental passivity and transcendental activity, passive doxa and modalized certainty, and so forth. This moment is perhaps the moment of genesis itself.[47] Negation belongs in its purity to none of the defined mo-ments. However, it remains linked to every constitution. Without the possi-bility of negation or disappointment, intention and intentionality would be impossible. Is not neutralization originarily a "disappointment," that is to say, the moment when the "I" "removes itself" from facticity, without however denying its existence? Does not the predicative judgment presuppose a certain negation of the sensuous antepredicative, subsumed under one or several concepts? Is not the transition of passivity to transcendental activity originarily a negation? In all these "transfers," which are so difficult to conceive if one stays with Husserl's analyses, negation carries out the role of mediation. As such, it seems to be the motor and movement of every genesis. It is because it is mediation that its status is ambiguous and partakes both of activity and passivity and of all the pairs of contraries that can appear. Since Husserl does not elucidate the "duplicity" of negation and abandons it to confusion, he does not allow himself to thematize the real genetic movement. Since he throws light only on the two extreme moments, he gets caught up in *the* contradictions without perceiving that it is *the* contradiction itself which defines and promotes genesis. In the same way that it was not known whether it was the real world, in its natural and cultural totality, which engendered the idea of a possible world in general, whether it is the essence which precedes fact, whether it is a sense which constitutes a genesis or a genesis which produces sense, in the same way, it is not known at this point whether negation was *a priori* possible in order to allow the passive "disappointment" or whether, conversely, it is disappointment that founds and produces negation. To grant an absolute priority to one or the other, that is to say, to the transcendental or to the ontological, is to immobilize genesis.

The Already Constituted Temporality

To the degree that the analyses of Husserl do not respond to this difficulty, they are disappointing. Genesis is never met with in them. It is because once more temporality is treated there as an accessory. It in no wise intervenes as such in the origin of negation. And yet, what founds the presence of negation in every intentional act, in every reduction, in every predicative activity, and so on is the originarity of time. It is because every absolute present is at the same time negation and assimilation of the past moment in retention; it is because this retention itself is immediately of a piece with a protention that preserves and denies the present as future in the past, because all the movements of intentionality are constituted by this dialectic of time, that negation appears here as what essentially animates any genesis.

Now all the texts of *Experience and Judgment* concerned with time bring us nothing. In the same way as the unities of the sensuous substrates, so "[sound for instance] is *passively pregiven* as unity of duration"[48] "If we apprehend the sound as enduring, in short as 'this sound,' we are not turned toward the momentary and yet continuously changing present [...] but *through* and beyond this present, in its change, toward the sound as a unity which by its essence *(wesensmäßig)* presents itself in this change, in this flux of appearances."[49] This essential unity of tone, pregiven as such to our passivity, is thus already constituted in its temporality. To the degree that it is this temporal unity which founds the appearance of every individual, sensitive, or other substrate, it can be said that the genesis of these substrates and of their unity has *already* taken place. The supposed transcendental passivity is thus not absolutely originary here and refers us to a preceding moment of constitution. Husserl, in some very detailed and remarkably complex analyses, shows in effect that, for example, the activity of apprehending a tone, which depends on a passive constitution of living duration, possesses a very complicated structure. It belongs to the very essence of activity: it is a continuously fluid activity united with an activity that has been modified and that has the character of a "holding which is still grasped" *(Noch-im-Griff-halten)*, and [moving] toward the future, that of a "pregrasping" activity. While the active grasping of sound is taking place, this activity emanates from the Me; but in it a distinction must be made between *"the active ray actually springing up continuously"* and "a fixed *passive regularity,* which, however is a *regularity pertaining to the activity itself."*[50] There is thus, Husserl adds, not a passivity before activity, as a passivity of preconstituting temporal flux, but as well and in addition, a sedimented passivity, properly objectivating, "namely, one which thematizes or cothematizes objects; [...] a kind of *passivity in activity."*[51] The foundation of this dialectic which refers us to the deepest layer of the constitution of time is absolutely not brought to light by Husserl, who merely indicates the impossibility of a "language" that would distinguish strictly between passivity and activity. Discourse must be adapted to the subtlety of concrete description, to its nuances, its contrasts. "This remark is valid for all descriptions of intentional phenomena." But Husserl maintains this difficulty at a descriptive, almost rhetorical level. Why is intentionality at the same time active and passive? Why does any constitution start with a synthesis of passivity and activity? Why are the units of time passively preconstituted before their thematization in the *Im-Griff-behalten?* These questions, which were being posed from the very first moments of phenomenology, are still without an answer. By many allusions and anticipations, like those in *Lectures* and *Ideas,* Husserl presents antepredicative temporal units as "achievements of the passive synthesis of time-consciousness."[52] Individuation and identity of the individual become possible on the foundations of the "absolute temporal position."[53] Or again "individual objects of perception have their reciprocal spatial situation on the basis of their being-together in a single time" But the origin of this absolute time, which is neither a subjectivity's passivity nor its activity, remains veiled. Antepredicative time, in opposition to noematic time in the *Lectures,* is still the foundation of absolute temporality; but this latter involving the couple passivity-activity, it is not known what is the first condition of its constitution and of the agreement between the time of the transcendental subject and of the real substrates. What is the foundation of the "being together" of objects in a *same* time? Husserl emphasizes that the time of perception is not enough to define absolute time. "More precisely, the time by which objects are united is not the subjective time of perceptual lived experience but the *objective time* conjointly belonging to the objective sense of this experience *(zu ihrem gegenständlichen Sinn mitgehörig);* not only are the lived experiences of perception immanently simultaneous, in other words, in general linked to a single perception of the plurality, but the objectivities intended in these experiences as actually being are also intended as objectively and simultaneously enduring."[54]

There is thus a unity of objective time which is imposed on consciousness and which thus appears to it as preconstituted. Although we are very far away from the *Lectures,* where objective time appears either as already constituted by the act of consciousness, or as a transcendental time not intervening in lived immanence, it is still the case that this objective time is not comparable to the worldly or transcendent time "bracketed" in the *Lectures.* The reduction is not explicitly removed and, in Husserl's eyes, this objective unity of time, as preconstituted by a transcendental activity "in general"[55] is passively received by consciousness. This widening of transcendental activity and of the "ego-world" correlation is appropriate for the intentional being of consciousness. It is thus that the absolute temporal position[56] is granted to the perceived object because it is given "in person" and because the intentional act, fully completed, accedes to being *qua* being of the object; the objects of the imagination do not have the same privilege.

Since this widening brings out only the ambiguity of transcendental activity in general, the unity of objective time is [has to be] dialectically produced by a historical genesis of which the ego is no longer the only source. Insisting on the necessity of an auto-constitution of objective time, Husserl notes that "Objective time, objective being, and all determinations of existents as objective certainly designate a being not only for me but for others."[57] There is a "necessary connection, on the basis of time as the form of sensibility, between the intentional objects of all perceptions and positional presentifications of an ego* and a community of egos."[58] This universal form of sensibility founds the unity of time. Every perception has its horizon of anteriority and of future. Now, if a memory brings me back to my own past, this past, as belonging to me myself, belongs to the world in which I live at present. From the intersubjective point of view, if another describes his past experiences to me, what is remembered in them belongs to the objective world of our common present. All the moments which we remember are the moments of a self-same world: "our earth." In a single world, everything I perceive, that I have perceived, about which others inform me, all that has a place, the one that objective time determines for it. So "the sensuously constituted temporal series is unique."[59] Every object of intention, as constituted in sensibility, that is to say, in its originary appearance, is subject to it. Hence, anything that appears originarily has a determinate temporal place, that is to say, not only a time given as such in an intentional objectivity, but also a fixed place in [an] objective time. The Kantian proposition is thus true: time is the form of sensibility and hence of every possible world of objective experience.[60] Before any question about the objective reality of certain phenomena, the essential property of any phenomenon in general is imposed: they give time and all given times are united in one and the same time. In the same way, every experience and perception of every "I" are "put in harmony" in relation to their intentional objects; this harmony is originarily one of "an objective time being constituted in all their subjective times and of an objective world itself being constituted in objective time."[61]

The Presupposition of the Theoretical Attitude

Objective time, final foundation of any genealogy of logic and of any transcendental activity that presides over it, is thus the product of a genesis in which the real or natural world, the world of intersubjectivity, the world of the pure ego, seem to have participated continuously as if belonging to one and the same world. But throughout *Experience and Judgment*, Husserl will not push the investigation or the genetic description farther than that suite of [moments of] objective time, whose genesis is already completed. As in the *Lectures* and in *Ideas* I, the temporality described is fixed; it interrupts the

---

*Derrida translates as "I." *Trans.*

whole movement of constitution at a certain moment. This latter, then, is no longer transcendental and originary.

But in the analyses prior to 1919, this insufficiency appeared in a way to be conscious; it was presented as provisory and methodical. The absence of radical genesis was, according to Husserl, purely "thematic."[62] But the argument in *Experience and Judgment* is explicitly genetic. Now Husserl alludes in it again to later investigations where a deepening analysis of genesis would come to found the present analyses in a definitive way. Certain scattered phrases in *Experience and Judgment* as in *Ideas* I translate all Husserl's disquiet and prolong the programmatic sense of these considerations. What is noteworthy here is that any formal program always stops before the actual genesis; yet any philosophy not attaining the actuality of genesis is condemned to remain immobilized at the level of a formal idealism.

In § 14, at the end of his introduction,[63] Husserl announces a "limitation" *(Bregrenzung)* of research; it is because the unities of the substrates are already constituted that it is going to be possible to retrace a "second" genesis of categoric judgment. We must, Husserl says, orient ourselves toward perceptive judgment in order to study in it the structures of predicative judgment in general. This latter is based on sensible perception. Yet sensible perception and later explication presuppose the purely contemplative interest granted to bodies as the last pregiven substrates that affect us. Hence, at first one obtains in the antepredicative sphere a perceptive interest that is already "fulfilled." But this fulfillment has itself necessitated a genesis which Husserl leaves deliberately aside here. The movement which has led consciousness from a noncontemplative interest to a theoretical interest still remains hidden from our gaze. Husserl, however, admits that "the ego,* living in its concrete environing world *(Umwelt)*, given over to its practical ends, is in no way a subject which is contemplative above all."[64] "For the ego in its concrete lifeworld, the contemplation of what exists is an *attitude* which can be assumed on occasion and in passing, as an attitude not having any special distinction." The theoretical attitude, which in the end is not even an attitude in the psychological sense of the term, is thus not primitive. However, it is from it that there must start a radical becoming-aware which Husserl recognizes to be always "later" *(die nachkommende philosophische Besinnung)*. The Absolute beginning can be the object of philosophical thematization only at the absolute

---

*Derrida translates as *moi*. Trans.

end of philosophy. This philosophical reflection being always unfinished, it seems that, in spite of what Husserl says, the race toward the originary is permanently and essentially condemned to failure. The indefinite of this dialectic, which forbids any "first philosophy" systematizing and founding phenomenology,[65] seems not to worry Husserl for the moment. According to him, the privilege of the theoretical attitude is uncontestable and uncontested, to the degree that it "reveals the structures of the world, and has them as a theme. These structures also underlie all practical activity, although they do not usually become thematic."[66]

The contradiction which follows is that, under pretext of a methodological requirement which would oblige him to start from the simplest, that is, from the constituted self-evidence in the antepredicative perception of objects at rest,[67] Husserl in fact starts out from the most complicated, the most developed, the most fulfilled. The domain of completed constitution, methodologically the most accessible, is in reality the most complex and the most "sedimented." To give in to methodological demand is to refuse to take into consideration the actual genesis which leads from the simple to the complex; it is still to reduce genesis under the pretext of taking it in and of thematizing it in its "final" formally "originary" historical sense.

Thus, we are not surprised when Husserl admits that, in proposing to attain those most fundamental and most originary pieces of self-evidence from out of which any predicative judgment arises, his "theme" is only the constitution of the perceived thing and of the external world; there is recourse to perceived structures only in order to understand how logical operations are constructed on perceptive experience; by thus limiting himself to a relatively superficial degree of research, Husserl cannot give account either of the total historical genesis of the life-world "in the most comprehensive sense of the word" or of the relations or the possible agreement between phenomenology thus defined and real nature or sciences whose object it constitutes. In a note,[68] Husserl writes: "In our context we can disregard the problem of knowing how the world, taken concretely as the life-world of humanity, stands with regard to the objective world in the strict sense, i.e., to the world as determined in the sense of natural science." Thus, on the one hand, the originarity of predicative structures, however widely one conceives it, seems autonomous in its foundation and can be thematized on its own; but, on the other hand, they are presented by Husserl as belonging to a constituted layer whose description alludes to a more originary domain. For Husserl declares very clearly that "various constitutive strata and operations are therefore presupposed. In particular, it is presupposed that a *field* of spatial things is already constituted and, along with it, the entire layer of investigations which have reference to the constitution of the perception of things in all of its levels."[69] These lower layers are those of the constitutive formation of the sensory field, the putting into relation of these singular fields, the kinestheses, the relation to a body of the perceiving subject in its normal functioning, the constitution by stages of the sensible object in itself and in relation with other things. "Equally presupposed with this is the constitution, already carried out, of things as temporal, as extended in time, and from another aspect, the constitution of individual acts in which the spatiality of things is constituted in the internal consciousness of time. All these are dimensions of constitutive investigations which lie still deeper than those conducted here."[70] Farther on, Husserl declares that "the problems of the constitution of time [...] are not to be treated here in their full compass."[71]

At the moment when Husserl claims he is treating it, the genetic problem is thus once more bracketed. Yet here *Experience and Judgment* cannot take on the appearance of an "introduction" to a new problematics of genesis and announce the later researches. Though *Experience and Judgment* was edited by Landgrebe from manuscripts dating from 1919, this elaboration, which was made under the attentive direction of Husserl himself, lasted until 1938, one year before the publication of the work. On the eve of his death, Husserl, always reticent when the publishing of writings with which he was not entirely satisfied was proposed to him, consented to the publication of this book.

In fact, this reduction of genesis is not just "thematic" here. It will continue up to the moment when Husserl will make of historical becoming the central, almost exclusive, theme of his meditation. Feeling how much any true genesis ran the risk of compromising phenomenological and philosophical discourse in general and even of making it fail completely, Husserl seems to have ceaselessly and tirelessly prepared a vast methodical access to a sphere so little accessible to phenomenological elucidation. *Experience and Judgment* is a book that was composed and meditated on for twenty years. *Formal and Transcendental Logic, Cartesian Meditations,* and *Crisis,* all texts where genesis seems to receive constant attention, were published without the essential features of *Experience and Judgment* being modified. That is a piece of evidence. There are others. Thus, for example, Husserl never published some very important manuscripts attacking directly the problem of the originary composition of time.[72] Having entrusted a certain number of them to E. Fink, right up to his death he showed himself dissatisfied with the versions which his assistant proposed to him.[73]

It is because in questioning time immediately in its most denuded and most originary existence, the phenomenological attitude as Husserl conceived it ran up against insurmountable difficulties. Husserl not having begun by a pure description of genesis, his methodological propaedeutics in fact betrays the presuppositions of a whole philosophy of genesis which assimilates the creative becoming of essences to an "idea" or to a sense of becoming that Husserl will confuse later with the very idea of philosophy. This teleological idea will be revealed to us later as a veritable reduction of actual genesis to its finality, that is to say, to what in it is stripped of every historical facticity and whose becoming "does not exist"; it will only be clearly brought to light and envisaged as such starting from the 30s. Before this date, two powerful attempts to systematize genetic phenomenology as it is sketched in *Experience and Judgment* seem bound to fail.

Transcendental Genesis and Absolute Logic

The first of these attempts is to found a genuine *Critique of Pure Reason* on a transcendental genesis. It is the aim of *Formal and Transcendental Logic*, which we will not examine here closely[74]; this work adds nothing essential to the theses of *Experience and Judgment* on the problem which interests us here. We will be satisfied with referring to a magisterial essay where Cavaillès, in a couple of pages of rare depth, shows—for the domain of mathematics' development, which is more than an example here—the antinomies in which genetic phenomenology constantly gets caught up, needing ceaselessly to choose between a "progress of consciousness" and a "consciousness of progress."[75]

Wishing to found the supposed absolute logic, that is to say, one not genetic and formal, on a genetic science of transcendental consciousness and on a transcendental logic or a constitutive phenomenology, Husserl is always stopped by the same dilemma: "[...] absolute and last science, writes Cavaillès, also demands a doctrine which may govern it." This doctrine—which also furnishes *a priori* norms (or at least, a "guiding thread" or a "transcendental guide") in founding a transcendental logic or a creative subjectivity—will precede them; these latter will not be able to

> understand it starting from itself; it is perhaps taking advantage of the uniqueness of the absolute if one singles out for it the coincidence between constituting and constituted moment. Besides there is not even coincidence but insertion of the first in the second, since the norms of the constituting constitution are nothing but a part of the constituted

constitutions. Now it seems that it is particularly difficult for phenomenology to admit such an identification of level, where precisely the motor of research and the foundation of objectivities are the relation to a creative subjectivity. If these are also given norms, then there has to be a new transcendental search to relate these norms back to a superior subjectivity since no content except consciousness has the authority to posit itself in itself. If transcendental logic really founds logic, there is no absolute logic (that is to say, one which governs the absolute subjective activity). If there is an absolute logic, it can only draw its authority from itself, it is not transcendental.[76]

To make the whole development and all the syntheses of logic into a transcendental genesis which refers to the becoming of a creative subjectivity, is not that in fact to make the absolute of logical truths into something fleeting, contingent, and out of date?

Perhaps this objection is valid only for an empirical and psychological subjectivity which is not originarily and intentionally oriented toward objective truth, which it creates only through "intuition." But it is then truth grasped intuitively which no longer participates in genetic becoming. If transcendental subjectivity is intentional, it must be asked where genesis is situated: in the act of consciousness or in its correlate? Is genetic animation in the object of the intuition—which is at the same time a product of the creation—or else in the act of production—which is at the same time intuitive passivity? To install the sense and the origin of genesis in one or the other is to forbid oneself the possibility of a necessary and *a priori* synthesis and of a becoming of logic. This is why the absolute of genesis is the opposite of the absolute. It is a temporal absolute, a synthetic becoming in the clear evidence of the "living Present" of the transcendental subjectivity which retains what has already become and no longer passes away, and which anticipates what is not yet there. The essential of transcendental genesis is to produce the becoming of the Absolute in clear evidence. The absolute logic of which Cavaillès speaks is a necessity that rules the operations of transcendental subjectivity in its intuitive movement; it is at the same time a historical product of this subjectivity to the degree that no synthesis and no clear evidence would be *a priori* possible without it. This ambiguity of genesis, where each pole appears as genetic only by assimilating and presupposing the other pole as atemporal absolute, only "reproduces" the ontological dialectic of time. It would be absurd and opaque if precisely both poles were simultaneous or ordered in an irreversible unilinear and absolute successivity in relation one to the other. In a word, the contradiction would only be philosophically incoherent or insufficient if the intentionality of consciousness were not originary temporality itself.[77]

To be aware of the identity of temporality and intentionality is, first of all, to reject the hypothesis of an absolute simultaneity of objective logical truth with the act which produces it or grasps it. If it is temporal, transcendental consciousness always appears as preceding *a priori* the truth which is given it in clear evidence and "for itself," as succeeding the truth which it has just constituted and which, as a product already endowed with meaning, is given as an autonomous value that is "in itself," as foundation of the movement which is constituting "for itself." The apparent simultaneity of consciousness and of truth in clear evidence is thus *always already synthetic,* that is to say, *a priori* synthetic. The absolute simultaneity, that is to say, the analytic identity of two moments or of a moment with itself, is incompatible with *a priori* synthesis, that is to say, with the *truth of being.*

Now, the absolute foundation of phenomenological clear evidence, the last authority for all language, all logic, all philosophical discourse, is that intentionality is merged with the temporality of consciousness. I can think, aim at, perceive only what is foreign to consciousness; because this intentional movement is originally synthetic, it is originarily temporal. Thus, every relation between absolute logic and transcendental logic, as Cavaillès shows, ends in a formal antinomy precisely if account is no longer taken of the "temporal-intentionality"[78] of consciousness or if out of intentionality or temporality there are made reciprocal determinations or psychological and accidental characters of some absolute consciousness whose myth is said to be entertained secretly.[79] Conversely, if as phenomenological certainty teaches us, the very being of consciousness is temporal-intentionality, absolute logic will be the absolute norm of transcendental logic only to the extent that transcendental logic will recognize it in the certainty of the "living Present" as already constituted by it in a "retained" past and as susceptible to be transformed into it and through it in its future clear evidence; it will then recognize *itself* as constituting. The astonishing coincidence of the constituting and the constituted astonishes Cavaillès, who thinks that Husserl is making bad use of the singularity of the absolute. But is it not Cavaillès himself who makes bad use of it? Indeed, when Husserl makes the absolute of constituted formal logic out of transcendental logic or consciousness, it seems that precisely the very temporality of this absolute takes away from it any theological aspect. The unthinkable and impossible coincidence of constituting and constituted is not analytic here, but *a priori* synthetic and temporal. It is a dialectic coincidence. The criticisms of Cavaillès are addressed only to a "perfect" absolute (these two terms are not synonymous for Husserl. The perfect absolute is only a constituted absolute, a reality dependent on the absolute transcendental consciousness), closed on itself, maintaining external relations with what is not it. It is finally a "factitious" absolute, a logical or psychological consciousness or, correlatively, a formal logic, a set of norms that have been turned into canons. After having posed the problem of the becoming of logic with the greatest acuity, Cavaillès seems to have stopped in his criticism of Husserl at the idealist level of the noetico-noematic[80] correlation, that is to say, at the moment of the static constitution.

To say that intentionality and temporality overlap originarily is—secondly—to put aside the possibility of a succession and of an absolute and irreversible subordination. It is to recognize that consciousness is no more outside time than in time. No temporal order can impose itself on it from the exterior or absolutely envelop it; it itself cannot orient the becoming or the creation of logical truths in an absolutely free way. The absolute clear evidence is that the synthetic correlation between consciousness and truth is originarily [a] production of what was already there; that is to say, that the originary time cannot take on the aspect of a spatial continuous line; it is uneven; its progression is a return; its instants are more and less than points, in the purity of their clear evidence, still and already their past and their future. It is through an effective protention that the past can be freely reproduced; through a retention that the future appears as future of a past present, and so forth. To be surprised by the unheard-of coincidence of the constituting and the constituted, of transcendental logic and formal logic, is to be surprised by the clear evidence of temporality. This surprise is itself founded on a temporal evidence. Thus it is, in spite of itself, the victim of the idealist and psychological prejudice according to which a theoretical consciousness of temporality and existence is *a priori* possible. It participates in an attitude through which, since the sense of the temporal existence of consciousness is not probed, the "point of view" of one temporal instance on another is taken for a liberation and a being pulled out of time; through which an atemporal point of view is believed possible, since the temporal sense of every clear evidence and of every view point have not been elucidated.

When Cavaillès, at the end of his analysis, invokes the necessity of a dialectic against what he believes to be the unilinear genesis of formal logic from out of transcendental logic, when he writes that "the generating necessity is not that of an activity, but of a dialectic,"[81] he is only clarifying the temporal being of consciousness and stripping Husserl's thought of its old idealist and formalist prejudices.[82]

Old prejudices? That is neither so clear nor so simple. On the one hand, indeed, it is serious that the theme of temporality, the only foundation of a transcendental genesis of logic, should be absent from *Formal and Transcendental Logic*. In supposing, as was done just now, all the constituting temporality, one can run the danger of a formal idealism or an empiricism through this supposedly methodological implication. On the other hand, the originarily synthetic and ontological identification of consciousness and time leads rigorously to the abandoning of idealism, be it methodical or transcendental. Yet Husserl is less than ever resolved to [do] this.

For the originarily synthetic identification of consciousness and time is equivalent to confusing the pure subject with an originarily historical existence that is neither the psychic double, nor the constituted event, nor the empirical facticity of the transcendental "I."[83] It is the very "existence" of the subject. This existence, as originarily temporal and finite, is "in the world." Intentionality is no longer then an aiming at being and the noetic synthesis of its different moments, operated by a pure subject. The intentional lived experience is no longer a simple "unreal" constituting the meaning of the "real." The subject is an "existence" even though one of a radically original and originary type. The noetico-noematic synthesis is not theoretical. It is existential experience. Intentionality is then no longer what links an ideal "ego" to the world. It is the mediating moment of a properly ontological synthesis. It is being itself which takes possession of its sense. The *a priori* synthesis is the synthesis of being and of sense: that is the only condition of possibility of a predicative synthesis carried out by a knowing subject. The passive constitution of the theoretical transcendental subject is then only the reversed idealist expression of the originary movement of existence.

All these consequences, schematically defined, are clearly extremely grave. They lead us by a strange reversal to put intentionality itself in brackets, from which we had nevertheless started out. Because existence is no longer originarily constituted by a transcendental gaze, the theoretical consciousness of existence itself is no more than a modified moment of existence. It has "started out" from the ontological synthesis. It is no longer absolutely originary. It is understandable that Husserl steps back from such consequences. All this signifies nothing less than the collapse of phenomenological transcendental idealism. Phenomenology, the science of self-evidences given to a theoretical consciousness is methodologically first; but it needs beforehand a whole ontology. It is a moment of the autoconstitution of being, which is synthetically and originarily identical to time.

The only way for Husserl to escape from all the dilemmas that he has constantly put off was to comprehend them in their foundation. For that, it was necessary to clarify the transcendental temporality whose thematization he always announced. Now, this thematization, if it were total, would upset the initial givens of phenomenology itself. So much so that Husserl's possible answer to Cavaillès, such as we have sketched it, would be at the same time rigorous and mistaken, unfaithful and conforming to the published works of Husserl. The second of the systematic attempts which were announced above, the *Cartesian Meditations,* presenting in a way that intends to be definitive the idea of an ultimate genetic constitution in general, whether active or passive, has consistently as its aim the foundation of a transcendental idealism, first philosophy of transcendental phenomenology. Under what condition can such an enterprise escape failure, or at least continue? And what new sense must be given to transcendental idealism to merge it or conciliate it with an authentic philosophy of genesis?

7

The Genetic Constitution of the Ego and the
Passage to a New Form of Transcendental Idealism

The Infinite Idea of "Theory"
and the Repetition of the Difficulties

The *Cartesian Meditations*[1] offer us the most systematic expression of
Husserl's thought. Prepared and written around 1930, they do more than
translate the continuity of the phenomenological method, all of whose principles are taken up and synthesized in a remarkable way. They announce the
new orientation of the research. The mastery and depth with which Husserl,
leaving none of the earlier themes aside, takes stock of how far he has gotten
and sketches out the later movements without ever at any moment making
reference to a regression or to a revolution, to a rupture or to a lack of progress, have to be admired. All the dilemmas and the impasses with which we
have tried to mark out the itinerary of his thought, all the thematic or systematic conversions whose necessity we have tried to indicate, the impossibility of a philosophy of genesis faithful to the pure principles of phenomenology, would all that have only an illusory sense? That is what, at first
reading, *Cartesian Meditations* might let one think. The genetic theme,
which receives here its greatest light, appears to fit in harmoniously with all
of the past of phenomenology. As it is presented, it takes on the appearance
of an implication which is fundamental, which a method well conducted
through necessary meditations finishes by bringing to light. Nothing is
brought into question again, nor, even more, renounced. In fact, the ample
philosophical discourse which is pursued here hides a profound malaise behind serene and powerful gestures.

First of all, as a reprise and deepening of the preceding stages, there reappear in the first three *Meditations* the same difficulties as before, in a form that

is hardly renewed. It will be remembered that in *Logical Investigations,* in *Ideas,* and in *Experience and Judgment,* the status of certain infinite ideas, the idea of an infinite becoming of logic, the idea of an infinite time of pieces of lived evidence, the idea of a world as a horizon of infinite possibilities of experience, remained very obscure. In order to conform to the mode of clear evidence in which they are presented to us, these ideas must be neither founded essences nor constructed concepts, nor predicates engendered from singular experiences nor individual substrates. Different from limit-concepts obtained by induction or absolute extension, they had, on the contrary, a sort of concrete and universal presence. In a word, their paradox was that, being merged with the most concrete and the most originary temporality, that is to say, with the pure temporality of the "I" or the antepredicative substrate of the world, they were at the same time the most formal. The absolute antepredicative is pure being, which has not yet received any determination, which has not yet given itself any and since it is situated this side of any constitution, at the limit remains inaccessible to any transcendental activity. It is not susceptible to any phenomenological "appearing." It never presents itself "in person." The only resource of the subject is then to form a concept of it whose extension will be absolute only by seeing itself purified, stripped of any concrete comprehension. Here is found once more in a very precise way the dialectic defined by Hegel: pure being is identical to nonbeing. Because he wished to escape from the finitude of singularity, because he wished to go beyond the negations bound up with determinations, one ends up in an abstract universal and a pure negation.

This is what happens to phenomenology. Being the only foundation of an *a priori* synthesis between fact and essence, the only mediation between the singularity of lived experience and the eidetic universality, the idea of an infinite totality becomes the ultimate concrete reference of all constitution in general. It was then converted quite naturally into a formal condition of possibility, itself having never been constituted by a concrete subject. It could at the limit be described as the *a priori* character of any transcendental experience and cause us thus to fall back into a transcendental psychologism. What is certain is that, making possible any genesis and any becoming, [this idea] itself has nothing historical or genetic and is not given in person in an originary clear evidence. So that the alternative is still there: either it is condition of possibility for any clear evidence without being itself concretely present as a singular; but on what basis can one then speak of the originarity of certainties since they are preceded and founded by this condition? Or else the concrete and simple certainties are really originary and then the infinite idea, by definition not being given in an intuition, remains a complication, a super-structure, a conceptual product. Losing its character of foundation, it is trans-formed into a predicate of all experience in general. Husserl thus could not make of it at the same time an infinite idea and an originary clear evidence ex-cept by putting himself at a constituted level where indeed the sedimented meaning is given immediately. But this constituted level was itself already no longer originary.

We have seen that only a dialectic of temporal existence could, if not ef-face the dilemma, at least illuminate its philosophical sense. Husserl seems to refuse this dialectic, which we will attempt to show is identical with the very idea of philosophy. At bottom, always faithful to an intention profoundly ide-alist and rationalist, he never wishes to stop at the stage of pure becoming, even though in probing it he meets it constantly. This becoming must be thought and reduced to its "eidos" by something other than itself.

Therefore let us not be surprised when in *Cartesian Meditations,* present-ing phenomenology as absolute science, as the foundation of every possible sci-ence, of every science that is existent in history and constituted in a culture, Husserl alludes to a new "idea," a teleological idea that will give him a sense of the becoming which in itself and as such is not constituted by any becoming. Section 3, where Husserl deals with the "idea-goal," regulator of a foundation of science, is one of the most awkward of the work. After having pushed as far as possible the "putting off line" of existing sciences, of the facts and of the ideas which they could deliver to us, after having attained a radicalism that is appar-ently not to be exceeded, and shown how Descartes missed his original project in giving himself in advance the scientific ideal of his time, Husserl writes: "As beginning philosophers we do not as yet accept any normative ideal of science; and only so far as we produce one newly for ourselves can we have such an ideal."[2] After such a total revolution, what will then be the guiding thread of the research? "Naturally we get the general idea of science from the sciences that are factually given. If they have become for us, in our radical critical atti-tude, merely alleged sciences, then, according to what has been already said, their general final idea has become, in a like sense, a mere supposition. Thus we do not yet know whether that idea is at all capable of becoming actualized. Nev-ertheless we do *have* it in this form [in the French translation: "we possess this idea"], and in a state of indeterminate fluid generality; accordingly we also have the idea of philosophy: as an idea about which we do not know whether or how it can be actualized"[3] Husserl admits that in this way he enters into "rather strange circumstantialities." But, he adds straightaway, they are inevitable if our radicalism is to move into action and not remain a simple gesture.

This idea, borrowed from existing sciences and admitted as a hypothesis, will never receive a concrete determination. It will always remain a formal intention, explained by leaving aside the historical facticity of the different sciences to allow their common "claim" to appear. Doubtless Husserl is careful about attaining the sense of this project by purely and simply stripping it of its empirical becoming: "The genuine concept of science, naturally, is not to be fashioned by a process of abstraction based on comparing the de facto sciences, i.e., the Objectively documented theoretical structures (propositions, theories,) that are in fact generally accepted as sciences. The sense of our whole meditation implies that sciences, as these facts of Objective culture, and sciences 'in the true and genuine sense' need not be identical and that the former, over and above being cultural facts, involve a claim, which ought to be established as one they already satisfy. Science as an idea—as the idea, genuine science—'lies,' still undisclosed, precisely in this claim."[4] This claim or intention, in order to be revealed as such, must be rigorously distinct from a concept and must be lived or relived in some way. "Even though we must not take any position with respect to the *validity* of the de facto sciences (the ones 'claiming' validity)—i.e., with respect to the genuineness of their theories and, correlatively, the competence of their methods of theorizing—there is nothing to keep us from 'immersing ourselves' *(erleben)* in the scientific striving *(Streben)* and doing *(Handeln)* that pertain to them, in order to see clearly and distinctly what is really being aimed at. If we do so, if we immerse ourselves progressively in the characteristic intention of scientific endeavor, the constituent parts of the general final idea, genuine science, become explicated for us, though at first the differentiation is itself general."[5] The sense of the title, on which no other light is shed during the paragraph, is then understood: the "revelation of the final sense" of science is obtained by the "act of living it as noematic phenomenon."[6] In other words, the pure scientific intention animating all the factitious moments of sciences remains hidden from the gaze of the simple historian or the simple scientist who lives his or her activity spontaneously. By the phenomenological reduction which "suspends" the facticity of scientific activity, the deep intention, buried or perverted in the real results or in the facts whose sense they supply, is seen to be recognized now as such and in its purity. Instead of being the hidden noetic source of every science, it becomes, after the reduction, the noematic or thematic object for a consciousness. The constituting movement of every science is thus supposed to have been revealed. But just as the temporality of the ego and the transcendental becoming of science had invited us to consider no longer the pure "I" as the first moment of constitution, it is now a teleological idea

(*Zweckidee*) which plays this role: not that there is attributed to the ego a secondary or mediate role: at the limit, and it is already a strange transformation, the pure transcendental ego will have to merge itself with the pure life of this teleology. The true transcendental power will be the infinite totality of an oriented becoming or of the orientation of becomings.

In spite of the very seductive character of the experience to which Husserl invites us, one has the right to have doubts about its possibility. How can one "live" as such an intention or a teleologically pure idea? On the one hand, the expression "noematic phenomenon" can be thought infelicitous—and perhaps that is an external reproach. A noematic phenomenon or a phenomenological theme is constituted for and by a transcendental consciousness to which it always refers. What will be the status of the subject which intentionally lives the "effort of science"? Will it itself be originary? Would it be the absolute of this tendency which would occur in its history like an event? It is probably not like this that Husserl means it. The pure "I" is merged in Husserl's eyes with the theoretical intention of science defined as a pretension to the universal and to absolute foundation.[7] Beyond the fact that this theoretical attitude was not originary, Husserl confesses so himself,[8] it is impossible to see what this "living" of a pure scientific intention can be, in which no moment constituted as a scientific fact would be comprehended. Either this intention or this teleological sense are formal concepts and *a priori* conditions of possibility. As such, they cannot be "lived." Or else, the purity of this "living" is concrete, like every phenomenological purity. But then it is synthetic; it is developed in a pure and concrete time about which eidetics has revealed to us that every constituting moment—the one which one wishes to attain here—brings with it a constituted moment in the intimacy of its foundation. This essential intrusion of constituted time into constituting time does not then allow us to make the distinction rigorously between the pure intentional teleology and the facticity of existing sciences. The passive synthesis of time, which always precedes the active synthesis, is an *a priori synthesis* of fact and intention, being and sense. The intention of the passed moment, retained in the living Present whose constitution it participates in, is at the same time constituted existence and constituting intention, that is to say, protention. In a word, any grasping of the pure teleological intention is essentially part and parcel of a constituted moment of real science. This constituted moment is at the same time its foundation. The apprehension of the pure sense of the becoming of science, since it is itself a becoming, never touches its absolute limit. The sense of genesis is a genetic product. This dialectic leads us to an indefinite progression or regression. While, in our opinion, it is the very possibility of a "living" or of a "reliving" of the scientific intention in historical facticity and of anticipating it, for Husserl the regression to the infinite remains a formal obstacle. He alludes to this as if it were a difficulty of systematics, but does not spend time on it.[9] Thus, he displaces that irreducible existence which time institutes at the heart of any lived experience that would intend to be theoretical. The doctrine of the intuition of essences which, right from the establishing of phenomenology, translated the dream of an "existence" or of a "theoretical expression," is prolonged here, with the intention of "living" an absolute teleological idea. It is the impossible analytical confusion but [also] that necessary synthetic identity of experience and knowledge which the idea of dialectic "signifies." Having distinguished between the transcendental and the existential, Husserl had to preserve at the same time an absolute dissociation of empirical and theoretical as the foundation of his philosophy and an analytic identity of knowledge and the concrete in intentionality, that is, in the effort to live science as noematic phenomenon. This is why Husserl was abandoned by most of his disciples, who accused him—in part rightly—of psychologistic idealism: the concrete life of the transcendental "I" not being originarily an "existence," it became psychological fact, constituted event. It would be enough just to push things a little in order to transform Husserl's philosophy into a transcendental psychologism, the accusation that he himself leveled against Kant. Evidently it is not that simple, and the explicitation of the dialectical theme which underlies all the developments of Husserl's thought would here provide us with some very vigorous rejoinders.

This teleological idea of an absolute science, this experience of a limitless theoretic intention, where the whole fate of phenomenology is played out in this way, hence only brings back the difficulties and the dilemmas encountered earlier. The pure activity of experience cannot be clarified as such except by a meditation and a mediation which are infinite. But this idea, to the very degree that it is "lived" as a noematic phenomenon, is a possible experience for a transcendental ego. Thus Husserl situates it on the methodical path that leads to the synthesis of the constitution of the transcendental ego (*Der Weg zum transzendentalen Ego*). Once again the apparent foundation of constitution is only a "transcendental guide" according to which we must follow the half-visible actual and deep movement of the constitution. It is only a question of a mediate stage, insufficient but necessary, and one can imagine that the ultimate foundation of teleology is going to be delivered to us at last. At least, that is what the fourth *Meditation* claims to do, where the "constitutive problems of the transcendental ego itself" are treated. It would be interesting to comment in detail on the admirable analyses with which Husserl precedes this meditation. We would be able to follow there at every instant the same difficulty reproduced, reduced, and diversified at every paragraph and every line. But the limits of the present work do not permit this. Since teleology was lived as noema and presupposed a subject which itself was constituted in a genesis, let us be content with studying this genesis, the theme of the whole *Fourth Meditation*.

The Contradiction of Active Genesis

Up to now, in our quest for an ultimate genetic source, we have encountered only constituted moments: facts, essences, noematic time, noetico-noematic correlation, transcendental activity, all presupposed the originary temporal layer. Basically, we have still not attained a genesis that is transcendental in the strict sense of the word. The most originary factor in genetic constitution was always fleeing in front of us, and the progress of our way of proceeding was being measured by the indefinite marking out of mediations toward an absolute transcendental ego. This latter could, in its mysterious indetermination, be, as we were supposing, either a logical and formal subject or the totality of intersubjectivities, or infinite history, or an originary temporal existence, and so forth. Only the constitution of this ego could give us further information. If Husserl put off its thematization for so long, it is because the whole phenomenological edifice then ran the risk of shaking, as he sensed very keenly. Was this autoconstitution of the subject not going to put into question again the very sense of its phenomenological and theoretic activity? Would it not reduce it to the concrete existence of a living being in general? Especially and to this very degree, would we not be referred once again to a universal teleology, by means of an ideal "sense" of concrete constitution? Would not the transcendental idealism whose theme Husserl associates with that of the egological genesis be enlarged to the dimensions of an absolute idealism of a Hegelian type?

The first paragraphs of the *Fourth Meditation* give us much to hope for. Husserl begins by recognizing that we have been immobilized up till now at the level of a constituted correlation and of the "intentional relation [...] cogito to cogitatum."[10] Now "the ego is himself *existent for himself* in continuous evidence; thus, in himself, he is *continuously constituting himself as existing.*"[11] "Heretofore we have touched on only one side of this self-constitution, we have looked at only the *flowing cogito*. The ego grasps himself not only as a flowing life but also as *I*, who live this and that subjective process, who live through this and that cogito, *as the same I.*"[12]

Thus, we are touching here, it seems, the final stage of our research, with this identical Me, absolute reference of any possible signification which engenders itself in a "*conscious activity or in the passive affecting*" *(bewußtseins-tätiges und affiziertes)*. Everything that is said about this Me will be passed on through the mediate spheres of constitution, because equally everything is constituted in it and for it. "Since the monadically concrete ego includes also the whole of actual and potential conscious life, it is clear that the problem of *explicating this monadic ego phenomenologically* (the problem of his constitution for himself) must include *all constitutional problems without exception.* Consequently the phenomenology of this *self-constitution* coincides with *phenomenology as a whole.*"[13]

It would be legitimate to expect now a total change of method. The eidetic reduction, the transcendental reduction, and the eidetic intuition that they made possible were applied to moments constituted for a subject. Obstacles had already been met with in wishing to take these reductions to their final end. Now it seems that the Me being recognized as absolute constituting source and at the same time as temporal synthesis, it cannot by essence be reduced to any putting between brackets (the essence here is just merged with existence). It is its very existence which carries out and authorizes the reduction. To reduce it to an eidetic generality is to lose what there is in it that is both originarily temporal and constituting. In separating once again existence and essence in it, and in being interested only in this latter, it runs the risk of falling definitively into an eidetic psychology or in a transcendental psychologism, the two shortcomings denounced by Husserl himself. For one last time, it is to miss the description of an authentic transcendental genesis. In separating the transcendental from pure existence, a constituted "eidos" is made out of the first. We remain on this side of absolute originarity.

Yet this is what Husserl does; the transcendental analysis which leads us toward the egologic genesis is an eidetic analysis.[14] This is the sense of the whole of § 34. "If we think of *a phenomenology* developed as an intuitively *a priori* science *purely according to the eidetic method,* all its eidetic researches are nothing else but *uncoverings of the all-embracing eidos, transcendental ego as such,* which comprises all pure possibility-variants of my de facto ego and this ego itself qua possibility."[15] The necessities of this preparatory eidetics are methodological ones in Husserl's eyes, it must not be forgotten. If one does not begin by a description of the *a priori* essence, there can never be a claim to any rigor. Existence itself, in its most originary coming forth, will not be able to appear to a philosophical gaze. So any reproach addressed to this Husserlian essentialism in the name of an empirical or existential originarity or in the name of some preceding moment of genesis will, in order to have a sense, have to suppose an already constituted eidetics. It is this postulate of all philosophy that the first steps of phenomenology had brought out in all its depth. The absolute beginning of philosophy must be essentialist. This law, to the extent that it is "methodological," to the extent that it is not founded on the actual movement of constituting genesis, one prior to essences and to the extent that it rules over any philosophical elucidation, makes out of formalism and idealism, or one can say, of eidetism, the inaugural moment of any actual or possible philosophy. Any reflection must begin by assuming this idealism, without which it will always remain in confusion and in inauthenticity. It is this which authorizes us to speak of a dialectic philosophy as the only possible philosophy of genesis. In fact, it is by knowing that the eidetic moments are themselves constituted beforehand by a genesis, thus that they come second, that one relates to it as to an absolute beginning of a phenomenological revelation of genesis. The sense of the genesis is produced by a genesis, but the genesis is accessible in its being, possible in its appearance, only if one starts from the originality of its sense. Every philosophy is condemned to work back along the actual itinerary of every becoming. All the criticisms addressed to Husserl (those, notably, of Heidegger and of Trân Duc Thao, very different from each other, by the way) tend to a radical reversal which, though this is not seen, presupposes the set of problems defined and resolved by Husserl.

So let us not be surprised, let us measure all the depth of Husserl's fidelity to the absolute necessity of the eidetic reduction, when we see that what has actually required a historical and singular genesis is being described on the level of "essential generality." All philosophical rigor is paid for at the price of this shortcoming. The becoming conscious of this necessary shortcoming and of this possible rigor, whether simultaneous or *a priori* synthetic, constitutes, it seems to us, the very idea of philosophy as infinite dialectic. The absolute beginning of reflection is a formal beginning but without it one stays on this side of any meaning, any philosophy, and any science. The historico-psychological becoming is thus reduced *a priori* to its eidetic form. Thus, Husserl indeed writes, "Manifestly I cannot imagine the theorizing I do or can do now as shifted arbitrarily within the unity of my life; and this too carries over into the eidetic. Eidetic apprehension of my (transcendentally reduced) childhood life and its possibilities of constitution produces a type, such that in its further development, but not in its own nexus, the type 'scientific theorizing' can occur. Restriction of this kind has its grounds in an a priori universal structure, in a conformity to universal eidetic laws of coexistence and succession in egological time."[16] In the same way, the originary time itself will not be envisaged except as the "universal form of every ego-logical genesis" and one must begin with the definition of the *"formal regu-larity pertaining to a universal genesis,* which is such that past, present, and future, become unitarily constituted over and over again, in a certain noetic-noematic formal structure of flowing modes of givenness."[17] All this is disap-pointing and Husserl seems to agree himself:

> Access to the ultimate universalities involved in problems of eidetic
> phenomenology is, however, very difficult. This is particularly true
> with respect to an *ultimate genesis.* The beginning phenomenologist is
> bound involuntarily by the circumstance that he takes himself as his
> initial example. Transcendentally he finds himself as the ego, then as
> generically an ego, who *already* has (in conscious fashion) a world—a
> world of our universally familiar ontological type, with Nature, with
> culture (sciences, fine art, mechanical art, and so forth), with personal-
> ities of a higher order (state, church), and the rest. The phenomenol-
> ogy developed at first is merely "static"; its descriptions are analogous
> to those of natural history, which concern particular types and, at best,
> arrange them in their systematic order. Questions of universal genesis
> and the genetic structure of the ego in his universality, so far as that
> structure is more than temporal formation, are still far away; and, in-
> deed, they belong to a higher level. But even when they are raised, it
> is with a restriction. At first, even eidetic observation will consider an
> ego as such with the restriction that a constituted world already exists
> for him. This, moreover, is a necessary level; only by laying open the
> law-forms of the genesis pertaining to this level can one see the possi-
> bilities of a *maximally universal* eidetic phenomenology. In the latter
> the ego varies himself so freely that he does not keep even the ideal re-
> strictive presupposition that a world having the ontological structure
> accepted by us as obvious is essentially constituted for him.[18]

In this declaration, which in a certain sense marks the essential and defini-tive limit of all eidetic phenomenology of genesis, we perceive two short-comings; one confessed shortcoming: the eidetic elucidation is established only from mediate moments of genesis. It gives account only of what is not genesis itself, but merely its phenomenological sense constituted right away on the foundations of a world whose ontological structures, themselves pro-duced in the unity of a history, are neither put into question nor thematized as such. We have seen why it was necessary to begin there and this failure appeared to us linked to the very vocation of philosophy. In this sense, we had tried to define in this way the limits of the inescapable idealism of any philosophy: *always and essentially,* eidetic reflection will presuppose an already constituted ontology. This was at once a temporal and ontological necessity. Idealism being constituted by the finitude of temporal existence, a universal pure eidetics of genetics will never be possible. The dialectical constitution of original time is such that the ego, contrary to what Husserl says, "cannot carry out variations of the self with a freedom such that it does not even maintain the ideal supposition of a familiar ontological structure." Now, where we see an absolute existential limit, Husserl sees only a methodological limit; at the moment when we believe that any idealism must be converted into its opposite, Husserl believes he is merely getting through a stage. Not only does he think that an absolute eidetic reduction of ontology is possible and that it will found a universal phenomenology of genesis, but he holds that within the provisional limits that he has just set for his research, an eidetics of genesis is already possible in all its rigor. It is here that a graver inadequacy is hidden.

As if he were through with methodological reservations and precautions, Husserl develops straight afterward the results of his first eidetic analysis. "Principles of constitutive genesis that have universal significance for us [are] divided according to two fundamental forms, into principles of *active* and principles of *passive* genesis."[19] That the active genesis inaugurated and pursued by a continuous intervention of the subject can be used in an eidetic inventory, can be considered as always possible, at least in principle. All the moments of active constitution, still animated by the intentional sense that has produced them, can be "reproduced" at each moment, as Husserl notes himself, or, as he will say later, "reactualized" or "reactivated" in the purity of their originary meaning. To the degree that what is "constituted" in this genesis is reduced by the very subject of the constitution, their pure meaning, which is intentional meaning, is respected in this way. To the degree that it is myself who produces in some way the sense of my history, this sense is perfectly transparent for me. Between the facticity and intentional meaning of my becoming, the separation will be made in complete clear evidence, and since I appear to myself, identical and monadic subject, me, as the only absolute source of meaning for my history, I will make this history perfectly intelligible to myself. I will be the absolute eidetic sense of the relative multiplicity of the moments of my experience, the "same" constituent to which the becoming of all the "others" will have to be referred. That is clear and easy. Let us not insist on it; let us simply note that two difficulties are already be-

ing announced. First of all, when it is a question of active genesis, eidetic reduction should no longer be thought necessary. All the moments of active
genesis are constituents by essence and at that level the separation between
the transcendental and the empirical has no sense. Is it not here that this core
of originary existence is met with, merging itself dialectically with its essence
and resisting any "imaginary variation," any eidetic reduction? Then, certain
objects, inside the sphere of activity itself are by essence constituted by a totality of subjects. Even the clear evidence in which they are constituted by a
monadic ego implies their preceding, simultaneous or even future, constitution, by an "alter ego" or by a multiplicity of egos. These are also powers of
transcendental activity and thus introduce an irreducible passivity into the
very intimacy of its activity. The problem is capital. Husserl, concerning himself here only with the eidos ego,[20] is content with pointing it out and announces that he will come back to it (which he will do in the *Fifth Meditation*). Once again, this division through method can compromise the sense of
each of his developments. It is only in referring to another analysis which will
illuminate the sense of transcendental intersubjectivity that Husserl can present the egologic genesis he is talking about here as "active." However let us
follow him and seek to illuminate the gaps in the analysis from the inside.

The more Husserl's thought progresses, the more it tends to present active genesis as superficial and secondary. It necessarily presupposes its foundation in passive genesis. This is what appears to us in the last analysis irreducible to every concrete eidetics. It is this that will be integrated into the
transcendental constitution only in a formal and a conceptual way. It is this,
finally, that will run the risk of altering the original project of a transcendental idealism and of leading to a formal idealism with all its avatars. The way in
which Husserl was tempted to save this idealism by reference to a teleology
and a philosophy of history is what we should like to begin to speak of now.

The Passive Genesis
Necessity of a Philosophy of History

After having defined the principles of active genesis, Husserl writes: "In any
case, anything built by activity necessarily presupposes, as the lowest level, a
passivity that gives something beforehand; and, when we trace anything built
actively, we run into constitution by passive generation."[21] Now, to the degree that any "eidos" appears as such and exists as such[22] only if it is aimed at
by an *a priori* intuition and if it is the intentional correlate of a conscious activity, one might ask what will be the eidetic status of passive genesis. To say

that it is the essence of the passively constituted object not to be intentionally constituted, to limit the intentionality here in exclusive fashion to its passive movement, is that not precisely to include formally in the activity what is
really and "in itself" foreign to the constituting intentionality?[23] To say, as
Husserl does in the manuscripts and in *Experience and Judgment,* that passivity is a moment of activity is to make use of an abstract concept of activity,
which does not refer to any originary clear evidence. It is to stay prisoner of a
formal idealism. Why might not activity itself be a modification of passivity?
To reduce one of the moments to the other is to privilege either a subjectivism
that, being close to a psychologism, does not recognize objectivity except as
linked to a factitious act of my consciousness, or a materialism, itself also psychologistic, that makes of the intentional act the prolongation of a "worldly"
determinism. Under both hypotheses, there is unfaithfulness to the pure
principle of transcendental intentionality. Instead of describing passive synthesis as pure existential experience, preceding any transcendental constitution by a theoretic subject, irreducible as such to any eidetic elucidation, instead of making of it the core of existence and of precategorial objectivity,
Husserl envisages it only as condition of possibility of active genesis proper;
in the last analysis, any transcendental genesis is reduced to this latter in his
eyes. While passive synthesis appears, once the transcendental reduction has
been carried out, as the absolutely originary constitutive layer, Husserl seems,
implicitly and in contradiction to his initial intentions, to put passive synthesis, pure and as such, in its turn into brackets.

The second part of § 38 bears witness to this subtle deviation. Certain
phrases doubtless situate and define the whole primordiality of passive synthesis: "The 'ready-made' object that confronts us in life as an existent mere
physical thing *(als daseiendes blosses Ding)* (when we disregard all the 'spiritual' or 'cultural' characteristics [*«geistige» Charaktere*] that make it knowable as, for example, a hammer, a table, an aesthetic creation) is given, with the
originality of the 'it itself,' in the synthesis of a passive experience."[24] This passive synthesis of the existent with the existent,[25] which is *a priori* synthesis and
purely ontological, involves a becoming that is always preconstituted and
that, for sure, will not be understood *as such* and originarily except through
an activity of the subject but always *understood with its sense of "already there."*
The time of any constitution of sense is structured by these infinite referrals.
The transcendental activity will not at any moment have absolutely assimilated the existence preconstituted in passive synthesis—and that is an eidetic
necessity as well. If it managed to do so, on the one hand, the sense that it
would thus produce would not have its foundation in any existence, on the

other, it would mark the end of its own becoming: two mythical or meta-physical consequences that would suspend the originary intentionality and temporality of lived experience—and Husserl recognizes it: "while these ['spiritual' activities] are making their synthetic products, the passive synthesis that supplies all their 'material' still goes on. The physical thing given beforehand in passive intuition continues to appear in a unitary intuition; and, no matter how much the thing may be modified therein by the activity of explication, of grasping parts and features, it continues to be given beforehand during and in this activity."[26] The passive synthesis which here is synonymous with the hyletic structure of intentional consciousness—[a structure] already so obscure in *Ideas* I—is thus a constituting moment of the unity of intuition. But as Husserl presents it here, this unity is not simple; the absolute is divided in it; there is present in it a composition which is essential and by which the purity of any phenomenology and any philosophy will be definitively affected. In fact, this unity of intuition cannot be *totally* constituted in a passive synthesis. The passive synthesis does not appear as a synthesis except insofar as it is a phenomenon for an intentional consciousness. No transcendental activity would be possible if the unity of the object were totally constituted in a passivity. The real *(real)* unity of the substrate, temporal or sensible, would never bring about a unity of the sense of the object. But conversely, the transcendental activity is above all explicitation, unveiling: it participates in the constitution of that unity of sense which refers essentially to the real *(real)* unity of the empirical or sensible substrate. The unity of the intuition is thus originarily synthetic. It is possible only through a dialectic of antepredicative time and phenomenological time; since it is essentially complex, to be grasped in its pure simplicity, which can only be formal,[27] it refers to a genesis indefinite in its past and in its future. "This synthesis [...] has its 'history' evinced in the synthesis itself."[28] That this history is "evinced"[29] in the moment of transcendental activity is incontestable, since this activity is above all revelation and intuition of what is pregiven to the consciousness. The history that is announced there is by definition already endowed with its intentional sense. It is phenomenological history. Yet we have just seen that phenomenological history presupposes real history, of which it is the constitution and explicitation. Now, at the moment when Husserl writes that the history presupposed by the passive genesis "is itself announced," he has interrupted this dialectic between phenomenology and ontology. Every history announcing itself is reduced *a priori* to its phenomenological and intentional sense, to a sense which it did not create in its authentic genesis but which preexists it, envelops it, and continually informs it. Its possibility is the modification of an originary constituting activity. The eidetic rigor is saved in this way, but it is by altering or suppressing genesis.

What follows in the text only turns the description in this direction. Admitting that it is "is owing to an essentially *(wesensmäßig*)* necessary genesis that I, the ego, can experience a physical thing," that "this is true, moreover, not only as regards phenomenological genesis but also as regards genesis in the usual sense, psychological genesis," Husserl means explicitly, in some way, that it is always possible to keep to the active and intentional moment of the historical or genetic constitution. Which is what he himself does: "Yet, without putting ourselves back into the realm of passivity, to say nothing of using the external psychophysical point of view of psychology, we can, the meditating ego can, penetrate into the intentional constituents of experiential phenomena themselves—thing-experiencing phenomena and all others—and thus find intentional references leading back to a 'history' and accordingly making these phenomena knowable as formations subsequent to other, essentially antecedent formations (even if the latter cannot be related to precisely the same constituted object)."[30] From the exclusively phenomenological viewpoint that is maintained here, history will thus be only the intentional chain of meanings, the series of moments where passive synthesis, "animated" by active synthesis, is "recognized" as passive synthesis. History will be but history endowed with lived sense, history for a transcendental subject. But these intentional referrals are in principle infinite and, to that degree, never take on the absolute of their sense; now they are infinite because the active synthesis that inaugurates the possibility of a piece of eidetic research is always preceded by a passive synthesis. So to be rigorous, an eidetic analysis must suppose the absolute of sense to be *already* known, and institute the absolute intentional sense and the transcendental activity on the threshold of passivity itself by a decree or a certainty of an exceptional and nonphenomenological type. No doubt there is then the risk of transforming the passive synthesis, the only foundation of objectivity so far, the only certainty of an access to being as being, into a pure activity of the subject and into a purely productive intentionality whose dangers we have confirmed. But this is the only way, it seems, for Husserl to save the absolute rigor of his descriptions. It is thus that the becoming is *a priori* stripped of facticity and of its effectiveness, to the advantage of its rationality. "There," writes Husserl, "we soon

---

*Insertion of German by J. D. *Trans.*

encounter eidetic laws governing a passive forming of perpetually new syntheses (a forming that, in part, lies prior to all activity and, in part, takes in all
activity itself). [...] Even the circumstance that everything affecting me, *as a*
[*fully*] *'developed' ego,** is apperceived as an 'object,' a substrate of predicates
with which I may become acquainted, belongs here."[31] But since this synthesis is always incomplete in both directions, since it has always already started
and has never finished, the "fully developed" ego is the subject of an infinite
history. The absolute intentional sense by which it is wished to found the genetic eidos is pushed back to an infinite limit. Which does not prevent Husserl
from specifying, and defining with the greatest clarity, the idealism that ori-
entates his whole reflection: "This is an already familiar goal-form *(eine im
voraus bekannte mögliche Zielform)* for possible explications as acquaintive explications—explications that would constitute an object as an abiding possession, as something accessible again and again; and this goal-form is understandable in advance having arisen from a genesis. It itself points back
to a 'primal instituting' *(Urstiftung)* of this form. Everything known to us
points to *an original becoming acquainted; what we call unknown has, nevertheless, a known structural form:*[†] the form 'object' and, more particularly, the
form 'spatial thing,' 'cultural Object,' 'tool,' and so forth."[32]

With genesis being reduced to its intentional and eidetic meaning, its passivity integrated *a priori* into a transcendental activity, one has no reason to be
surprised at statements as paradoxical as these. It will be understood that it is
at the price of the actual originality of becoming that the final form is not only
"known beforehand" but in a way that is even more precise and more complex, "known beforehand as the product of a genesis." Husserl is interested
only in the *a priori* and ideal form of the constituted product of genesis. It is
from this form that he starts off. It is no longer here a transcendental act of genetic constitution that gives its sense to itself, but forms and conditions of *a
priori* possibility that make genesis itself intelligible. Defined in these terms,
genesis in its irreducible actuality is understood, as in a Kantianism, in the form
of an empirical genesis or of a manifold of sensibility—here object of a purely
passive synthesis—which becomes possible and intelligible through the transcendental activity of a subject that, in the last analysis, is not actually engendered. "The structural forms of the known" are perhaps themselves produced

---

*Derrida's italics. *Trans.*

†Derrida: "structural form of the known." *Trans.*

in Husserl's eyes in a genesis, but they intervene in philosophical reflection and in eidetic description only at the moment when they can define *a priori* the sense of every possible genesis. For that, they must in their specific moment be autonomous and transcendent in relation to the very content of the effective genesis. Whatever may be the product of any genesis whatsoever, it will be comprehended and organized by the structural form of the known. That is to say that this latter is universal and *a priori*. As such, it is originarily taken out of genesis. Husserl would be able to reply that here the whole difference separating him from Kant is that the *a priori* is *phenomenological*, that is to say, concrete. [This *a priori*] is given to an intuition, and thus is distinguished from a form or a category. And that is what he writes in passing in § 39, while reiterating the conclusion of § 38: "Nor should it be overlooked here that '*fact*,' with its '*irrationality*,' is itself a structural concept within the system of the *concrete a priori*."[33]

But for us, this is now only a decree. Since any concrete is constituted according to a temporality, it is originarily complicated with *a priori* and *a posteriori*, with truth and with being, with unveiling and enrichment. The pure *a priori*, whether it is formal or not, would have to define itself by an atemporality or an absolute temporal antecedence.[34] We know that these two possibilities are forbidden us because of the irreducible temporality of the transcendental. So the very idea of an *a priori* intuition of essences, guiding principle of every phenomenology, must be profoundly transformed in the light of the dialectic whose necessity we are verifying at each step. Because the concrete *a priori* of genesis, the final forms of the known, and so on are founded on their own passive synthesis, because they are negotiating with their opposite and are only genetic to the degree that they do so, it is again by an irreducible prejudice, and in disagreement with the very results of his analysis, that Husserl defines the method and the first philosophy of phenomenology as a transcendental idealism.[35]

This transcendental idealism, whose originality Husserl underlines in a couple of pages of a remarkable force and density, constantly leaves the impression of an overhasty systematization. In presenting phenomenology as a "transcendental theory of knowledge"[36] Husserl ratifies the formalism which he used to integrate passivity into a transcendental activity in general. Husserl defends himself on this score; having nothing in common with a Kantian idealism or a psychologist idealism,[37] transcendental idealism is "nothing more than [...] an explication of my ego as subject of every possible cognition."[38] Now, to the degree that it refers at the limit to an ultimate passive synthesis where the ego has not yet taken possession of its sense as an ego—and here comes the compromising of phenomenology with psychology, sociology, biology, and so forth—the egologic science, thus defined, is not autonomous in its foundation; it causes the frames of an idealism to burst asunder. *"The proof of this idealism is therefore phenomenology itself,"* Husserl tells us.[39] But this proof is only mediate. Any phenomenology supposes, according to Husserl himself, an already constituted ontology. Whilst transcendental idealism does not found itself explicitly, and in its own moment, on an ontology, it risks being confused with a classical idealism.

Husserl remains very conscious of all these difficulties. The problem of passive genesis, thematized in three forms, the hylé, transcendental intersubjectivity, and originary temporalization, does not stop worrying Husserl. All the manuscripts dating from this period bear witness to this. In very rich analyses,[40] stripped of any concern to systematize, Husserl's thought oscillates constantly between an idealism and an "existentialism" (in the deep sense of that term) which would overturn any phenomenology or would make it superficial and purely methodological.

Thus, in the meditations on the theme of the "Living Present" *(lebendige Gegenwart)*[41] Husserl, analyzing the passive constitution of the time of the ego, will run into insurmountable difficulties: how to define passivity inside the "vigilant" and active "I"?[42] A little later, going back over the same text,[43] he thinks he has found the "solution of the difficulty" by merging the "transcendental phenomenological I with actual temporality." It follows rigorously that the "phenomenological theme is always already constituted for the 'existent I' *(ich seiendes)*."[44] Would the phenomenological "I," to which the existent "I" appears, not then itself be a transcendental constituent? Turning back again once more, Husserl asks himself "whether the transcendental I is not atemporal."[45] In another very rich text, Husserl asks himself whether, since time and being are always passively preconstituted, pretemporality *(Vorzeit)* and preexistence *(Vorsein)* are not beyond any possible experience *(unerfahrbar)* and any possible discourse *(unsagbar)* for the "phenomenologizing I."[46] Finally, in a text of 1932 Husserl asks himself about the very possibility of a reduction to the Living Present.[47] If there is a self-temporalization *(Selbstzeitigung)*, what can be the transcendental sense of a reduction and an eidetics of the temporal genesis?[48] All the manuscripts of this period combine the problem of time, of the hylé and of intersubjectivity. At bottom, their meaning from the point of view of a transcendental idealism is the same: a simple explicitation of the transcendental ego as such, in its monadicity, cannot account for their existence and for the constitution of their sense. Better, the objectivity of knowledge, of which transcendental phenomenology is the "theory," is only possible—and Husserl insists on this himself—through the passive synthesis of the temporal and sensible hylé and through the originarity of transcendental intersubjectivity.[49] The common root of these three themes is again brought to light by Husserl, who defines the originary hylé *(Urhyle)* as the kernel of the alter ego *(ichfremde Kern)*.[50] In fact, it is starting from the originary impression of time (and, on its foundation, of that of space) that, in the experience of the Living Present, there appears to me, the theoretical transcendental subject, the irreducible alterity of the moments of past and future time, retained and anticipated, from the surrounding world, from history, from "egos." It is on this foundation that transcendental intersubjectivity sets itself up, condition of possibility for objectivity in general. If transcendental intersubjectivity is only possible starting from the single common world, existence and essence are given to us in a passive genesis that runs the risk of reducing the explicitation of the monadic transcendental ego—and thus the whole of transcendental idealism—to being only a second moment of a veritable constitutive analysis, indispensable but insufficient: this analysis must be instituted starting from an ontology.

It is no accident if Husserl never showed himself satisfied with the manuscripts relating to these problems. The *Fifth Cartesian Meditation,* which explicitly tackles the question of transcendental intersubjectivity, psychology and history, *Ideas* II, which describes the constitution of material nature, of animated nature, and of the spiritual world, are only a repeat of the difficulty. In fact, all the systematic and apparently definitive positions that Husserl takes after 1930 remain faithful to this transcendental idealism for which being remains "a practical idea, that of the infinity of theoretically determining work."[51]

The development of this idealism was neither serene nor continuous. With passive genesis, historical time had been introduced in the transcendental sphere. If passive genesis, forcing us into an infinite regression, seems unable to be assimilated to an egological activity, must there not be an attempt to reconquer it by enlarging the transcendental to the dimensions of history in general, and through a teleological idea, to give back to passive genesis itself an intentional sense that the ego alone could not confer on it? Thus, once again all the anterior eidetic analyses would be newly founded.

The problem of teleology that appears in the manuscripts of 1925 had profound roots in Husserl's philosophy. Linked to the theme of intentionality in general, to the idea of a philosophical "task," it was also implicitly of a piece with the infinite idea in all its forms: the infinite becoming of logic, the idea of an infinite totality of lived experiences of the pure me, the idea of the world as infinite possibility and infinite foundation of experience, and so forth. After *Cartesian Meditations,* where it makes its first appearance, philosophical teleology will occupy a privileged place in Husserl's thought. In the important cycle of the *Krisis* and in the *Origin of Geometry,* it develops into a veritable philosophy of history. It is this which we must examine to conclude, asking ourselves to what degree this philosophy of history, bringing to a close the system of transcendental phenomenology, at the same time and at the same moment sanctions the unsurpassable depth and the irreducible insufficiency of Husserl's philosophy of genesis.

Appendix

We choose here those of the unpublished texts that we have been able to consult in the "Husserl Archives" at Louvain which immediately interest us and which we could have integrated directly into our argument if we had had the time. We will refer to these texts by their themes.[52]

Group D of the unpublished work: "Primordial Constitution" (*Urkonstitution*)

~ The difficulty of a distinction between static analysis and genetic analysis on the subject of the kinestheses (D 12, 1930–31, pp. 19–27).
~ Originary association and temporalization—Constitution of the real (*Realen*), of time, of space, of causality:
  • Analysis of originary association as pretemporalization, p. 1;
  • Movement of the originary impression as synthetic unity, p. 3;
  • Problem of the constitution of a time that is homogeneous in spite of "perspectivity" (*Perspectivierung*), p. 4;
  • If there is neither a necessary beginning of time nor atemporality of the beginning, what will be the apodictic foundation of the "I am"? p. 5;
  • The flux of lived experience is "during," immanent, but not in the sense of "experimentable," p. 6 9d15, 1–3 November 1932).
~ Covering (*Verdeckung*) and fusion (*Verschmelzung*) as "originary phenomena" (*Urphänomen*) in the genesis of a "being in itself" in the sphere of immanence (D 9, 1926).
~ Meaning of a dissociation between the period of sleep and the period of dreaming. Enigma of the unconscious; is the hypothesis of a nothing of retention verifiable? (D1, before 1930, pp. 3–7).

Group B: "The Reduction"

~ Universal constitutive phenomenology must be transformed into a universal theory of genesis:

- Is there a genesis of the monad? p. 58
- The *Lectures* [*The Phenomenology of Internal Time Consciousness*] did not go beyond a static phenomenology, p. 62;
- Domain of passive genesis: constitution of an anthropological world. Physiological evolution and its conditions in the unity of the physical world, p. 63;
- Domain of active genesis: motivation of my thought. Value. Willing, p. 63 (B III, 10, 1921–1923).

Group C "Constitution of Time"

~ Difficulty of dissociating "real" analysis and intentional analysis in relation to the reflexive experience of the flux of lived experience (C 12, 1 F, no date).

~ Idea of a transcendental "instinct"—Instinct and universal teleology being developed as constitution of the world (C 13, 1 January 1934).

~ Inauguration of a methodical reduction of the proto-phenomenal present, as method of a reduction of the pregiven world as such in the regression *(Rückfrage)* toward the essential phenomena of subjectivity, substituted for the method of an ontology of the world of experience; this latter is the transcendental guide in the description of the originary structures *(Urstrukturen)* of the Living Present: hylé, egological structure, primordiality, layers of temporalization, originary temporalization of nature, of the world. . . .

- The world as "pregiven," but in the form of an open horizon, p. 1;
- Appearance of the constituted (types, children, babies, animals) in the horizon of an unfilled experience. Problem of a universal worldly psychology and its possible method. Idea of normality, p. 2;
- The constituting origin of transcendences as constituted in a "present," p. 2;
- Constitution and passive temporalization of the "I-person," p. 8 (C 6, August 1930).

PART IV

TELEOLOGY

THE SENSE OF HISTORY AND

THE HISTORY OF SENSE

8

The Birth and Crises of Philosophy

Furtively reintroducing the constituted world into the transcendental sphere, passive genesis rendered an elucidation of history necessary. The problem of history had always been considered by Husserl as belonging to the empirical sciences dealing with causality and "worldly" events. In this respect, phenomenology had in some respects ostracized historical man. The unveiling of passive synthesis in the temporal constitution of the ego and of intersubjectivity was the unveiling of man originarily caught in his historical environment. We have seen how difficult it was by a simple explicitation of the monadic ego to give an account of its passive genesis. This latter was, as such, bereft of any intentional sense produced by the activity of the ego. Thus, it was indispensable, in order to save transcendental idealism, that it be originarily animated by some intentionality which transformed it from a pure inert and "real" datum into a preactive and preconscious project of theoretical meaning. This was the role of transcendental teleology; the idea of an explicitation of the ego as infinite task of philosophy seemed to be bound to save phenomenology once again.

But it saved phenomenology by contradicting it. This teleology could not by essence be given to a concrete subject in an originary clear evidence. To be faithful to its mission, it had to precede any active constitution and, in itself, any becoming conscious of the subject. This was the danger of metaphysics and *a priori* formalism apparently so feared by Husserl. To make a suprasubjective, supra- or omnitemporal activity out of intentionality, is this not to deny all the preceding results of phenomenology? The problem, so grave, so dangerous, had not been directly tackled in *Cartesian Meditations*. The teleological idea cropped up at the very moment when the difficulties seemed insuperable. But nothing was yet known about its origin. What was the transcendental subject pertaining to this idea? Was it constituted in a "noema" or did it merge with the noetic movement of the subject itself? Husserl merely let these questions be guessed at. He seemed to think that the mode of clear evidence of the teleological idea was absolutely exceptional, that, truth to tell, this idea was the only one not to be founded in something other than itself, for the good reason that it stayed veiled, hidden, under the apparent movement of philosophy. Because nothing could put it in doubt, or merely reduce it, "neutralize" it, the true philosopher felt its sense, verified it and authenticated it by the very exercise of philosophy. In mysterious fashion, phenomenology was also the "proof" of teleology.

But for this, the necessity of this teleology must not have been compromised by the empirical event of which it was the foundation. Presiding over the very constitution of "worldly" history, it had to be imperturbable and incorruptible by essence. To be a transcendental evidence and not an empirico-psychological one, it was all the more indispensable that it be or could be recognized by every possible transcendental subject. So that, putting aside the objections that might be addressed from the outside to a phenomenological teleology, one sees that Husserl himself had to ask himself the fundamental question: How can the teleological idea be refuted, ignored, perverted, or hidden, nonexistent or "forgotten" for certain subjects, at certain moments of history, in certain places of the world? How is the "crisis" of a transcendental teleological idea possible? How can the empirical event, if it is only constituted, "cover up" and "veil" the very act of its constitution? Will not the simple existence of "crises" oblige us to make the idea of philosophy come down into a "worldly" history and lend a constituting role to the empirical event itself? Teleology would be thus at the same time production and product of history, still according to the same dialectics of time and the same *a priori* synthesis of being and time. At least that is the answer that we would be right to expect from Husserl. It is not the one that he gives us, explicitly at least.

In the "Vienna Lecture,"[1] it is Europe which takes on the role of mediation between the pure transcendental ego and the empirical incarnation of the teleological idea. Of course, it must be further said quickly with Husserl, Europe is not thus understood in a "worldly" sense that it might acquire from a geographical, political, or other specification. The empirical Europe also has itself its genesis, which one would have the greatest difficulty in understanding in a transcendental infinite teleology. Starting from geographical political or economical facticity, the eidetic unity of Europe cannot be defined by anything rigorous. To take in Europe, one must begin from an idea, from a pure and *a priori* meaning. This idea of Europe is the idea that is born in Europe;

it is the idea of philosophy that is, in its absolute originality, Husserl tells us, a European idea. Truth to tell, Europe is not the cradle of philosophy, it is itself born as a spiritual meaning from the idea of philosophy.

> Spiritual Europe has a birthplace. By this I mean not a geographical birthplace in one land, though this is also true, but rather a spiritual birthplace in a nation or in individual men and human groups of this nation. It is the ancient Greek nation in the seventh and sixth centuries B.C. Here there arises a *new sort of attitude* of individuals toward their surrounding world. And its consequence is the breakthrough of a completely new sort of spiritual structure (*geistiger Gebilde*) rapidly growing into a systematically self-enclosed cultural form; the Greeks called it *philosophy*. Correctly translated, in the original sense, that means nothing other than universal science, science of the universe, of the all-encompassing unity of all that is. [...] In the breakthrough of philosophy in this sense, in which all sciences are thus contained, I see, paradoxical as it may sound, the primal phenomenon (*Urphänomen*) of spiritual Europe.[2]

This is a strange declaration which betrays the persistence of all the preceding obscurities. The idea of philosophy is not carried or produced by a "real" empirical history. In this sense, European facticity must be put in brackets. In order to detect the idea of philosophy in its purity and its necessity, one must, through the classical "imaginary variation," suppose it rooted in thousands of geographical and historical ways. In this respect, Europe should be able to be replaced by Asia or by Africa. Husserl would not dispute that Europe in its empirical facticity has no privileged relation to the idea of philosophy. And yet, Europe, philosophy's spiritual place of birth, its mysterious and immaterial residence, resists variation. There is a European *eidos* merging itself with the idea of philosophy. But since this *eidos* is neither an event nor an empirical localization, do the precise allusions to the "Greece of the seventh century B.C.," the expression of "nation," the homage paid to "certain isolated men" have only a fictional and metaphorical sense? Is it only a question of contingent examples? Certainly not. As in numerous texts having the same inspiration, such precision in the evocation shows clearly that it is indeed a question of real and irreplaceable facts and of a history that is effectively historical. For actually real history gives a very particular status to essences. These are no longer obtained by an imaginary variation, by a fiction and eidetic reduction. They are *a priori* and synthetically linked to existence. What one cannot cause to vary, what cannot be neutralized here is the finite existence of pre-Socratic thinkers to whom the idea of truth appeared one day. At a certain moment, the pure idea of philosophy came and merged itself with the destiny and the existence of a people or of a group of men. Can it even be said that this idea came and was identified with an existence? That would presuppose that this idea had preexisted the existence in some way. Must it not be said, on the contrary, that it is existence which has produced philosophy? But if the originary unveiling of truth is posterior to a movement of existence, is one not led to conceive this existence as purely empirical, real, psychological, and so on? All originary evidence, every access to truth, every manifestation of being as being would then be forbidden it. The transcendental and the empirical must then be originarily implied in an existence that would still be opened to the truth of being, while still being "in-the-world." It is in the existence of the Greek people that there would thus appear this "human reality" whose essence is confused with existence and which is the object of an "existential analysis" and of an "anthropology" in the Heideggerian sense (which obviously has nothing in common with the worldly science rejected by Husserl).

Because Husserl does not start from this "human reality" and because he still believes an eidetic reduction of the totality of human existence is possible, one cannot help but see a contradiction[3] between the refusal of an empirical definition of Europe (in the first phrase of the cited text) and the presenting of philosophy as borne in "the heart of certain men" and as an originary historical phenomenon. If the idea of philosophy or the *eidos* Europe have only one spiritual birthplace, then while staying rigorous, one can bring together this place with a Hellenic phenomenon, localized in real time and space. The idea of philosophy is thus reduced to a fact.

For the genetic problem is still not cleared up. If the idea of philosophy as infinite *telos*, if the *eidos* Europe have [each] been brought into the world, and if this birth can be situated and dated, it can be asked what might have preceded or surrounded it. The same question was asked for the transcendental reduction: Either the possibility of reduction was present, although hidden, dissimulated in the temporality of the natural attitude. Then one wonders why it appeared at one moment of empirical becoming rather than another. The pure meaning of the reduction cannot teach us this and we are obliged to have recourse to a "worldly" causality. Explaining the transcendental reduction by natural causality, one makes it lose all its originary sense. Or else the reduction marks an absolute beginning in temporality. But then its situation on the inside of the "naive" experience that it is reducing no longer has any sense. One is still forced to explain it by what is not it. In both cases, the essential distinction between originary moment and constituted moment obliges us to interchange their role and reverse their definition.

On the level of teleology, the question is analogous: Does the establishing of philosophy divide humanity in its geographical and historical extension into two families, of which one would be limited to an empirical group, comprising on the one hand the Europeans who preceded the spiritual advent of Europe, on the other hand, the non-Europeans? The hypothesis is laughable. Yet Husserl writes in the reworked text of the Vienna Lecture[4] that "Only Europe has an 'immanent teleology,' a sense. While India, China have only an empirical sociological type, Europe has the unity of a spiritual figure." Taken seriously, this proposition is contradictory; if humanity, conscious of the philosophical telos, has had a past, if at a certain moment it has inaugurated the philosophical attitude, then the historical temporality of man has known a rupture. How did humanity pass from ignorance to the consciousness of an infinite task of philosophy? From a purely empirical subjectivity to a transcendental subjectivity? For the idea of philosophy to have an infinite sense originarily, was it not necessary for ignorance to be only a forgetting, for empirical subjectivity to be only the burying of an original transcendental subjectivity? But then how can one distinguish rigorously between the empirical types of human groups and the transcendental types? Because the transcendental possibility is always *already there*, is the act by which it is awakened a transcendental or an empirical "birth"? Is it more than a historical accident? If, in accordance with its essence, the infinite task is always originarily present or possible, the act by which one "becomes aware" of it is not itself originary. That ruins the whole foundation of this teleology.

The realization of this becoming is thus very obscure. How is it still possible, since India or China or at least Indians or Chinese, as empirical individuals, can become aware of this infinite task and assume it by participating in Western culture? Two hypotheses can be envisaged: Either the idea of philosophy in one form or another is buried but present in the empirical becoming that precedes its advent. As absolute idea, it is not produced by an empirical genesis and precedes its anthropological incarnation. But then two questions have to asked: First, why does it appear at one moment and in one place in human history? And, at the limit, why is it necessary that it appears? This is a mystery that cannot by definition be revealed either by the idea as such, whose temporality is not "finite," or by empirical subjectivity, which as such does not know the idea. Then, if the idea really is infinite, can its taking root be only an accident? It seems not. The teleological idea is the very being of transcendental subjectivity or its noematic correlate. To this extent, it is not linked by accident to an anthropological subjectivity. But if, conversely this rooting is made into an absolute and essential event, then one admits that a supposedly infinite idea is lacking some complement, some possible enrichment. In the same way, if the birth of the idea to history is of an empirical and worldly order, by what right is Europe defined as a spiritual birthplace? By what right is it stripped of its facticity and distinguished from another empirical world? What existential determination can then be given to an *eidos* Europe which has not in itself, as Husserl underlines, any "real" determination? "I mean that we feel (and in spite of all obscurity this feeling is probably legitimate) that an entelechy is inborn in our European civilization that holds sway throughout all the changing shapes of Europe and accords to them the sense of a development toward an ideal shape of life and being as an eternal pole. Not that this is a case of one of those well-known types of purposeful striving which give the organic beings their character in the physical realm; thus it is not something like a biological development from a seminal form through stages to maturity with succeeding ages and dying-out. There is, for essential reasons, no zoology of peoples."[5] The paradox is that, by wanting to discriminate absolutely between the empirical sense of the idea and its transcendental sense, the teleological finality which one hopes to keep absolutely pure is transformed into an empirical finality. For in both cases the European genesis of the idea takes on the figure of an accident. If this genesis is completely spiritual, it is not clear why it is a genesis: the infinity and eternity of the idea ought really to do without a human becoming. This becoming then remains, as such, exclusively empirical and exterior to the life of the teleology.

Husserl would doubtless reply that the teleological idea is not transcendent to the becoming of the transcendental subjectivity. The dilemma in the face of which one tries to immobilize one's thought is only possible by a "separate" realization of the idea. But once this idea is hypostasized, human subjectivity can only be worldly. In fact, the idea of philosophy is the noetic motor and the noematic correlate of transcendental subjectivity; it is an intentional finality: "the spiritual *telos* of European humanity, in which the particular telos of particular nations and of individual men is contained, lies in the infinite, is an infinite idea toward which, in concealment, the whole spiritual becoming aims, so to speak. As soon as it becomes consciously recognized in the development as telos, it necessarily also becomes practical as a goal of the will; and thereby a new, higher stage of development is introduced which is under the guidance of norms, normative ideas. Now all this is not intended as a speculative interpretation of our historical development but as the expression of a vital presentiment which arises through unprejudiced reflection *(Besinnung)*."[6]

We encounter, then, a second hypothesis: the idea does not exist outside transcendental experience. Beyond the fact that the way the idea is announced in experience remains very mysterious, beyond the fact that all the illusions are lying in wait for this "felt signpost,"[7] this presentiment, "this presentiment that we all have and which, in the absence of any clear notion, is quite justified" (a declaration whose style is very unusual with Husserl), the constitution of the transcendental becoming of the idea reproduces on a hardly different level all the aporias to which the couple of passive genesis and active genesis had led us. Indeed, for the becoming of the idea to be constituted in a transcendental experience, the idea before being actively aimed at and assumed by the "I" or by a community of "I"s, must produce itself in a passive synthesis. The alternative is thus the following: either the passive moment of genesis is already animated by the idea; it is then integrated to a transcendental activity in general whose subject is no longer an ego but an infinite totality of egos or a suprahuman ego. The division between the spiritual family of Europe and the families of an empirical type, between the past of ancient Greece and its birth to philosophy, loses all its sense.

Transcendental genesis is then preceded by nothing. One comes back to the preceding hypothesis. Or, and this is the most plausible, the passive movement refers to a pretranscendental domain. But, the passive synthesis ensuring continuity between the worldly and the transcendental, it is no longer possible to distinguish rigorously between empirical constitution and transcendental constitution. There would thus be a genesis of the idea of philosophy out of what is not it, a knowledge of what is not it starting from the philosophical coming to awareness. But then how can the idea of an infinite task be instituted in a pure finitude? Is it not necessary that, in some way, the infinite was *already* present in human finitude? And if it was thus, why should it be revealed in the finite? These are just some of the questions that a simple "eidetics" founded on a phenomenological idealism cannot resolve and that should motivate a radical conversion. It is only by abandoning the point of view of an eidetics incapable of giving account of a genesis of the idea and by turning toward a new ontology that one will be able to try to describe faithfully and to live this genesis—since it is indeed a question of a theoretical "task"—or to relive it. This ontology, far from ignoring the essential moment of eidetic phenomenology, one that cannot be gone beyond, will show, by deepening the phenomenology of temporality, that at the level of the originary temporal existence, fact and essence, the empirical and the transcendental, are inseparable and dialectically of a piece. This identity is the originarily dialectical identity of being and time, where being, constituting itself by itself, goes beyond itself in its constituted moments as empirical fact and appears to itself as transcendental subject in its constituting productivity. Human existence, where being becomes dialectically a subject "for itself," assumes originary temporality and becomes aware of the necessity of dialectics as of its original finitude, is the starting point of an ontological reflection.[8]

Husserl now seems to have definitively missed this starting point. The Vienna Lecture, leaving the eidetic brackets always closed in some way, starting out from an idea of history, constantly fails to give account of the actual genesis of this idea and of its historical rootedness. No doubt Husserl notices the dialectic movement of genesis: "that which is so acquired as valid, as truth, is serviceable as material for the possible production of idealities on a higher level, and so on again and again"[9]; or again, "it also means a revolutionization of [its] historicity, which is now the history of the cutting-off of finite mankind's development as it becomes mankind with infinite tasks."[10] But this is noticed incidentally; Husserl never describes this revolution as such and in its conditions of possibility. The theme of his reflection remains the theoretical attitude which he has nevertheless recognized as not being originarily constituting. He devotes some very beautiful pages to this life of the theoretical attitude and to its correlate. The crisis of this teleology is interpreted as a momentary victory of the naive objectivism of science,[11] which, taking what is only a formal objectivity for an absolute objectivity, falls back into the naturalism of the prephilosophical period when man, by his whole concern and his whole activity, is spontaneously and naively in the world. Thus, a "naturalization of mind [*esprit*]" is arrived at and a covering up of pure subjectivity. But the origin of this crisis is not gone into more deeply, precisely because, on the one hand, there is no teleological reason for the crisis and, on the other, because the crisis itself cannot by definition reveal us anything originary. If objectivist naturalism, in Husserl's eyes, comes from an ignorance or a forgetting of the transcendental genesis by which subjectivity has created *(Leisten)* the ideal objects which have been taken afterward for autonomous absolutes, is not it to be guilty of the same sin and the same "prejudice" to start out absolutely from a theoretical attitude whose originary existential constitution has not been made explicit? But perhaps there is still time to do this.

9

The First Task of Philosophy:
The Reactivation of Genesis

If the "teleologico-historical realization applied to the origins of the critical situation we are in" constitutes an "independent introduction to transcendental phenomenology,"[1] if, in other words, it can serve as an intentional guide for a return to transcendental subjectivity, perhaps expliciting the idea of philosophy will make us at last come near that existential constitution of the theoretical attitude; then, if it is sure that every apodictic meaning is accessible only by starting from this attitude, to elucidate the genesis of this attitude is perhaps to accede to the apodictic sense of every genesis. Yet even so, will that be to grasp its ontological sense?[2]

Up till now the idea of philosophy remained defined in a formal way as idea of an infinite task,[3] *theoria*.[4] Could a history of this infinite theoretical life, which merges itself in its efforts and failures with a simple *realization of the self*, take on the value of a genetic description? Will the history of the "transcendental motive," through all the stages of European philosophy, enlighten us at last on the genesis of transcendental subjectivity? But such a history presupposes the possibility of a going backward, the possibility of finding again the originary sense of the former presents as such. It implies the possibility of a transcendental "regression" *(Rückfrage)* through a history that is intelligible and transparent to consciousness, a history whose sedimentations can be unmade and remade without alteration.

All the texts that followed the Vienna Lecture develop the same line of questioning: How can one, starting from a historico-intentional analysis, "reactivate" the originary sense of the acts or the historical productions of consciousness? The theme of historico-intentional analysis occupies many very important manuscripts, but the technique for this analysis is only presented in the *Origin of Geometry* (1938). In this text of twenty pages, one of

Husserl's most beautiful, the author proposes[5] to retrace the intentional genesis of Geometry and thus to define, through this example, the type of analysis by which it must always be possible to grasp again the transcendental originality of a historical production of consciousness at its very birth.

As Fink says in his introduction, this point is not entirely new; in *Formal and Transcendental Logic* one had to penetrate right through to the very origin of logic. In appearance, this origin could claim to be absolutely eternal and autonomous in relation to a pure logical consciousness, a system of constituted syntheses, a finished product closed in on itself. In fact, it was only possible by starting from a transcendental genesis whose sense had to be found again. However, was not this sense buried under the infinite history of logical acts and structures whose sedimentations, superposed one on the other, seemed, at first sight, to be impenetrable once and for all?

This impenetrability would make any philosophy of history and, at the limit, any historical truth impossible. Whether the facticity of the sedimentations is opaque or not is a point that does not interest Husserl. But the intentional and transcendental sense of every human past, of every act and of every production of consciousness, must be originarily accessible provided one knows how to investigate it.

> The question of the origin of geometry [...] shall not be considered here as the philological-historical question, i.e., as the search for the first geometers *(faktisch)* who actually *(wirklich)* uttered pure geometrical propositions, proofs, theories, or for the particular propositions they discovered, or the like. Rather than this, our interest shall be the inquiry back *(Rückfrage)* into the most original sense in which geometry once arose, was present *(da war)* as the tradition of millennia, is still present for us, and is still being worked on in a lively forward development; we inquire into that sense in which it appeared in history *for the first time*—in which it had to appear, even though we know nothing of the first creators and are not even asking after them. Starting from what we know, from our geometry or rather from the older handed-down forms [...], there is an inquiry back into the *submerged (versunkenen)* original beginnings of geometry as they necessarily must have been in their "primally establishing" *(urstiftende)* function.[6]

It is once again a question of searching for the originary sense by the method of transcendental reduction; a reduction that no longer has a simply egological sense but that is practiced with the transcendental community as its starting point. The constituted facticity of history being "neutralized," the very act of producing sense from a transcendental subjectivity is allowed to appear. At the same time, this operation will lay bare the transcendental foundations of geometry. It is through a becoming aware of the whole genetic movement which has been instituted starting from these fundamental productions of consciousness that, through a radical return to subjectivity, the idea of teleology will be brought back to life and the crises of naturalist objectivism will be overcome. "The whole cultural world, in all its forms," says Husserl, "exists through tradition. These forms have arisen as such not merely causally; we also know already that tradition is precisely tradition, having arisen within our human space through human activity," and it is to that degree that one has to be able to bring back life to the sense even if one is ignorant of the factitious reality of the culture. The empirico-historical "non-knowledge" essentially brings with it the possibility of a knowledge whose evidence is irreducible. Thus, for example, to take the most superficial evidence, we know through an absolute knowledge that any tradition is born from a human activity. As such, "tradition is open in this general way to continued inquiry *(läßt sich befragen)*."[7] "With every form the reference to an earlier one is repeated. Clearly, then, geometry must have arisen out of a *first* acquisition, out of first creative activities."[8]

Starting from this creative origin, genesis does not consist in a causal chain, whether inductive or deductive; it is not a question of a historical connection of elements created or deduced from preceding elements, but rather of a "continual synthesis" in which all the productions are present and valid and form a totality, in such a way that in each present the "whole production" *(Totalerwerb)* is, so to say, a total premise for the production of the superior stage. This movement is that of any science, and it is the one that has to be remade in order to find once more the transcendental originarity of any science and any intentional history.

But this originarity being just as much that of a first historical moment as that of the absolute foundation of a science, "In the finally immense proliferation of a science like geometry, what has become of the claim and the capacity for reactivation *(-alité) (Reaktivierbarkeit)?*"[9] Does every researcher who wishes to give foundation to a proposition have to run through in its totality *"the whole immense chain of groundings back to the original premises (Urprämissen) and actually reactivate (wirklich reaktivieren) the whole thing?"*[10] That would make the development of science impossible. In fact, it is enough, at the level of simple scientific activity and before any philosophical "becoming aware" of this activity, for there to be a reactivation that is "mediate and implicit."

It is here that the *a priori* possibility or the possibility in principle of reactivation is converted into an *a priori* impossibility or impossibility in principle, or at least negotiates dialectically with it. First, it is hard to see what separates rigorously implicit and mediate reactivation operated by the "naive" scientist, living spontaneously and naturally his activity of scientist, from the absolute reactivation operated by the phenomenologist. From what moment is the reactivation made totally and immediately explicit? Probably it is not a question of a regression that arrives at its endpoint only after having worked through the series of mediate foundations where the reactivation remains implicit. The reactivation must be *a priori* immediate and radical in some way thanks to a total conversion of attitude. This attitude, which is that of the reduction, must suspend every mediate and constituted moment of science. In other words, it is the whole tradition of geometry, the scientist's whole activity and even his implicit regression, that must be put in brackets. Now, this tradition and the "traditionality in general" are *a priori* conditions of the possibility of reactivation. The traditional sedimentations must be reduced in order for us to be able to return to the originary foundation; but at the same time it is because there is sedimentation and tradition that this return is possible. "It is," said Husserl, "from what we know about our geometry as a scientific tradition that a regression towards the primordial origin is possible in principle." In the same way, Husserl recognized in *Krisis* II that "we find ourselves in a sort of circle. The understanding of the beginnings is to be gained fully only by starting with science as given in its present-day form, looking back at its development. But in the absence of an understanding of the *beginnings*, the development is mute as a *development of meaning*. Thus we have no other choice than to proceed forward and backward in a zigzag pattern; the one must help the other in an interplay."[11] If this zigzag method is essential and indispensable, it is because at the moment when we get to the most originary constituting source, the constituted is always already there. The supposed *a priori* possibility of reactualization will always suppose a constituted tradition in some form or other. This conforms anyway very precisely with the dialectic of temporal constitution, where the originarity of the "now" and the "Living Present" in its original and creative appearance is founded on the retention of the constituted moment beforehand. However, the "traditionality" as such is always defined by Husserl as an empirical phenomenon: it is, for example, the acquisition of the techniques through which the transmission and the inheritance of ideas become easier and easier.[12] If Husserl does not show us how the genesis of this technique happens, one still knows that it is founded on the temporal continuity of every constitution. Every originary moment of a creating of sense presupposes a "tradition," that is to say, a being already constituted in facticity. At the limit, if this pure facticity is not constituted by a human activity, the first moment of this activity is an originary synthesis of constituted sense and of preconstituted fact. This synthesis is not undone. What then is pure originarity? Is it transcendental or factitious? If the synthesis between the transcendental and facticity is originary, is not then the necessity of the regressive method in a zigzag an indefinite one?

This is a question that cannot be posed at the level of the *Origin of Geometry*. This latter—and this is true of the whole of Husserl's philosophy of history—remains finally below the constitutive analyses which have nevertheless preceded it. It is a question here of the constitution of a geometric science by a transcendental subject whose genesis is supposed completed and starting out from a world whose ontological structure is sometimes *already there* with its own meaning, sometimes merged, as antepredicative substrate, with an *a priori* constituted as an infinite horizon of the possibilities of theoretical determination. The subject and the world are already there as such when geometry begins. In a word, we stay in the eidetic sphere of the constitution of noematic sense or of what Husserl calls, in the *Origin*, ideal objectivities. This constitution takes place at the level of the noetico-noematic correlation, which, we have seen, was static and was itself founded on a genetic constitution. So that the constitution of geometry, in the way it is thematized here, stays very visibly postgenetic, in spite of a pretension to originarity.

Only a genetic elucidation could found absolutely the distinction between real analysis and intentional analysis: to know in which case and from which moment a purely intentional analysis is possible, it must first be known from which moment the intentionality of the subject—here of the geometer—appeared as such. Is it from the moment when this intentionality became self-positing, that is to say, began actively to be engendered by itself? Or is the passive genesis of the subject already intentional?[13] If that were so, it would be necessary to enlarge the concept of intentionality, to make of it a teleological movement that would no longer be only transcendental, but ontological in the broad sense of the word. Then the transcendental activity of man and, even more, that of European man, would be only a mediate, modified moment of the originary fulfilling of this teleology. It would a question of a mediation and of a mission whose sense would not be originarily produced by the transcendental or theoretical vocation of man as such. With this teleologico-cosmic intentionality, the value of a distinction between intentional analysis and real analysis is compromised for good. It is so in two cases:

whether the questioning is purely eidetic or whether it implicitly refers to a transcendental genesis.

In fact, the two points of view are mixed up and confused in the *Origin of Geometry*. Hence, in spite of the seductive project that gives life to these few pages, their actual content and the results of the analysis are most disappointing. While recognizing that "the *total* meaning of geometry [...] could not have been present as a *project*," that is to say, that it was constantly produced in a history, Husserl nevertheless claims to have access to its appearance in the originary evidence of "a more primitive formation of meaning [*sens**]."[14] Is it not by supposing that the total sense of geometry is known and completed, that its originary sense can be discerned? Is it not from actual clear evidence that I discover the originary evidence? And do I not do that still according to the dialectic method of the "zigzag"? If I admit that the absolute sense of the geometrical project is not yet fully completed, how will I be able to decide that it is indeed geometry which begins with a particular act of subjectivity or that this act itself does not get its meaning from a preceding constitution? If I empty geometry of its traditional, present, effective content, nothing will remain for me, or only a formal concept of geometry that will itself be constituted or derived. And it is according to this concept that I will attempt to define the original or originary sense of geometry. Thus, I will get to a description that will oscillate between an *a priori* formalism and an absolute empiricism, according to whether I am going to consider the concept as absolute or as itself constituted by the act of a subjectivity.

In effect this is what happens. Sometimes the originary evidence, as such and in general, is evoked as "grasping an entity with the consciousness of its original being-itself-there."[15] The intuition or the production (intentionality is this double movement) of geometrical being in its own specificity is that of an "ideal objectivity," one that is "super-temporal"[16] and universally valid *(für jedermann)*. How does one go from an absolutely originary individual antepredicative state (as we have seen in *Experience and Judgment*) to the existence of a geometric being in its ideal objectivity? If ideality is a logical predicate of the antepredicative being, it is produced by a logical genesis of which we are told nothing here.[17] If, on the contrary, the ideal objectivity is grasped as such originarily, it is always already there, as *a priori* ideal form, before any explicitation by a transcendental subjectivity.

---

*Derrida's translation uses *sens*. Trans.

Sometimes, on the contrary, it is indeed a question of giving an account of the actual genesis of geometric essences. Only the description of the processes of idealization allows the escape from an *a priori* evidence of the order of formal logic.[18] Hence, it is necessary to return to the prescientific situation and to the production of originary idealities *(Uridealitäten)* from the "prescientific data of the environment of life *(Lebensumwelt)*." It is then, it seems, that the transcendental intentional analysis falls into a surprising interpretation whose poverty links in a way that is rather laughable all the inadequacies of an overbold explicative hypothesis, of a confused probabilism, and of a prephilosophical empiricism. "In the first oral cooperation *(Zusammenarbeiten)* of the beginning geometers, the need was understandably lacking for an exact fixing of descriptions of the prescientific primal material and of the ways in which, in relation to this material, geometrical idealities arose together with the first 'axiomatic' propositions."[19] This technicist explanation is of the same order as the two images, the most empirical and the most "relativist" that Husserl has used; images that people never lose the opportunity of holding against him: one is that of "a garb of ideas thrown over the world of immediate intuition and experience, the life-world";[20] the other is that of "The trader in the market [who] has his market truth. In the relationship in which it stands, is his truth not a good one, and the best that a trader can use? Is it a pseudo-truth, merely because the scientist, involved in a different relativity and judging with other aims and ideas, looks for other truths—with which a great many more things can be done, but not the one thing that has to be done in a market?"[21] Not that such an explicitation or such a perspective is false, properly speaking. Simply, it is necessary to recognize that it shuts us up in the domain of the purely empirical facticity, precisely what we wanted to "suspend." It is highly likely that "matters" happened like this, that the "events" unfolded in this way. But in no case—and it is on this certainty that the very project of phenomenology is founded—will these empirical events as such be able to explain the genesis of essences. At the most they can help us determine a structure or a conceptual evolution. Not only is this a constant theme of Husserlian philosophy, but in the *Origin of Geometry*, whose fundamental postulate it is, Husserl writes: "All [merely] factual history remains incomprehensible."[22] Every historical fact has its "internal structure of meaning," and it is from the chain of motivations[23] and implications of sense that history becomes intelligible. It is only by recourse to the "historical *a priori*" that the sense of our set of problems must be grasped. The problem of the origin of geometry, to be developed at least as a problem, must be guided by a knowledge of the structures of principle such as originary foundation *(Urstiftung)*,

originary material *(Urmaterial)*, originary certainty *(Urevidenz)*, sedimentation, reactivation, and so forth.[24]

We admit that we do not see the continuity between this apriorism and the
technological explanation which has just been evoked. No doubt this explanation is not presented as technological. That would be to deny the whole
initial movement of phenomenology. No doubt, it is in intention a question
of an absolutely original description, where the *a priori* is grasped in an originary empirical evidence. In a certain sense, Husserl has always given himself
out to be an empiricist. Hence, one must not, in a systematic way and from a
Kantian point of view constantly refused by Husserl, divide each of the experiences described into an *a priori* element, formal, atemporal, and so forth,
and an empirical element (empirical in the Kantian sense), the one derived
from a pure theory of knowledge, the other from a psychology and from a
history. These two points of view are precisely empirical as such (in the
Husserlian sense), that is to say, "worldly." Husserl insists: "The ruling *dogma*
of the separation in principle between epistemological elucidation and historical, even humanistic-psychological explanation, between epistemological
and genetic origin, is fundamentally mistaken, unless one inadmissably limits, in the usual way, the concepts of 'history,' 'historical explanation,' and
'genesis.'"[25]

But being once again referred to a concrete intuition of *a priori* essences,
we encounter two questions; the first, the most important, is of a transcendental order; the intuition of essences is possible for a transcendental ego that
produces itself in a genesis. This intuition is thus possible *a priori* only at the
level of a constituted subject. It is thus not originary, and we are thus brought
back to the difficulties already mentioned and that we will not come back to.
The other question, a secondary one, which we know cannot be absolutely
resolved in itself, is posed at the level of the *Origin of Geometry:* If the possibility of ideal objectivities is at the same time *a priori* and empirical, if it is
given in the temporality of an originary evidence, why is it only at a certain
objective moment that the idealities appear in their rigorous exactness? Why
and how are this rigor or this exactness engendered out of an inexactness?
Again, one wonders what experience can reconcile the continuous temporality with the production or the intuition of an *a priori* absolute. Once more,
Husserl's description betrays his principles. Rigorous "measurability" is born
from the world of spatio-temporal things. Its origin in human activity is
purely technical;[26] it is a "polishing" that gave us the pure idea of surface; out
of lines and points that are "more or less pure" that geometric lines and points
appeared. Again, the empirical technical and psychological act of "compari-

son" gave birth to identity. All the details of this curious analysis[27] describe a purely technical genesis. As such, this genesis is not intelligible and brings us back to the level of the debate between psychologism and logicism, which has been long since left behind. Either it is an empirical operation that founds ideal significations, and these are then bereft of objectivity and rigor, or else the ideal objectivities are *a priori* possible and the sense or the necessity of their historical becoming is no longer understood.

Because he did not start from an *a priori* that was ontological rather than phenomenological ([a phenomenological one] which at the end becomes formal), because he did not unite synthetically and dialectically being and time, which might have allowed him to understand the genesis of the *a priori* and the *a priori* of genesis, Husserl is obliged to bring together in confusion an empiricism and a metaphysics, the two ghosts of phenomenology.

In fact, failing to seize the *a priori* concrete sense of the technological genesis, Husserl must invoke a hidden reason in history,[28] which every reactivation of genesis will unveil. But as such and in its purity, this reason which is found again in every genetic origin is not itself engendered. In this perspective, which, from the point of view of Husserl himself, must be called metaphysical and formal, genesis is no more than a stratification of factitious sediments dissimulating the originary sense of history. And yet, history is not only a covering up of originary certainties: How does it happen that this movement of covering up is also a movement of revelation? Husserl invokes an eternal nature of man who understands himself and recognizes himself as an *"animal rationale."*[29]

At the end of this attempt at a historico-intentional analysis, we fail then to found the intentional analysis that alone could have made possible a pure philosophy of history. Let us not be surprised to see Husserl, after having invoked a *Reason hidden in history,* confuse his project of philosophy of history with that of a history of philosophy. This latter retraces the itinerary of an idea of philosophy whose genetic origin is not yet known, and will never be. We know now what the shortcomings of this enterprise are; we will not come back to them, and will concentrate only on the internal difficulties of this history of philosophy.

10

The History of Philosophy and the Transcendental Motive

History borrows all its sense from the intentional rationality which thus secretly animates it; the idea of philosophy, indefinite unveiling of this *ratio,* burst into European humanity. In its project, transcendental phenomenology is at one with the very life of this idea. So how is it possible that the concrete idea of phenomenology, whose sense was originarily antecedent to *homo europeanus,* should have appeared so late in the history of Europe, how can one explain that its motivation has "taken its time" to be completed and to appear to itself? Why does it clearly take possession of its sense at the moment when there is a crisis in which it runs the risk of being buried for [all] eternity? What is the sense of this crisis? What is its condition of possibility? If the idea of philosophy is present to itself from its birth (let us leave to one side the grave problem of a world antecedent to this idea), it is impossible that it should make itself a stranger to itself at a given moment of empirical becoming; if it does that, it is because it is no longer mistress of the sense and the condition of possibility of such an alienation. It is thus not purely originary; from its birth, it negotiates with what is not it. Its fulfillment is an indefinite synthesis that makes the crisis possible; the critical moment itself is constitutive of the synthesis and founds the pathway that the idea takes. In other words, if the idea is not originarily absolute, that is to say, analytically identical to itself, it will never be so; except in appearance, if it has been confused with its concept, which is identical to itself because it is formal. But for the idea to be *a priori* idea *of* philosophy and idea *of* history, it is necessary that it should be indefinitely synthetic, and that it takes the absolute of its sense from itself as well as from what is not it. Through a necessary movement, it loses itself in order to find itself in what is not it. If the idea allows access to the sense of its correlate, the reverse is true immediately. There is a crisis of mind [*esprit*] as soon as what is only the product of a transcendental subjectivity is isolated and made into an autonomous absolute through "objectivism" or "naturalism."

But in Husserl's eyes this is the only interpretation of the crisis of philosophy and the sciences. Is not Husserl in this way unfaithful to his very intention? Is he not missing the sense of any crisis and any history? This question, which we were already posing about teleology in general, is produced again here about the transcendental idea as the only intentional motivation of history. Does not Husserl, wanting to derive the principle of explanation of the crisis and of the going beyond it from the constituting subjectivity alone, and thus limiting intentionality to its active movement, deny himself the possibility of understanding by which essential movement the idea of philosophy is led to alienation? To escape in a last effort from temporal dialectics, is he not condemned to leave the very foundation of phenomenology: transcendental intentionality, the return to the things themselves, *a priori* intuition of essences, *a priori* synthesis of sense and being, and so on?

In *Krisis* II[1] Husserl takes on all these problems. The movement and the being of history are oriented by the "ideal of universal philosophy." But

> *Can reason and that-which-is be separated, where reason, as knowing, de-termines what being is?* This question suffices to make clear in advance that the whole historical process has a remarkable form, one which becomes visible only through an interpretation of its hidden, innermost motivation. Its form is not that of a smooth development, not that of a continual growth of lasting spiritual acquisitions nor that of a transformation of spiritual configurations—concepts, theories, systems—which can be explained by means of the accidental historical situations. A *definite ideal of a universal philosophy* and its method forms the beginning; this is, so to speak, the *primal establishment of the philosophical modern age* and all its lines of development. But instead of being able to work itself out, in fact, this ideal suffers an inner dissolution.[2]

The principle of this internal decomposition* is always the same: the "forgetting" or "covering up" of transcendental subjectivity as absolute constituting source. It is always because at a certain moment a simple constituted product

---

*"Dissolution" is Carr's translation. *Trans.*

has been taken for absolute, originary and constituting, that the movement of the idea has been interrupted or corrupted in a crisis. The crisis is thus, contrary to what Husserl says, an internal necessity of history. The transcendental constitution of meanings in some way produces the very occasions and conditions of its alienation. The naturalist naïveté would finally consist in the ending of the constitution of the mind by itself. In the end, any attention or any intention aiming at a product constituted as such will be an instant of crisis, where the subjectivity not only runs the risk of losing itself, but must necessarily lose itself; so that any intentionality brings with it in essence an objectivist naïveté and postulation. This belongs to its synthetic character: it is consciousness of something; this [in turn] more deeply depends on the temporality which alone makes this synthesis possible: every temporal constitution comprises the "retained" sedimentation of the constituted past in the originarity of the "Living Present." Time is perpetual promotion of crises and a leaving behind of them, where the passively constituted moment participates in the originary movement of active constitution. Hence the sense of Husserl's surprise must be reversed, an idealist surprise that presupposes an already constituted idea of history as well as a purity of mind; if it were thus, the intentional act that testified to our "faith" in these ideas would be "naive." Here one is faithful to the whole point of phenomenology in refusing idealism as a "worldly" philosophy. In being surprised by the idea's deterioration, one must not ask oneself how "this sort of naïveté actually became possible and is still possible as a living historical fact" but rather how such a naïveté is always necessary. It is only from the point of view of the philosopher's subjectivity, or of philosophy as already constituted, that the constituted, the alienation, the "outside," and so forth appear as simply possible. There is a something of psychologism and of objectivism in Husserl's question.

Hence, a radical critique of the Husserlian project of a history of philosophy can be already founded at this level: it is known from now on that this history will unfold an idea that might not have been corrupted; it is known that this idea is in itself a traditional meaning and sedimentation. The transcendental *motive* by whose light Husserl conducts his analysis should have merged itself with the idea of this necessary alteration, of an alteration whose very necessity shows that it is, in the same moment, fulfillment and authentic constitution of history. In fact, this *motive* remains the completed idea of a philosophy which recognizes itself, more or less thematized, through a series of imperfect sketches. These only have sense to the degree that in them one perceives the transcendental project. Right up to Husserl himself, this project has always been sent off course, perverted, dissimulated at any given moment. Because Husserl places himself on the level of philosophical teleology and because his "type of investigation [...] is not that of a historical investigation in the usual sense,"[3] the necessity of the movement of decomposition is not attained at any moment. The decomposition being essentially a constituted, factitious moment, historical in the "real" sense of the word, it constantly escapes our gaze and remains stripped of any meaning.

It is not an accident if Husserl envisages only the history of modern philosophy. This is because the whole history of philosophy takes its sense in its last moment. This latter, allowing us to understand the intentional or teleological sense of the totality of the preceding moments, will take on the shape of a revolution; that is because in the end a veritable phenomenology of time has not been reached, where every moment continuing, taking in, and exceeding its past in the same movement appears at once as revolution and as tradition.

Modern philosophy manifests itself as such through its effort to found a "theory of knowledge." "Thus world-enigmas *(Welträtsel)* now enter the stage, of a sort previously never imagined, and they bring about a completely new manner of philosophizing, the 'epistemological' philosophy, that of the 'the theory of reason.' Soon they also give rise to systematic philosophies with completely novel goals and methods. This greatest of all revolutions must be characterized as *the transformations of scientific objectivism*—not only modern objectivism but also that of *all the earlier philosophies of the millennia—into a transcendental subjectivism.*"[4] The idea of a theory of knowledge and of transcendental subjectivism is "the *unity* running through all the philosophical projects of history that oppose one another and work together in their changing forms"; it is "the hidden unity of an intentional interiority which alone constitutes the unity of history." But this unity of sense with itself has been constituted in a history; only the genesis of the unity of sense, which refers to a past of transcendental philosophy, could enlighten us here. It would help us to understand both the principle of its deterioration and the principle of the conflict that opposes it to its contrary. If Husserl evokes so well the unity of transcendental *eidos,* it is because he envisages it in its purity, in its originary or final sense. The moments of its being in tension with the empirical multiplicity of its accidents and of its alterations are always "absurd."

The whole history of philosophy since the appearance of 'epistemology' and the serious attempts at a transcendental philosophy is a history of tremendous tensions between objectivist and transcendental philosophy. It is a history of constant attempts to maintain objectivism and to develop it in a new form and, on the other side, of attempts by transcendentalism to overcome the difficulties entailed by the idea of transcendental subjectivity and the method it requires. The clarification of the origin of this internal split in the philosophical development, the analysis of the ultimate motives for this most radical transformation of the idea of philosophy, is of the utmost importance. It affords the first insight into the thoroughgoing *meaningfulness* [*Sinnhaftigkeit*] which unifies the whole movement of philosophical history in the modern period: a unity of purpose binding generations of philosophers together, and through this a direction for all the efforts of individual subjects and schools. It is a direction, as I shall try to show here, toward a *final form* of transcendental philosophy—as *phenomenology.*[5]

Now, in starting from a knowledge of the teleological unity that is already fulfilled, how could Husserl indeed "elucidate the origin of this internal division"? Not only does nothing explain to us why the Western idea of a universal philosophy and the discovery of the infinite came about with the Renaissance and Galileo's mathematization of nature, but again this sort of "intentional psychoanalysis"[6] to which Husserl submits thinkers, leaves aside those reasons for their failure that precisely are by definition not comprised in the unity of teleology. Galileo, who is not to be confused here with the real historical personage, no more than is the Renaissance with its real epoch, has by an "extraordinary" invention, made possible an infinite eidetics of nature; this invention is totally and originarily intelligible to us in its teleological sense because it completes the idea of philosophy as infinite task, an idea that is not born with Galileo but with the European mind. But what is totally unintelligible to us and what we must attribute to a simple empirical or psychological causality, a technical, economic or personal situation of the thinker, is that Galileo did not himself perceive the originary and teleological sense of his revolution. Having in fact brought about "the surreptitious substitution of the mathematically substructed world of idealities for the only real world, the one that is actually given through perception, that is ever experienced and experienceable—our everyday life-world,"[7] Galileo hid the activity of transcendental subjectivity operating on the basis of the life-world. Taking the evidence of the mathematical type to be the only absolute evidence, he forgets that this latter is formal and constituted from a transcendental evidence. "Galileo lives in the naivety of apodeictic certainty."[8]

Galileo, the discoverer—or, in order to do justice to his precursors, the consummating discoverer—of physics, or physical nature, is at once a *discovering and a concealing genius* [*entdeckender und verdeckender Genius*]. He discovers mathematical nature, the methodical idea, he blazes the trail for the infinite number of physical discoveries and discoverers. By contrast to the *universal causality of the intuitively given world* (as its invariant form), he discovers what has since been called simply the *law of causality*, the "a priori form" of the "true" (idealized and mathematized) world, the "law of exact lawfulness" according to which *every occurrence* in "nature"—idealized nature— must come under *exact laws*. All this is discovery-concealment.[9]

If the covering up has not a necessary *motive* in this double movement, one may as well say it would have been preferable to go back constantly to the act of transcendental subjectivity constituting the life-world as such. At that moment, would the progress have been pure and simple? On the contrary, would it not have become impossible? Without a work that was naively operating on constituted idealities, the development of mathematics and physics would have been inconceivable. Failing to analyze the necessary movement of the crises of the transcendental motive, Husserl fails to grasp the necessity of the teleological progress. The "ambiguous" destiny of Galileo will also be that of Descartes, of Hume, of Kant. Descartes was at the same time the founder of the modern idea of objectivist rationalism and of the transcendental motive. But after having worked out this latter by a powerful initiative that Husserl traces here, he falls victim to Galileo's prejudice about the possibility of a universal deduction from an absolute apodictic ground. The ego thus becomes substance through a philosophical falsification that identifies it with the soul; it is no more than a logical motor inside a metaphysical system. The transcendental motive has been downgraded into an objectivist psychologism.

Hume remains the most revolutionary European philosopher for Husserl; he caught sight of the sense of transcendental phenomenology. Escaping from the objectivist and scientistic naïveté of Galileo and Descartes, he put in question the whole value of constituted idealities. In this sense he had started a return to the constituting subjectivity and made dogmatic objectivism shake. But coming to an irrationalist skepticism, he got lost in a "misinterpretation." A philosophy cannot be irrationalist without ruining its own foundation. "Astounding as Hume's genius is, it is the more regrettable that a correspondingly great philosophical ethos is not joined with it."[10]

In spite of what he claims is a return to transcendental subjectivism, Kant falls short of Hume's deep intention. The transcendental ego and the Kantian understanding are categories and concepts; Kant's empirical world hides a world in itself; the transcendental activity is thus neither concrete nor originary; it comes about from a logical or psychological subject and from a nature understood by a given science and logic "[...] for Kant, now, *objective science,* as an accomplishment[11] remaining within subjectivity, is separated off from his *philosophical* theory. The latter, as a theory of the accomplishments necessarily carried out within subjectivity, and thus as a theory of the possibility and scope of objective knowledge, reveals the naïveté of the *supposed rational philosophy of nature-in-itself.*"[12]

Thus, the authentic leading idea of the transcendental has always been missed. Truth to tell, this idea is not to be met with as such in a particular philosophy. It cannot be backed up by texts; it cannot be found by the immanent interpretation of particular systems and by their comparison. It is, rather, an idea acquired by the deepening of the history of the whole philosophy of modern times seen as a whole: the idea of its task, which can be shown only in this way, which is in it like the driving idea of its evolution, which starts from a vague *dynamis* and which tends toward its *energeia.*[13] The sense of this task has "only now been discovered."[14]

Why is it today that the task of philosophy appears to us clearly? Why has Husserl chosen one or other thinker to illustrate the becoming of the transcendental motive? Why does this history of philosophy stop after Kant and a very vague German idealism? It seems that the thematic sense of all these facts is purely accidental. "The history of philosophy is not a novel" is the first sentence of an important unpublished text of this period. In his lectures, Husserl often talked about his history of philosophy as a composition or a novel-like creation. But if he puts aside, on principle, a purely historical method, historical in the "real" sense of the word, his history of philosophy claims to reach an absolute eidetic rigor beyond the systematic interpretation in general and the one that the author gives of his work in particular. It is the originary sense *of* the history of philosophy, as an introduction to a philosophy of history itself founding any phenomenology, which Husserl wants to determine. In spite of the unifying strength of certain of his analyses, their poverty and their formalism are surprising. The sense is rich and rigorous at the same time only to the degree that it is already completed and refers only to itself, that is to say, to the degree that it is not the sense of the history of philosophy. To the degree that philosophy is an infinite task, the concrete idea of philosophy as transcendental motive must not be already constituted as a noema.

In fact, one of two things:

~ Either it is supposed that the sense is definitively constituted; one has the right retrospectively to run through the whole of its history in order to unveil its teleology. This is what Husserl does. But then there are two dangers lurking: on the one hand, this constituted unity of philosophy is closed on itself. It cannot be opened to an infinite task. It is no longer an intentional movement, but a concept. On the other hand, it is implicitly recognized that, constituted and founded on a constituted idea, the philosophy of philosophy, or the philosophy of history is itself a critical moment; it is a moment of alienation since it is the naïveté of a constituted evidence which wrecked philosophy. We are at the opposite pole to a veritable transcendental genesis as authentic *motif* of all philosophy.

~ Or else the idea of philosophy is an intentional movement whose unity is indefinitely constituted by an uninterrupted series of alienations and "comings to awareness." Every system of history of philosophy is then an "interpretation," a hypothesis that is always premature. Husserl's procedure must not be given as a theoretical gaze on a history that has taken possession of its sense; it must be presented as a simple moment of the constitution of philosophy and of history by themselves. Without abandoning the project of an infinite theory, philosophy, reflecting on itself, in this way completes an existential act and comes to an awareness of its finitude.

It would remain to show how, in a form that is here more than symbolic, the thought of Husserl is the "repetition" of the genetic movement of all philosophy and all history. All the methodical mediations, all the false starts that Husserl has made, correspond exactly to the critical moments as he himself defines them: psychologistic starting point, reduction starting from the natural attitude, reduction that is eidetic then transcendental, static constitution, eidetics of genesis, noematic unity of history—these are all moments that are constituted and secondary, and Husserl had to start from them in his regression to a transcendental primordiality. All these moments can be considered as crises and coverings of the originary sense, and yet, in the light of the later themes, in the initial hesitations and slips, the final aim of philosophy is recognized.

From the point of view of the transcendental motivation itself, this final aim is also and essentially a failure of an objectivist or idealist type. We have ceaselessly approached absolute genetic originarity, without ever attaining it: the empirical facts of psychology and of the natural sciences referred us to constituted essences. These have become noemata, were thematized in the analyses of the static constitution, were themselves already constituted by a transcendental subject whose fixity and eidetic atemporality implied a genetic constitution. Yet the transcendental genesis itself was already described, in its very passivity, in terms of universal eidetic structures. The genesis of these structures, to be accessible to a theoretic gaze, had to be shaped by a teleology. Finally, the unity of this teleology is always already there; its genesis remains exterior to the sphere defined by the transcendental reduction.

At the end of philosophy, the most far-going reduction has not been lifted. The ontological genesis, which alone could produce and found a phenomenology, remains "neutralized" in the name of a teleological *eidos* that should itself have been reduced. Husserl's philosophy of history, becoming merged with the most dubious history of philosophy, remains less than the phenomenological project. The naïveté of the eidetic evidence as it was defined in *Ideas* I has not been got over. The existential "originary synthesis" of the transcendental subject is still hidden. A new radical explicitation, a new beginning, is necessary. It is from this indefinite necessity that genesis must be dialectically lived and understood.

> I did not know that it might be so hard to die. And yet I have tried so hard right through my life to take out all futility . . . ! Right up to the moment when I am so penetrated with the feeling that I am responsible for a task, to the moment when, in the Vienna and Prague lectures, then in my article *(Die Krisis)*, I have exteriorized myself with such complete spontaneity and where I have realized a weak start—it is at that moment that I have to interrupt things and leave my task incomplete. Just when I am getting to the end and when everything is finished for me, I know that I must start everything again from the beginning. . . .[15]

NOTES

The following abbreviations are used in the notes:

CM

Cartesian Meditations: An Introduction to Phenomenology, trans. Dorion Cairns (The Hague: Martinus Nijhoff, 1960).

Crisis

The Crisis of European Sciences and Transcendental Phenomenology: An Introduction to Phenomenological Philosophy, trans. David Carr (Evanston, Ill.: Northwestern University Press, 1970).

Experience

Experience and Judgment: Investigations in a Genealogy of Logic, rev. and ed. Ludwig Landgrebe, trans. J. S. Churchill and Karl Ameriks (Evanston, Ill.: Northwestern University Press, 1973).

Geometry

David Carr's English translation of *Die Frage nach dem Ursprung der Geometrie als intentional-historisches Problem,* in *Edmund Husserl's Origin of Geometry: An Introduction,* by Jacques Derrida, ed. David B. Allison, trans. John P. Leavey (Stony Brook, N.Y.: Nicholas Hays; Sussex: Harvester Press, 1978).

H.

Husserliana: Gesammelte Werke und Dokumenta (The Hague: Martinus Nijhoff; then Dordrecht: Kluwer, 1950–).

Ideas I

Ideas: General Introduction to Pure Phenomenology, trans. W. R. Boyce Gibson

(1931; 4th impression, London: Allen & Unwin; New York: Humanities Press, 1967).

Ideas II

Ideas Pertaining to a Pure Phenomenology and to a Phenomenological Philosophy, book 2: *Studies in the Phenomenology of Constitution,* trans. Richard Rojcewicz and André Schuwer, in *Collected Works,* vol. 3 (Dordrecht: Kluwer Academic, 1989).

Ideen I

Ideen zu einer reinen Phänomenologie und phänomenologischen Philosophie, vol. 1 (1913). Ricœur's French translation is referred to as *Idées* I; Boyce's English translation is referred to as *Ideas* I.

Ideen II

Ideen zu einer reinen Phänomenologie und phänomenologischen Philosophie, vol. 2: *Phänomenologische Untersuchungen zur Konstitution,* ed. Marly Biemel, *H.* 4 (The Hague, M. Nijhoff, 1952).

Idées I

Idées directrices pour une phénoménologie et une philosophie phénoménologiques pures, trans. Paul Ricœur (Paris: Éditions Gallimard, 1950).

Lectures

The Phenomenology of Internal Time Consciousness, ed. Martin Heidegger, trans. James S. Churchill (Bloomington: Indiana University Press, 1964).

LI

Logical Investigations, 2 vols., trans. J. N. Findlay from the 2d German ed. (London: Routledge & Kegan Paul; New York: Humanities Press, 1970).

LU

Logische Untersuchungen, Prolegomena zur reinen Logik, 1st ed., 1900.

RMM

Revue de métaphysique et de morale.

Vienna Lecture

La philosophie dans la crise de l'humanité européenne [Philosophy in the crisis of European humanity], lecture given at the Vienna Kulturbund, 7 May 1935; French trans. Paul Ricœur, *RMM,* 1950, no. 3, pp. 229–58; English trans. David Carr, *Crisis,* appendix 1.

Translator's Note

1. Edmund Husserl (1859–1938), *Husserliana: Gesammelte Werke und Dokumenta* (The Hague: Martinus Nijhoff; then Dordrecht: Kluwer, 1950–) [henceforward *H.*].

2. The chapters numbers have been changed, so as to run consecutively rather than beginning at "1" within each part.

I owe gratitude to Michael Naas and Pascale-Anne Brault for rereading the translation so carefully and for making suggestions; naturally, any mistakes are my responsibility. The quotations from Husserl were taken from the translations of Husserl available in English (see list, after the bibliography); Ann Troutman helped me with this.

3. This question has recently been the object of much more attention than in the past, no doubt in large part through Derrida's influence. A dictionary of philosophical "untranslatables" is being put together under the direction of Barbara Cassin. A visit to Husserlian websites shows that there is now much more interest in the question of the different language versions of Husserl's work. Earlier on, the concern with the problem in relation to Husserl gave rise to Dorion Cairns's *Guide for Translating Husserl, Phænomenologica* 55 (The Hague: Martinus Nijhoff, 1973).

4. For example, *Writing and Difference*, p. 33 n. 4; for other examples see M. Hobson, *Jacques Derrida: Opening Lines* (London: Routledge, 1998), pp. 211–19.

5. *The Origins of Analytical Philosophy* (London: Duckworth, 1993).

Preface to the 1990 Edition

1 P. xxv, below.

2. P. xl, below.

3. P. 211, below.

4. P. 124 ff., below.

5. Whether it be a matter of phenomenology or of dialectic, the distance has never been without remorse for me. Those who are interested by the trace of this remorse could find it everywhere, for instance in "La clôture de la représentation" [The theatre of cruelty and the closure of representation], in *L'écriture et la différence* (1967, Paris: Seuil), p. 364 [*Writing and Difference*, trans. Alan Bass (Chicago: University of Chicago Press, 1978)].

6. Except, I confess, for some typing errors or errors of grammar, and some awkwardnesses of punctuation.

Preface to the 1953/54 Dissertation

1. Originally these long preliminary considerations were not meant to introduce the present historical study. Rather, in their outline they get underway a more extended and more dogmatic piece of work which we may undertake later around the same problem. We thought that it was perhaps right to present them here, insofar as they might throw some light on the historical essay which is going to follow them.

2. We have to start here from a constituted science. But we will see later how this start is a "false start," a start which is essentially "naive." We will have to think about this problem often: Why is a false start always necessary for discourse? What is the sense of this necessity? It seems that it is not a merely rhetorical one, that it does not only answer the demands of a psychology or of a "pedagogy." These demands themselves refer to a deeper "moment" in the question: Why is it always starting from the constituted, that is to say, from the derived product, that one has to go back to the constituting source, that is to say, toward the most originary moment? We will see that it is the whole problem of genesis which is being posed here.

E. Fink raises a similar problem, in relation to the Husserlian texts which deal with the "phenomenological reduction" in *Ideen* I. <*Ideen zu einer reinen Phänomenologie und phänomenologischen Philosophie*, 1. Buch (1913). Reedited by W. Biemel in *H*. 3 (The Hague: Martinus Nijhoff, 1950).> [Edmund Husserl, *Ideas: General Introduction to Pure Phenomenology*, trans. W. R. Boyce Gibson (1931; 4th impression, London: Allen & Unwin; New York: Humanities Press, 1967); henceforward *Ideas* I.] See Fink, "Die phänomenologische Philosophie E. Husserls in der gegenwärtigen Kritik," *Kantstudien* 38, 3/4, Berlin, 1933, pp. 346–47.

3. Later, we will have to illuminate the meaning of this reality, using the distinction made by Husserl between worldly natural reality (*Reales, Realität*), and the reality of what is lived (*reell*).

4. Husserl would have liked to bring back the word "archaeology" in the phenomenological sense, which is not that of "worldly" science (see E. Fink, "Das Problem der Phänomenologie E. Husserls" [The problem of Husserl's phenomenology], *Revue internationale de philosophie* 1, Brussels, 1938–39, p. 246). The search for an absolute beginning is present throughout the whole of Husserl's work; see especially *Ideas* I, § 1, p. 44, and also Fink, *loc. cit.*, p. 338, which was thoroughly approved of by Husserl, and which defines Husserl's question as the question of the "origin of the world" (*die Frage nach dem Ursprung der Welt*).

5. *Passim*, especially *Vorlesungen zur Phänomenologie des inneres Zeitbewußtseins* <ed. Martin Heidegger, in *Jahrbuch für Philosophie und phänomeno-*

logische Forschung 9, 1928; separately published (Halle a.d.S.: Max Niemeyer, 1928); afterward in *H.* 10: *Zur Phänomenologie des inneren Zeitbewußtsein* (1893–1917), ed. Rudolf Boehm (The Hague, Martinus Nijhoff, 1966)> [*The Phenomenology of Internal Time Consciousness,* ed. Martin Heidegger, trans. James S. Churchill (Bloomington, Ind.: Indiana University Press, 1964); also cited as *Lectures*] and the whole of the C group of the manuscripts, one of the most important among those that have not been published.

6. *Passim,* especially "Die Philosophie als strenge Wissenschaft" (*Logos* I, 1911) <*Logos: Internationale Zeitschrift für Philosophie des Kultur* (Tübingen), reedited by Th. Nenon and H. R. Sepp, in *H.* 25 (The Hague: M. Nijhoff, 1987)> ["Philosophy as Rigorous Science," trans. Quentin Lauer (New York: Harper & Row, 1965), pp. 71–147; also in *Husserl: Shorter Works,* ed. Peter McCormick and Frederick Elliston (Notre Dame, Ind.: University of Notre Dame Press, 1981)].

7. *Passim,* especially *Logische Untersuchungen* [henceforward *LU*], vol. 1, *Prolegomena zur reinen Logik,* 1st ed. (1900–1901) <3 vols., reedited (Tübingen: Max Niemeyer, 1968)> [*Logical Investigations,* trans. J. N. Findlay from the 2d German ed., 2 vols. (London: Routledge & Kegan Paul; New York: Humanities Press, 1970); henceforward *LI*] and *Ideen* I (1913).

8. *Passim,* especially *Die Krisis der europäischen Wissenschaften und die transzendentale Phänomenologie* (1936) <reedited by Walter Biemel in *H.* 6 (The Hague: M. Nijhoff, 1954)> [*The Crisis of European Sciences and Transcendental Phenomenology: An Introduction to Phenomenological Philosophy,* trans. David Carr Evanston, Ill.: Northwestern University Press, 1970); henceforward *Crisis*]. *Die Frage nach dem Ursprung der Geometrie als intentional-historisches Problem,* published by Eugen Fink, *Revue internationale de Philosophie,* 1939, no. 2 <reedited by Walter Biemel in *H.* 6 (The Hague: M. Nijhoff, 1954). French translation with an introduction by Jacques Derrida, *L'Origine de la géométrie* (Paris: PUF, 1962)> [Jacques Derrida, *Edmund Husserl's Origin of Geometry: An Introduction,* ed. David B. Allison, trans. John P. Leavey, Husserl's text trans. David Carr (reprinted from *Crisis*) (Stony Brook, N.Y.: Nicholas Hays; Sussex: Harvester Press, 1978); henceforward *Geometry.*]

9. *Passim,* especially: *Ideen* II <*Ideen zu einer reinen Phänomenologie und phänomenologischen Philosophie,* ed. Marly Biemel, *H.* 4 (The Hague: M. Nijhoff, 1952) [*Ideas Pertaining to a Pure Phenomenology and to a Phenomenological Philosophy,* book 2: *Studies in the Phenomenology of Constitution,* trans. Richard Rojcewicz and André Schuwer, in *Collected Works,* vol. 3 (Dordrecht: Kluwer Academic, 1989); henceforward *Ideas* II]> and the group M of manuscripts, of which a short fragment has been published under the title of "Rapport entre la

phénoménologie et les sciences" [Relation between phenomenology and science], in *Les Etudes philosophiques* (Paris) 4, no. 1 (January–March 1949), pp. 3–6.

10. A reconquest that one must be careful not to assimilate to a deductive piece of work, in Cartesian style, after arriving at the absolute certainty of a "cogito."

11. This notion, absent until *Ideen* I (1913) is explicitly used in *Erfahrung und Urteil* (whose manuscripts date for the most part from 1919) and in all following works <*Erfahrung und Urteil: Untersuchungen zur Genealogie der Logik,* rev. and ed. Ludwig Landgrebe (Prague: Academia, 1969); 6th ed. (Hamburg: Meiner, 1985)> [*Experience and Judgment: Investigations in a Genealogy of Logic,* rev. and ed. Ludwig Landgrebe, trans. J. S. Churchill and Karl Ameriks (Evanston, Ill.: Northwestern University Press, 1973); henceforward *Experience*].

12. And especially to the Husserlian idea of philosophy as "infinite task," see *Crisis.*

13. The most interesting historical comparisons will very often seem to be necessary in the course of this work. We will refrain from treating them other than allusively, thus avoiding diverging from our subject, which is already very vast, and burdening it further. Can the immense ignorance of Husserl in matters of history of philosophy be used as authority here without irony?

14. We are using this word here because of the ambiguity of its sense; this latter has its echo in the double sphere of time and of being.

15. It is already possible to say of a dialectic of possibility and necessity what we say a little farther on about other terms coupled together like this.

16. Or protention, in Husserl's language. This protention is made possible originarily in an originary "now" [*maintenant*], by a "retention" of the past. It is on this originary dialectic of time that every synthesis is founded; it is through it that the synthesis remains irreducible as an *a priori* synthesis.

17. This latter is at the same time, and in the same movement, an activity and a passivity, a production and an intuition of sense, a "making" and a "seeing," taken in their deepest sense. On this ambiguity of intentionality, see *Idées* I, p. xxx, translator's note 1.

18. In mathematics, time is supposed to be only fictitious. Synthesis and mathematical discoveries are supposed to be inscribed in time only through a contingency in the nature of the mathematician; in a word, their time is only psychological and the whole work of the scientist is supposed to consist in "redoing" a synthesis already done, in "reproducing" a span of time, in imitating a genesis.

19. *Ibid.*

20. Hegel, *Glauben und Wissen.* <Georg Wilhelm Friedrich Hegel, *Werke in*

zwanzige Bänden, 2: *Jenaer Schriften 1801–1807* (Frankfurt: Suhrkamp, 1970), pp. 287–433> [*Faith and Knowledge,* trans. W. Cerf and H. S. Harris (1977)].

21. For Husserl's conception of a concrete *a priori* which makes itself one with originary experience, and for its opposition to Kantianism, see G. Berger, *Le Cogito dans la philosophie de Husserl* (Paris: Aubier-Montaigne, 1941), § 6, pp. 121–26; see also Trân Duc Thao, *Phénoménologie et matérialisme dialectique* (Paris, 1951), vol. 1, § 6, p. 54.

22. That is to say, with Kant, without reference to an intuitive content. We are here at the opposite of Husserl.

23. Precisely it is a question of an *a priori* synthesis of being and of sense. Each of these terms must be known at the same time immediately *a priori* and hence in its originality, but at the same time, because it is implicated in a synthesis, must refer to something other than itself.

It must be recognized that the apparently purely logical nature of the expression *"a priori* synthesis" does not fit Husserl's language; he would certainly have refused its use. But here it poses the problem quite clearly and translates quite well, it seems, the sense of intentional experience.

24. We will often make use of this rather heavy word. Once again, it is an idea of genesis that justifies it: thematization, in attaching itself to an object of study, no more creates this than it adds this to a construction. Thematization reveals the object in the status of an already present theme, and by giving it a sense, describes it. So it translates the sense of the intentional act and of the transcendental genesis, which are at the same time intuitions and productions, revelations and inventions. The word "thematization" seems to give an account of this essential ambiguity quite well.

On the contradiction of a "thematization" of genesis, see below, chap. 6, p. 102 ff.

25. The problem of primitive mentality that we are quoting here as an example interested Husserl a good deal in the last years of his life. Numerous manuscripts take as a pretext the work of [Lucien] Lévy-Bruhl. See the unpublished letter to Lévy-Bruhl (11 March 1935) and Group F of the manuscripts.

26. A word that must not be taken in either of the determinations cited above, p. xviii.

27. Or is purely passive.

28. Activity and passivity.

29. Though the published works may seem to lend themselves to a chronology of themes, the complex weaving together of the latter in the unpublished works is such that it is absolutely impossible to determine with rigor the birth or the disappearance of a problem.

30. See below, p. 1.

31. On this "demotivation" *(Unmotiviertheit)* of the reduction, see E. Fink, "Die phänomenologische Philosophie Edmund Husserls in der gegenwärtigen Kritik," *Kantstudien* 38, 3/4, Berlin, 1933, p. 346.

32. Fink, always with the agreement of Husserl, in the article already cited, for example.

33. In its antepredicative attitude.

34. It has to be acknowledged that all these temptations appear in Husserl himself, in a more or less explicit way.

35. But this distinction is at one dialectically with an inseparability. See *Ideas* I, first section, chap. 1, § 2 and § 4.

36. Or logical.

37. Or, more precisely, "synthesis."

38. Vol. 1 especially.

39. Manuscripts dating from 1910–11 begin this theme in an explicit way, whereas it is absent from *Ideen* I (1913). This is one of the most striking examples of the chronological errors inspired by the published work.

40. See especially *Ideas* II, part 3.

41. Especially in the C group of manuscripts and in the works coming after *Ideen* I.

42. For this movement from *Logical Investigations* to *Ideas* I, see the introduction of *Idées* I (pp. xxvi–xxvii) and, especially, W. Biemel, introduction to *Die Idee der Phänomenologie, H.* 3 (The Hague: M. Nijhoff, 1950) [*The Idea of Phenomenology: A Translation of Die Idee der Phänomenologie,* trans. Lee Hardy, *H.* 2 (London: Kluwer Academic, 1999)].

43. It has been possible to accuse Husserl himself of the faults we are denouncing here. It seems that a misunderstanding is always at the origin of this. We will deal with this problem more closely in chap. 5.

44. This is the problem of the reduction of a transcendent or "noematic" time that brings to light a primordial time of the reduction, and we will explicitly face it. This time supposes a new problem of genesis. Why does any reduction of an attitude suppose an attitude of reduction?

45. Temporality and alterity are syntheses always already constituted and irreducible as such. With them will be introduced the most important theme of passive synthesis and genesis, which will pose very grave problems for Husserl: How can the constitution of a transcendental "ego" or starting from a transcendental "ego" be done passively?

46. Here the Husserlian reduction would become "anguish" in the Heideggerian sense of the word.

47. And what then would be the criterion of a distinction between these two types or moments of existence?

48. It is in this perspective that one understands the passage from Husserlian phenomenology to Heideggerian ontology.

49. These two meanings are identified with their "worldliness."

50. *Phenomenology and Dialectic Materialism.*

51. This is the absolute of phenomenological meaning, the only "serious" point of departure for any thinking.

Introduction

1. See especially *Die Philosophie der Arithmetik,* 1891 <reedited by Lothar Eley in *H.* 12 (The Hague, M. Nijhoff, 1970)> and his *Psychologische Studien zur Elementaren Logik* (1894) <republished in *H.* 22, 1979, pp. 92–123>.

2. See *LI,* vol. 1 (1900).

3. See *LI,* vol. 2 (1901).

4. See *The Phenomenology of Internal Time Consciousness* (1904–5) [*Lectures*].

5. See *Ideen* I (1913).

6. Husserl's lectures dealing with this enlargement of reduction date from the years 1920–25; R. Boehm, who communicated this to us, is working on their edition at present. <Since this, Boehm's edition has appeared, *H.* 8 (1959).>

7. This is the date of the manuscripts out of which L. Landgrebe edited *Experience and Judgment.* <See the preface of 1953/54, n. 11. >

8. See *Experience and Judgment* (1919–39).

9. See *Formale und tranzendentale Logik* (1929). <*Versuch einer Kritik der logischen Vernunft* (Halle [Saale]: Max Niemeyer, 1929). > [English translation by Dorion Cairns, *Formal and Transcendental Logic* (The Hague: Martinus Nijhoff, 1969).]

10. See *Cartesianische Meditationen* (1929). <*Cartesianische Meditationen und Pariser Vorträge,* ed. S. Strasser, *H.* 1 (The Hague: Martinus Nijhoff, 1950).> [*Cartesian Meditations,* trans. Dorion Cairns (The Hague: Martinus Nijhoff, 1960).]

11. A good many manuscripts dating from this period bear witness to these attempts; we will cite them more precisely at the appropriate time.

12. It is the fourth form of this idea, in the Kantian sense, that saves phenomenology from an empiricism or an existentialism (in the broad sense of that word). It was in *Logical Investigations,* vol. 1, the idea of the infinite becoming of logic; in *Ideas* I, the idea of an infinite totality of temporal experiences; in *Experience and Judgment,* the idea of a world as an infinite ground of possible experiences. We will see how difficult it is to give a phenomenological status to

these ideas that by definition precede and envelop any experience and any genesis.

13. See "Philosophy and the Crisis of European Humanity" (1935) [Husserl's Vienna Lecture, in *Crisis* as appendix 1], *Origin of Geometry* (1938), and many unpublished works, some of which we will cite later.

14. Paradoxically, it is the same thing here: essence is the universal structure of human nature. As such, it is appearing to a gaze that understands it, to an atemporal subject, to an existence that is not totally merged in some way with it. In this sense, essence is an accident. In order for the temporal essence of man not to be an accident, it is necessary that it is merged with human existence: that it is absolutely merged with it, because it never escapes from it in any way: that it should be merged so synthetically and dialectically with it because human existence (which must not be thought of here in an empirical sense) is no more *outside* time than it is *in time* because it appears to itself as temporal.

Chapter One

1. On the state of philosophy in Germany at the moment when Husserl starts out on research into psychology and logic, abandoning his purely mathematical activity, see M. Farber, *The Foundations of Phenomenology* (Harvard, 1943), chap. 1.

2. [Carl] Stumpf, *Psychologie und Erkenntnistheorie* (Trier, 1891). In this chapter, we will try to cite only those authors of whom Husserl had knowledge. Besides the fact that their number is very reduced thereby, the fact that we have been able to have access to Husserl's library has allowed us to establish the list of these authors with certainty.

3. See, for example, "La crise des sciences européennes et la phénoménologie transcendentale" [The crisis of European sciences and transcendental philosophy], trans. R. Gerrer, *Les Études philosophiques,* 1949, *op. cit.,* pp. 288–91; and also the numerous manuscripts of the last period (group M). On the confrontation of Husserl and Hume (one of the few classical philosophers well known to Husserl), see G. Berger, "Husserl et Hume," *Revue internationale de Philosophie* 1, no. 2, January 1939, Brussels, pp. 340–53.

4. Thadeuz Lipps, *Grundtatsachen des Seelenlebens* (Bonn, 1883).

5. It is here that there could be introduced the difference drawn later by Husserl between "worldly" consciousness and transcendental consciousness. The objectivity of geometric meanings is founded on the fact that it keeps all its value outside of every "real" relation with a consciousness. However, it has no sense except *for a consciousness:* the transcendental consciousness, which has anyway no other "real" content than the "worldly" consciousness.

6. On all these antipsychologist theses which Natorp defends, see P[aul] Na-

torp, "Quantität und Qualität in Begriff, Urteil und gegenständlicher Erkenntnis," *Philosophische Monatshefte* 27 (Berlin, 1891), pp. 1–31/129–60; and *Einleitung in die Psychologie nach kritischer Methode* (1888).

7. Lipps's expression.

8. Husserl borrowed a good deal from Natorp, even while he was opposing him. Thus, for example, the idea of the vicious circle through which psychology loses objective value as soon as it wants to found logic. In *Logical Investigations,* Husserl will make much use of this argument and will turn it both against psychologism and against empiricism and skepticism. He will use it again against Hume in *Crisis of European Sciences.*

9. Respect for the "meaning" of logic does not lack implication in phenomenology. The way in which a logical law presents itself to consciousness, the original way in which it is known or lived, in its universality, in its atemporality (or rather as Husserl will say later, its omnitemporality, or its supertemporality), its autonomy in relation to a real consciousness, that is where the beginning must be made and which it will never be right to transform or to "forget."

10. See Natorp, "Über objektive und subjektive Begründung der Erkenntnis," *Philosophische Monatshefte* 23 (Berlin, 1887), pp. 257–86.

11. The whole purpose of the present work is to show how Husserl, right from the start, turns upside down the Kantian doctrine of the ideality of time and is finally obliged, after endless detours, precautions, and subtleties, to reintroduce an ideality of time in the form of a teleology. Thus, he will start out from a time constituted in its unity, that is, we will see, from a "worldly" time. It is the very reason for his philosophy which will thus be contradicted.

12. Chr[istoph] Sigwart, *Logik* (Tübingen, 1873–78).

13. In *Experience and Judgment* and *Formal and Transcendental Logic.*

14. We will come back to the similar passages in *Experience and Judgment* (1, § 21); see chap. 6 below. On this subject, there would be very interesting comparisons to be made with some Bergsonian themes, which are similar.

15. See *Crisis,* pp. 91–97 [§ 25], and various manuscripts belonging to group M.

16. Chap 7, § 32–§ 39.

17. A piece of forgetfulness that here must not be confused with the psychological deficiency of memory (even though at the limit, it is very difficult to distinguish fundamentally the two pieces of forgetfulness. We will come back to this below).

Chapter Two

1. *Philosophie der Arithmetik—psychologische und logische Untersuchungen* [The philosophy of arithmetic—psychological and logical investigations] (1891). The work is dedicated to Franz Brentano <see the introduction>.

2. *Philosophie der Arithmetik,* part 2, chap. 10 <*H.* 12, p. 181 ff.>.

3. *Ibid.,* preface, p. v <*H.* 12, p. 5> [trans. from J. D.'s French translation].

4. *LU,* 1st ed., vol. 1, p. vi [*LI,* vol. 1, p. 42].

5. *Philosophie der Arithmetik,* p. v <*H.* 12, p. 5>.

6. *Psychologische Studien zur elementaren Logik,* p. 187 <*H.* 22, p. 120>.

7. *Philosophie der Arithmetik,* p. 5 <*H.* 12, p. 12>. [Karl Weierstrass.]

8. *Ibid.,* vol. 1 <what J. D. here and in the following calls "vol. 1" or "vol. 2" corresponds to the chapters of the book>, pp. 9–10 <*H.* 12, pp. 15–16>.

9. *Ibid.,* vol. 1, p. 11 <*H.* 12, p. 16>.

10. *Ibid.,* vol. 1, p. 11 <*H.* 12, pp. 16–17>.

11. Here the radical inadequacy of a psychology of number that invokes the act of abstraction can be perceived. This latter supposes synthetic unities, totalities that are already constituted by a prior genesis about which nothing is yet known.

12. It was the moment when *Gestalttheorie* was being born. Although he found it later very inadequate, Husserl who was a receiver of the idea, in return exercised an undoubted influence on it.

13. *Philosophie der Arithmetik,* vol. 1, p. 16 <*H.* 12, p. 21>.

14. Chap. 9.

15. *Ibid.,* vol. 2, pp. 19–20 <*H.* 12, p. 25>.

16. *Ibid.,* vol. 2, p. 25 <*H.* 12, p. 28>.

17. *Ibid.,* vol. 2, p. 28 <*H.* 12, p. 31>. [Johann Friedrich Herbart.]

18. Husserl's position in this work is very often purely and simply assimilated to a psychologism. An error committed especially in France.

19. *Ibid.,* vol. 2, pp. 28–29 <*H.* 12, p. 31>.

20. *Ibid.,* vol. 2, pp. 19–20 <*H.* 12, pp. 24–25>.

21. *Ibid.,* vol. 2, pp. 70–71, 76–77 <*H.* 12, pp. 68–69, 71–72>.

22. *Ibid.,* vol. 3, p. 77 <*H.* 12, p. 72>.

23. *Ibid.,* vol. 3, p. 79 <*H.* 12, p. 74>.

24. It will be thematized only with the description of a transcendental intentionality.

25. Here there is announced the relation of "foundation" *(Fundierung)* of essences or of symbols on the originarily concrete presence of the object "in person" to the consciousness.

26. *Ibid.,* vol. 4, p. 85 <*H.* 12, p. 80>.

27. Chap. 5.

28. Chap. 6.

29. [Gottlob] Frege, *Grundlagen der Arithmetik.* Husserl will take back his opposition to Frege in *Logical Investigations,* vol. 1, p. 292, and will cite *Grundlagen* as a very rewarding book.

30. *Ibid.,* vol. 7, p. 130 <*H.* 12, p. 118 n.3>.

31. Here it is seen how the problem is still posed at the level of a psychological intentionality that the objective sense of being can well do without. But will being not also do without a transcendental intentionality? Probably, but to the degree that it has an objective sense for a transcendental subject and that one always has to start out from this sense, transcendental intentionality will indeed be originary. But this originarity is phenomenological and not ontological. It is the whole problem of Husserlian idealism which is going to be posed.

32. Already there is a referring, beyond psychological genesis, to a transcendental genesis of formal logic. It is this genesis that will provide the theme of *Experience and Judgment* and of *Formal and Transcendental Logic.*

33. *Ibid.,* vol. 7, p. 134 <*H.* 12, p. 119>.

34. The question is, at bottom, whether a nonbeing can be aimed at in intention. An intentional idealism seems to fail here and can only allow the "signification" of a particular absence to be attained. Heideggerian ontology turns this intentional phenomenology upside down. "Anguish" is originary and allows an existential "stepping back" in the face of absolute ontological indetermination. It is a nothing that founds the possibility of logical negation. With Husserl, on the contrary, negation will always be performed starting from an intuition in which being, giving itself concretely, comes to "disappoint." Negation is genetically secondary. We will come back to this to find there one of most serious stumbling blocks of Husserlian logic.

35. *Ibid.,* vol. 8, pp. 140–50 <*H.* 12, p. 130 ff.).

36. One cannot fail to evoke here—as in many other places—the Platonic dialectic of the One and the Many, nor to regret that Husserl and numerous of his interlocutors and his disciples were not questioned, at least once in their lives, by a Socrates.

37. Then one no longer understands why the synthesis appears to us originarily.

38. *Ibid.,* vol. 7, p. 121, and vol. 8, pp. 154–55 <*H.* 12, p. 111 ff. and p. 139 ff.>

39. *Ibid.*

40. It could be regretted, as does Farber (*Foundations of Phenomenology,* chap. 2) the use of the word "content." It is indeed ambiguous and appears to be in contradiction with the intentionality of consciousness. But one has again to remember the insufficient explanation of this latter and, following Trân Duc Thao, and as the usage of the notion of "object in general" confirms, remark that intentionality corresponds to the criticist concept of *objectivation* (*Phénoménologie et matérialisme dialectique,* chap. 2, § 8, p. 78). This is the best proof that, from the point of view of an authentic transcendental phenomenology, Kantian criticism and psychologism have been assimilated.

41. *Ibid.*, vol. 9, pp. 190–98 <*H.* 12, pp. 161–76>.

42. *Cartesianische Meditationen und Pariser Vorträge,* § 41, p. 119 [*Cartesian Meditations: An Introduction to Phenomenology,* trans. Dorion Cairns (The Hague: Martinus Nijhoff, 1960), p. 86; hereafter *CM*].

43. See *LI,* vol. 2, *passim,* especially § 136.

44. See *Experience and Judgment* and *Formal and Transcendental Logic.*

45. *Ideas* I, § 22, pp. 88–90.

46. Husserl deals with this formal symbolism in the second part of the work, which does not concern us directly here.

47. *Ibid.,* [*Philosophie der Arithmetik,* part] 2, 13, p. 294 <*H.* 12, p. 260>.

48. The book also received great praise. See M. Farber, *Foundations of Phenomenology,* p. 54.

49. See *Zeitschrift für Philosophie und philosophische Kritik,* vol. 103 (Halle, 1894), pp. 313–32.

50. *LU,* 1st ed., vol. 1, p. vii [*LI,* vol. 1, pp. 42–43].

51. *Ibid.*

52. Especially in vol. 1, which allowed at that time the classification of Husserl among the logicists—with fairly good reason, it seems.

Chapter Three

1. *LU,* vol. 1, *Prolegomena zur reinen Logik,* 1st ed. (1900) <see the preface of 1953/54, n. 7>. [The quotations from Husserl follow *LI.*]

2. These are, above all, reading notes published in different journals of the period, and which Farber gives account of in a quite detailed way, *Foundations of Phenomenology,* chap. 3, pp. 61–89.

3. *LU,* vol. 1, p. vii [*LI,* vol. 1, p. 42].

4. *Ibid.*

5. *LU,* vol. 1, p. viii [*LI,* 1, p. 43].

6. *LU,* vol. 1, chap. 1, § 4, p. 9 [*LI,* vol. 1, p. 58].

7. *LU,* vol. 1, chap. 1, § 6, p. 12 [*LI,* vol. 1, p. 64].

8. *LU,* vol. 1, chap. 1, § 10, p. 25 [*LI,* vol. 1, p. 70].

9. *LU,* vol. 1, chap. 1, §§ 13, 14, 15 [*LI,* vol. 1, pp. 74–87].

10. *Formal and Transcendental Logic* and, especially, *Origin of Geometry* will show this.

11. *LU,* vol. 1, chap. 3, § 17, pp. 50–51, § 18, p. 52 [*LI,* vol. 1, chap. 3, §§ 17, 18].

12. J[ohn] S[tuart] Mill, *An Examination of Sir William Hamilton's Philosophy,* p. 461; quoted in *LU,* vol. 1, chap. 3, § 17, p. 51 [*LI,* vol. 1, pp. 90–91].

13. Lipps, *Grundzüge der Logik* (Leipzig, 1893), § 3; quoted by Husserl, *LU*, vol. 1, § 17 [*LI*, vol. 1, p. 91].

14. *Ibid.*, § 19, p. 58 [*LI*, vol. 1, p. 94].

15. This is what [Gottlob Benjamin] Jäsche (see *LU*, vol. 1, chap. 3, § 19, p. 53) and [Johann Friedrich] Herbart (p. 54) do [*LI*, vol. 1, p. 92].

16. Lipps, *Die Aufgabe der Erkenntnistheorie;* cited in Husserl, *LU*, vol. 1, p. 55 [*LI*, vol. 1, p. 93].

17. *Ibid.*

18. *Ibid.*

19. Husserl, in taking up the defense of psychologism for rhetorical purposes, brings up a theme to which he will always remain faithful; the must-be or the "value," are moments of being, just like nonbeing. Ethical judgment, or the judgment "of value" and negation are modalizations of a "thetic" attitude of being, which later Husserl will call the "doxic thesis" or the "passive doxa," an absolutely original "antepredicative" layer of any logic. If it is kept in mind that the deep sense of psychologism, which not every holder of psychologism has attained, is in the reduction to being—which a scientism of value, of the possible and of nonbeing has lowered to a simple natural reality—then the steadfastness of Husserl's inspiration can be perceived, one that links his first psychologist themes to the phenomenological themes of his latest period, the theme of the "worldly" genesis to that of the "transcendental" genesis.

20. *Ibid., LU*, vol. 1, p. 56 [*LI*, vol. 1, p. 94].

21. *Ibid.*, p. 57 [*LI*, vol. 1, p. 95].

22. Natorp, "Über objective und subjective Begründung der Erkenntnis," *Philos. Monatshefte* 23, p. 264; Husserl's quotation.

23. *LU*, vol. 1, p. 58 [*LI*, vol. 1, p. 95].

24. Especially in the *Origin of Geometry.*

25. *LU*, vol. 1, chap. 3, § 20, p. 59 [*LI*, vol. 1, p. 96].

26. *Ibid.*, chap. 4, § 21, p. 60 [*LI*, vol. 1, p. 98].

27. *Ibid.*

28. *LU*, vol. 1, p. 61 [*LI*, vol. 1, p. 98].

29. *Ibid.*, author's note <p. 65> [*LI*, vol. 1, p. 98].

30. Husserl here opposes the rigor or exactitude of pure logical rules to the "vagueness" of empirical laws. Later, he will oppose the "rigor" of eidetic descriptions to the "exactness" of concepts in the empirical sciences such as psychology. See *Philosophie als strenge Wissenschaft* (*Logos* I, 1911, pp. 289–341) ["Philosophy as Rigorous Science," in *Phenomenology and the Crisis of Philosophy*, trans. Quentin Lauer (New York: Harper Torchbooks, 1965), pp. 71–147].

31. On the general differences between Kant and Husserl, see G[aston] Berger, *Le cogito dans la philosophie de Husserl*, chap. 6, pp. 132–133; and, especially, Fink, who aptly emphasizes the essential difference between the *positio quaestionis.* "Die phänomenologische Philosophie E. Husserls in der gegenwärtigen Kritik," *Kantstudien*, 38, 3/4, 1933, p. 336 ff.

32. *LU*, vol. 1, chap. 4, § 21, p. 60 [*LI*, vol. 1, pp. 98–99].

33. *Ibid.*, p. 61 [*LI*, vol. 1, p. 98].

34. *Ibid.*, pp. 61–62 [*LI*, vol. 1, p. 99].

35. *Ibid.*, p. 62 [*LI*, vol. 1, p. 99].

36. *Ibid.*, p. 62 [*LI*, vol. 1, p. 99].

37. *Ibid.*, p. 63 [*LI*, vol. 1, p. 100].

38. *Ibid.*, p. 63 [*LI*, vol. 1, p. 100].

39. *Ibid.*, p. 63 [*LI*, vol. 1, p. 100].

40. *Ibid.*, p. 63 [*LI*, vol. 1, p. 100].

41. *Ibid.*, p. 64 [*LI*, vol. 1, p. 101].

42. *Ibid.*, p. 66 [*LI*, vol. 1, p. 102].

43. This is why, later, while radically distinguishing between the empirical genesis and the transcendental genesis of the "ego," Husserl will strongly emphasize that there is no difference of "content" between the transcendental "I" and the empirical "I." Transcendental and empirical will be different "moments" of the constitution, the first being absolutely "originary," the second "always already constituted" *(immer schon konstitutiert*, an expression that is found in all Husserl's later analyses and, especially, in the manuscripts. It seems to reproduce itself indefinitely and marks the moment where the regression toward a more originary moment must overcome a new obstacle). Thus, it may be understood why every transcendental constitution will later appear as "genetic."

44. *Ibid.*, p. 66 <see p. 71> [*LI*, vol. 1, p. 102].

45. An expression that Husserl does not use and that Father Van Breda wants to use to replace the term, too frequent, of "constituted" or of "founded" ("Note sur réduction et authenticité d'après Husserl" [Note on reduction and authenticity according to Husserl], in *Phénoménologie-Existence, Recueil d'études* [Paris: Armand Colin, 1953]); reedited [Paris: Vrin-Reprise, 1985], p. 7). The systematic use of this expression, though acceptable in certain cases, does not appear very felicitous. In commenting on Husserl, there is a loss in rigor for every gain in elegance and variety of style. As his thought progressed, Husserl expressed himself in a more algebraic style. What is more, he sacrificed no detail of description or of demonstration to lightness of style.

46. Which made the logicians of that time believe that Husserl, after having appropriately defined the necessity of a "logical realism," fell back into a subjectivist

idealism. On this error of interpretation, see the preface by W. Biemel to *Die Idee der Phänomenologie* [*H.* 2; *The Idea of Phenomenology*].

47. *Ibid.*, p. 71 [*LI*, vol. 1, p. 106].

48. *Ibid.* This is the first approximation of this pure "eidos," which later will be tested by an "imaginary variation" of the "existential content" that has no longer any role except as example and "fiction." This "eidos," emptied of all real content, will not for all that be an idea in itself, detached from facticity. It is inseparable from the fact of which it is the essence; it is, as such, accessible to an "intuition." The doctrine of the intuition of essences not having yet been elaborated in *Logical Investigations,* vol. 1, the meanings remain formal concepts.

49. We owe an explanation on the subject of the constant assimilation in our discourse of "synthesis" and "genesis." Their identity is not immediate. The whole difference between a Kantianism and a Husserlianism appears here. However, that genesis which might be characterized at the same time by its temporality and its creativity can only be empirical, can only be assimilated to an *a posteriori* synthesis and be under a corresponding judgment. *A priori* synthesis excludes any genesis. It is not empirical, it necessarily requires no sensible intuition, it takes place according to an "ideal" temporality. With Husserl, on the contrary, every *a priori* synthesis being founded on a concrete intuition where being comes "to give itself in person," it is thus temporal and enriching. It becomes one with a genesis. What is true of the *a priori* synthesis is all the more true of the *a posteriori* synthesis. But only the *a priori* genesis poses a veritable transcendental problem.

50. *Ibid.*, p. 72. [*LI*, vol. 1, p. 106]. Our emphasis.

51. *Ibid.*, pp. 72–73 [*LI*, vol. 1, p. 107].

52. These fictions can be constructions, conceptual or imaginative fabrications (*fingere*) of the mind. They are said to have an empirico-technical sense.

53. *Ibid.*, chap. 5, §§ 25–29.

54. Quoted by Husserl, *ibid.*, p. 79 [*LI*, vol. 1, p. 112].

55. *Ibid.*

56. *Ibid.*, p. 81 [*LI*, vol. 1, p. 115].

57. *Ibid.*, p. 93 [*LI*, vol. 1, p. 122].

58. [Friedrich Albert Lange,] *Logische Studien, ein Beitrag zur Neubegründung der formalen Logik und Erkenntnistheorie* (1877), p. 130; quoted by Husserl.

59. *Ibid.*, p. 93 [*LI*, p. 122 n.1].

60. *Ibid.*, p. 99 [*LI*, pp. 125–26].

61. *Ibid.*, p. 97 [*LI*, p. 125].

62. *Ibid.*, p. 110 [*LI*, p. 135].

63. *Ibid.*, p. 154 [*LI*, p. 155].

196 Notes to Pages 45–46

64. *Ibid.*, p. 192 [*LI*, p. 197].

65. *Ibid.*, pp. 193–97 [*LI*, pp. 198–200].

66. Husserl always liked to acknowledge the value of the anthropological sciences in their specific activity. Only, he denies them any originarity. It is the more disturbing to see Husserl, almost forty years later and in a radically different discourse, mix together the most rigorous transcendental motive with the most suspicious empiricist explanations, ones bordering on the pragmatism here evoked. We will come back to this.

67. *Ibid.*, pp. 205–6 [*LI*, p. 207].

68. Our italics.

69. *Ibid.*, p. 206 [*LI*, p. 207].

70. *Ibid.*, p. 215 [*LI*, p. 215].

71. *Ibid.*, p. 215.

72. The idea of infinite logic here announces the idea of transcendental logic. Husserl will present them later *(Formal and Transcendental Logic)* as essentially of a piece.

73. It is strange that criticism in general omits the absolutely essential role of the idea of infinite in Husserl. This role is all the more interesting and important in that it is always played *sottovoce* [*en sourdine*]. It is the idea of the infinite that always comes, at the last moment, to straighten out a difficulty or to swallow it. Now [and] we will have occasion to come back to this, the phenomenological or transcendental status of this "idea" is, if not inconceivable, at least absolutely exceptional. It seems that in coming to save phenomenology, it will at the same time convert all its sense.

To our knowledge, the only authors who indicate the importance of the infinite in Husserl's work are:

1. G[eorges] Gurvitch (*Les tendances actuelles de la philosophie allemande* [The present tendencies of German philosophy], Paris, 1930, p. 60), who rightly insists on the negative character of the Husserlian infinite and who regrets the absence of an absolute and actual Infinite of a classical type. Probably the infinite is above all essential incompletion and in this sense, definitive negativity. But the idea of a "task" must not be neglected, which is absolutely inseparable, according to Husserl, from the idea of infinite. With Husserl, there is an axiological and teleological positivity in the idea of infinite. We will see how uncomfortable and even somewhat artificial is the situation of this "ethics" in the thought of Husserl.

2. Ricœur ("Husserl et le sens de l'histoire" [Husserl and the sense of history], in *Revue de métaphysique et de morale*, 1949, p. 282), who points up the

role of mediation between consciousness and history that Husserl assigns to *Ideas* "in a Kantian sense." But the idea of this mediation, a very interesting one, is treated only by preterition.

74. In spite of a thematizing of this becoming that is more and more sustained, Husserl will never succeed in giving it its real sense. At least, this is what we would like to show through this [present] work.

75. *Ibid.*, p. 206 [*LI*, vol. 1, p. 207: title of § 56].

76. *Ibid.*, §§ 62–72, pp. 228–54 [*LI*, vol. 1, pp. 225–47].

77. *Ibid.*, pp. 228–33 [*LI*, vol. 1, pp. 225–29].

78. *Ibid.*, p. 232 [*LI*, vol. 1, p. 228].

79. *Ibid.*, p. 233 [*LI*, vol. 1, pp. 228–29].

Chapter Four

1. *LU*, vol. 2 (1901).

2. Husserl always claimed to remain faithful to the content and the sense of *Logical Investigations*. He will always try to heave them up to the highest level of phenomenology and will work at their reedition right up to 1928.

3. See *Die Philosophie als strenge Wissenschaft*, p. 325 ["Philosophy as Rigorous Science"].

4. See above, pp. 182–83 n. 5. [The quotations in English follow *Lectures*].

5. *Vorlesungen*, p. 2. <This reference is to the edition of Heidegger. In the following, we indicate the edition in *H*. 10; here p. 3> [*Lectures*, pp. 21–22. J. D.'s insertions of the German are in parentheses; those from the English translation by Churchill in square brackets.]

6. § 1, p. 3; <*H*. 10, p. 4> [*Lectures*, p. 22].

7. *Ibid.* <*H*. 10, pp. 4–5> [*Lectures*, p. 23].

8. *Ibid.*

9. *Ibid.*, p. 4 <*H*. 10, p. 6> [*Lectures*, p. 24]. "Transcendence" evidently does not have a mystic sense here, as indeed Husserl emphasizes a little further on.

10. *Ibid.*, § 1, pp. 4–5 <*H*. 10, p. 6> [*Lectures*, pp. 24–25].

11. This is pointed out very aptly by Trân Duc Thao in a long and remarkable note, which he devotes to temporality, *Phénoménologie et matérialisme dialectique*, p. 140.

12. *Vorlesungen*, § 2, p. 7 <*H*. 10, p. 9> [*Lectures*, p. 28].

13. *Ibid.*, pp. 7–8 <*H*. 10, pp. 9–10> [*Lectures*, pp. 28–29].

14. *Ibid.*, p. 8 <*H*. 10, p. 10> [*Lectures*, p. 29].

15. *Ibid.*, § 3, p. 8 <*H*. 10, p. 10> [*Lectures*, p. 29].

16. A definition of Brentano's, quoted by Husserl, p. 8 <*H*. 10, p. 10>

[*Lectures,* pp. 29–30], extracted from a lecture by Brentano that was never published and of which Marty and Stumpf gave account in their works. See *Vorlesungen,* p. 3 <*H.* 10, p. 4> [*Lectures,* p. 29].

17. *Ibid.,* p. 9 <*H.* 10, p. 11> [*Lectures,* p. 30].

18. "The temporal predicates which qualify that to which they refer are, according to Brentano, non-real [*irreale*]; only the determination 'now' is real"; quoted by Husserl, *ibid.,* § 5, p. 12 <*H.* 10, p. 14> [*Lectures,* p. 34].

19. *Ibid.,* § 41, p. 72 <*H.* 10, pp. 84–85> [*Lectures,* pp. 112–13].

20. *Ibid.,* § 6, p. 13 <*H.* 10, pp. 15–16> [*Lectures,* p. 36].

21. *Ibid.,* § 6, p. 13 <*H.* 10, p. 15> [*Lectures,* p. 35].

22. *Ibid.,* § 7, p. 18 <*H.* 10, pp. 22–23> [*Lectures,* pp. 42–43].

23. *Urimpression.* [The English translation reads "Primal impression."]

24. *Vorlesungen,* § 11.

25. *Ibid.,* § 12, p. 26 <*H.* 10, p. 31> [*Lectures,* p. 53].

26. Here all the sources exploited by the French phenomenologists can be recognized.

27. Moreover it is because it is imperceptible in time that it is so in space. Here can be seen the birth of the idea of time's primordiality over space, on which Heidegger, after Husserl, will insist a great deal. But we will see that though this idea merges with the very foundation of Heideggerian ontology, it is rather difficult to justify in Husserlian phenomenology.

28. *Vorlesungen,* § 11, p. 25 <*H.* 10, p. 29> [*Lectures,* p. 50].

29. *Ibid.,* § 12, p. 26 <*H.* 10, p. 31> [*Lectures,* p. 52].

30. Later, we will come back at some length to this genetic problem and the situation of the *hylé* in general in transcendental constitution, see chap. 5.

31. *Vorlesungen,* § 13, p. 27 <*H.* 10, p. 33> [*Lectures,* p. 54].

32. *Ibid.,* § 13, p. 29 <*H.* 10, p. 34> [*Lectures,* p. 56].

33. *Ibid.,* § 43, p. 78 <*H.* 10, p. 91> [*Lectures,* pp. 118–19]; our emphases.

34. The theme of the object present "in flesh and blood" (the inelegant but traditional translation of the epithet *leibhaft* [bodily]) to the perception that is "originarily giving," is already to be met with in the *Vorlesungen,* § 11, p. 24, and § 17, p. 34 <*H.* 10, pp. 29, 40–41> [*Lectures,* pp. 50, 63–64].

35. See *Idées* I, Ricœur's translation of *Ideen* I, p. xxx, translator's note 1.

36. This would be to make any phenomenology impossible.

37. *Vorlesungen,* § 16, p. 34 <*H.* 10, p. 40> [*Lectures,* § 16, p. 63].

38. *Ibid.*

39. In her remarkable study on temporality in Heidegger and Husserl, Yvonne Picard emphasizes very clearly the dialectical character of temporality in Husserl. She rightly refers this dialectic to the Hegelian dialectic of the identity of identity

and nonidentity. However, Picard, judging the temporal dialectic to be more authentic in Husserl than in Heidegger, does not see that the dialectic is exclusively
"phenomenological" in Husserl and that the transcendental idealism of the latter
will always prevent him from founding it in an ontology of temporality or in a temporality of being—which Heidegger will mean to begin by doing. See Y. Picard,
"Le Temps chez Husserl et Heidegger," in *Deucalion* 1, 1946.

40. *Vorlesungen*, § 18, p. 36 <*H*. 10, p. 42> [*Lectures*, p. 65].

41. *Ibid.*, § 36, p. 63 <*H*. 10, pp. 74–75> [*Lectures*, p. 100].

42. He attempted to do this later, in texts that for the most part remain unpublished (Group C of the manuscripts). We will try to show how he fails in this.

43. This is the thesis opposed to the formalism mentioned earlier.

44. Husserl will present the idea of the "infinite task" of philosophy as a "practical ideal" in *Crisis* and in *Cartesian Meditations*. We will try, at the conclusion of
this work, to oppose a dialectical idea of phenomenology to Husserl, and to define the "theme" or the dialectical "motive," as the becoming conscious of philosophy, and its fulfillment.

45. *Ibid.*, § 36, p. 100.

46. *Ibid.*, § 31, p. 63 <*H*. 10, p. 67> [*Lectures*, p. 90].

47. *Ibid.*, § 32, p. 59 <*H*. 10, p. 70> [*Lectures*, p. 95].

48. *Ibid.*

49. *Ibid.*, § 33, p. 61 <*H*. 10, p. 72> [*Lectures*, p. 97].

50. *Ibid.*, § 39, pp. 70–71 <*H*. 10, p. 83> [*Lectures*, pp. 109–10]; our
emphases.

Chapter Five

1. On this subject, see W. Biemel, introduction to *Die Idee der Phänomenologie*, by Husserl; Trân Duc Thao, "Les origines de la réduction phénoménologique
chez Husserl," in *Deucalion* 3 (Paris, 1947); and Ricœur, introduction to his
translation of *Ideen* I.

2. *The Idea of Phenomenology* is the text of five lectures given in Göttingen in
1907 which present the first doctrine of the reduction. [See n. 42 in the preface
to the 1953/54 dissertation.]

3. The reduction will, however, remain the sole condition of any phenomenological "thematization." When phenomenology becomes genetic, the method of
the reduction will still seem valid to Husserl.

4. We now refer to *Ideen zu einer reinen Phänomenologie und phänomenologischen Philosophie I* (1913), the most worked out and most important writing of this
period. We will quote directly the excellent translation of Professor Ricœur. <*Idées
directrices pour une phénoménologie et une philosophie phénoménologiques pures,*

trans. Paul Ricœur (Paris: Éditions Gallimard, 1950).> [English translation by W. R. Boyce Gibson, *Ideas* I.]

5. *Idées* I, chap. 3, p. 13 [*Ideas* I, p. 51 n. 1].

6. Husserl is concerned to distinguish his conception of the *a priori* from that of Kant. He takes linguistic precautions about this: see *Idées* I, author's introduction, p. 9; § 17, p. 57 translator's note; and especially p. 70 translator's note 1 [*Ideas* I, p. 46 and § 17, pp. 78–79].

7. *Ibid.*, section II, chap. 1, § 27, p. 87 [*Ideas* I, p. 101].

8. Introduction to *Vorlesungen*, p. 2 <H. 10, p. 3> [*Lectures*, p. 21].

9. *Idées* I, § 27, pp. 89–90 [*Ideas* I, p. 102]. <Here, as in what follows, it is always Husserl who underlines.>

10. *Idées* I, § 27, p. 90 [*Ideas* I, p. 103].

11. *Ibid.*, § 28.

12. *Ibid.*, § 29.

13. *Ibid.*, § 31, p. 97 [*Ideas* I, p. 107].

14. *Ibid.*, § 31, p. 98 [*Ideas* I, p. 108].

15. *Ibid.* [*Ideas* I, p. 108].

16. *Ibid.*, § 31, p. 99 [*Ideas* I, p. 109].

17. *Ibid.*, § 31, pp. 98–99 [*Ideas* I, pp. 108–9].

18. On the sense and the necessity of such images, see the note by Professor Ricœur (p. 99 n. 5 [of his translation]).

19. See our [preface to the 1953/54 dissertation], pp. xxxiv–xxxv.

20. *Ibid.*, § 33, p. 105 [*Ideas* I, p. 112].

21. *Ibid.*, § 33, p, 106 [*Ideas* I, p. 112].

22. *Ibid.*

23. See § 39, p. 125 [*Ideas* I, p. 126].

24. *Ibid.*, § 57, p. 190 [*Ideas* I, p. 173].

25. *Ibid.*, § 76, p. 242 [*Ideas* I, p. 212].

26. *Ibid.*, § 33, pp. 108–10 [*Ideas* I, p. 114].

27. It is the same thing here, always according to the same motive. "Real" beginning and formal beginning are both deprived of absolute originarity. They are both founded by a phenomenological beginning.

28. § 50, pp. 154–55.

29. See § 31–62.

30. *Ibid.*, p. 106 in *Idées* I, translator's [Ricœur's] note 2.

31. § 33, p. 108 [*Ideas* I, p. 113].

32. § 34, p. 109 [*Ideas* I, p. 114].

33. A dissociation whose terms are inverted.

34. See § 44, pp. 140–44 [*Ideas* I, pp. 137–41].

35. § 46, p. 148 [*Ideas* I, p. 143].

36. *Ibid.*

37. This confusion between the reality *(reell)* of lived experience and its "appearance" seems to forbid *a priori* any "reduction" in this sphere by which existence and essence are merged *a priori*.

38. *Ibid.*, p. 150 [*Ideas* I, p. 144].

39. *Ibid.*, § 46, p. 150 [*Ideas* I, pp. 144–45].

40. The texts we are quoting are extracted from the 3d ed. (1928). This is a simple reproduction of the first.

41. *Ibid.*, § 46, p. 149 [*Ideas* I, p. 143].

42. *Ibid.*, § 135, p. 457 [*Ideas* I, p. 377]; and § 143, p. 480 [*Ideas* I, p. 397].

43. Probably it is not a subjectivist idealism, of the classical type; but it can nevertheless be said that what separates it rigorously from such an idealism stays very inexplicit.

44. § 47, p. 154 [*Ideas* I, p. 147].

45. § 49, p. 160 [*Ideas* I, p. 150].

46. *Ibid.*, pp. 160–61 [*Ideas* I, pp. 150–51.

47. *Idées* I, p. 160, translator's [Ricœur's] n. 1.

48. *Ibid.*, p. 162, translator's n. 1.

49. Even at the moment when, later, Husserl seemed to have returned to the antepredicative world, to the world prior to any meaning and any "determination," cultural, logical, [or] practical, he will preserve a noematic sense for this "antepredicative" and thus compromise what some have wanted to call the realism of Husserl—we will come back to this.

50. § 49, pp. 163–64 [*Ideas* I, pp. 152–53].

51. We will be satisfied with specifying *real* or *reell* without making the adjective agree every time it is not a question of a quotation.

52. *Ideas* I, *passim*.

53. How can the object in person be noematic *a priori?*

54. *Ibid.*, § 57, pp. 189, 190 [*Ideas* I, pp. 172–73; Boyce Gibson translates as "Ego" what in Ricœur's French is *moi*].

55. *Ibid.*, p. 190 [*Ideas* I, p. 173; Boyce Gibson translates as "quite peculiar" what is "original" in the German].

56. § 49, p. 162 [*Ideas* I, p. 152]; Husserl's italics.

57. There is absolutely no "atemporality" in Husserl. Historical becoming or the multiplicity of temporal lived experiences can be escaped from only by an "omnitemporality"—this will be the case for the "ideal objectivities" of

mathematics, of logic, of traditional culture in general, etc. Here we bring together omnitemporality and atemporality of the "I" because neither one nor the other, as such, is originarily "actual."

58. The morphé is an intentional and real element of lived experience; the noema is, for its part, an unreal element of lived experience.

59. § 36, p. 117 [*Ideas* I, p. 120].

60. § 36, p. 117 [*Ideas* I, p. 120].

61. *Ibid.*, translator's note 1.

62. *Ibid.*, § 36, p. 118 [*Ideas* I, p. 120].

63. § 97, p. 335 [*Ideas* I, p. 282].

64. § 41, p. 137 [*Ideas* I, p. 132; the German in brackets was inserted by Boyce Gibson].

65. § 42, p. 137 [*Ideas* I, pp. 134–35].

66. This is the group D of the manuscripts, to which we shall return.

67. § 85, p. 290 [*Ideas* I, p. 247].

68. § 85, p. 289 [*Ideas* I, p. 247].

69. A capitally important parenthesis, whose sense we shall come back to a little later.

70. § 85, p. 289 [*Ideas* I, p. 247].

71. The temporal hylé makes up the theme of many of the later manuscripts (group C), which we will need to come back to.

72. § 86, p. 298 [*Ideas* I, pp. 253–54].

73. § 85, p. 288 [*Ideas* I, p. 246].

74. § 81, p. 272 [*Ideas* I, p. 234].

75. § 81, p. 273 [*Ideas* I, p. 235].

76. § 81, p. 274 [*Ideas* I, p. 235].

77. Husserl is speaking of the unique flux of lived experience as "originary form of consciousness" (*Urform*, which P. Ricœur translates by "forme mère" of consciousness).

78. § 81, pp. 274–75 [*Ideas* I, p. 236].

79. *Ibid.*, p. 275 [*Ideas* I, p. 236].

80. § 150, p. 503 [*Ideas* I, p. 415].

81. § 81, p. 275 [*Ideas* I, p. 236].

82. *Ibid.*

83. *Ibid.*, pp. 275–76 [*Ideas* I, p. 237].

84. *Ibid.*

85. *Ibid.*

86. § 82, p. 277 [*Ideas* I, p. 238].

87. § 83, p. 280 [*Ideas* I, p. 239].

88. *Ibid.*

89. It is the strange idea of an intuition of the indefinite that seems contradictory here. Instead of recognizing this indefinite as a limit inaccessible to any intuition, Husserl wants to render it immanent and present to the lived experience in concrete form. Instead of unveiling the absolute consciousness of an essential finitude, out of idealism he gives a concrete content to an indefinite. The intuition of the indefinite is intuition of the possible infinite. It is here that the split is made between Husserlian idealism and a philosophy of existence. This latter, starting at the same time from the possibility or from the existential necessity of death and from the idea of an indefinite possibility of time, leads us to bring together the impossibility of the possible and the possibility of the impossible. The inauthenticity of a supposed intuition of the indefinite in the face of the noncompletion of the present and indetermination of the future is exceeded in "anguish" faced with the absolutely indeterminate.

90. *Ibid.* [*Ideas* I, p. 240.]

91. It is this "always already" that constitutes originary finitude appearing to itself.

92. It would remain to make clear how such a piece of lived experience is possible in a pure immanence.

93. § 82, p. 279 [*Ideas* I, p. 239].

94. § 118, p. 403 [*Ideas* I, p. 334; Derrida's commentary has taken care of the omitted phrase outside his actual quotation]. See, in addition, the translator's note 1 [in *Idées* I, p. 403].

Chapter Six

1. Which besides is at the same time implied in it.

2. It seems that once again the influence of Natorp, who had determined Husserl to give up his initial psychologism, was important here. Natorp had advised Husserl, we are told, "to introduce movement" into phenomenology.

3. On the history of these texts, their elaboration and their publication, see L. Landgrebe's foreword to Husserl's *Erfahrung und Urteil: Untersuchungen zur Genealogie der Logik,* 1948 edition, pp. v–vii [in *Experience*] <see the preface of 1953/54, n. 11.>

4. Besides, this ontology is "monotypical." Human "existence" and empirical "existence" are not to be distinguished essentially. Both can be "objectivated" when faced with a theoretical intuition. But this ontology is, above all, that of the first moments of phenomenology. Hence, it is difficult to agree with E. Levinas that the whole of Husserl's thought is motivated by such an ontological presupposition. Besides, the thesis of Levinas is based only on texts that precede

Cartesian Meditations. Already certain discourses of *Ideas* I on the subject of the originarily "evaluating" and "practical," even "ethical" attitude, brought nuances into a univocal ontology (See Levinas, *La Théorie de l'intuition dans la phénoménologie de Husserl*) <4th ed. (same as 1st ed., 1930) Paris: Vrin, 1978> [*The Theory of Intuition in Husserl's Phenomenology*, trans. A. Orianne (1973, Evanston, Ill.: Northwestern University Press, 1995).]

5. A participle Husserl often uses in the manuscripts.

6. *Erfahrung und Urteil,* § 4, p. 11 [*Experience,* p. 19.]

7. *Ibid.,* § 3, p7 [*Experience,* p. 16.]

8. *Ibid.,* § 3, p. 8 [*Experience,* p. 17].

9. *Ibid.,* § 3, p. 9 [*Experience,* p. 17].

10. *Ibid.,* § 3, pp. 9–10 [*Experience,* pp. 17–18]; we are summarizing here these pages where the condemnation of a psychologism is confirmed. It is clear that it is not a question here, as it has often been thought (a), of a return to an empiricism or to a "realism" pure and simple.

(a) This is what Jean Wahl does, in the notes on the first part of *Erfahrung und Urteil,* and "Aspects empiristes de la pensée de Husserl" [Empirical aspects of Husserl's thought], in *Phénoménologie-Existence, op. cit.,* pp. 77–135. It could be said that Husserl's philosophy aims to be empiricist and realist in the unconventional and narrow sense of the word. In that case it is a truism. That is to find out in 1952 that Husserl wanted to return to "the things themselves" as early as 1900 and presented his philosophy as an authentic "positivism."

11. L. Landgrebe speaks of Husserl's "sensualist" prejudice (letter to J. Wahl, in *Phénoménologie-Existence, op. cit.,* p. 206).

12. *Ibid.,* § 4, p. 11 [*Experience,* p. 19].

13. *Ibid.,* § 4, p. 11 [*Experience,* pp. 19–20].

14. *Ibid.,* § 4, p. 14 [*Experience,* p. 21].

15. *Ibid.*

16. *Ibid.,* § 5, p. 15 [*Experience,* p. 23].

17. *Ibid.,* § 5, p. 16 [*Experience,* p. 23].

18. *Ibid.,* § 5, pp. 16–17 [*Experience,* p. 24].

19. *Ibid.,* § 5, p. 16 [*Experience,* p. 23].

20. *Ibid.,* § 5 p. 17 [*Experience,* p. 24].

21. This is the moment when the theme of teleology makes its appearance in the manuscripts in the form that it will take later in the *Krisis.* The theme of transcendental intersubjectivity is one of the oldest (1910–11).

22. *Ibid.,* § 7, p. 26 [see *Experience,* p. 30].

23. *Ibid.,* § 7, p. 25 [*Experience,* p. 30; there is a phrase missing from the English translation, replaced here from Derrida's translation and marked by square brackets].

24. *Ibid.,* § 9, p. 36 [*Experience,* p. 39].

25. We are glad to have come across, in something just read, the same idea, presented with a great deal of precision and exactitude by L. Landgrebe (in the letter quoted above [note 11, this chapter]).

26. An ambiguity that is very close to that of the pure me as originary "now" and as totality (in the Kantian sense) of lived experiences, form, and infinite and absolute matter (*Experience,* part 2, chap. 3). The meaning of these two ambiguities is identical and reveals the same difficulty.

27. In the sense at the same time philosophical and usual of the term.

28. *Ibid.,* § 10, p. 38 [*Experience,* p. 41].

29. *Ibid.,* § 10, pp. 38–44 [*Experience,* pp. 41–46].

30. *Ibid.,* § 10, p. 41 [*Experience,* pp. 43–44].

31. *Ibid.,* § 10, pp. 42–43 [*Experience,* pp. 44–45]. The phrase will be repeated in *Crisis.* [*Experience,* in a note, gives the location in *Crisis,* p. 52].

32. *Ibid.,* § 12, p. 51 [*Experience,* p. 52].

33. *Ibid.,* § 12, p. 52 [*Experience,* p. 52].

34. *Ibid.,* § 12, p. 54 [*Experience,* p. 54].

35. *Ibid.,* § 29, pp. 157–58. [*Experience,* pp. 137–38; "mundane" has been replaced by "worldly."]

36. *Ibid.,* § 31, p. 165 [*Experience,* p. 144].

37. "This phenomenologically necessary concept of receptivity is in no way exclusively opposed to that of the *activity of the 'ego'* ['I' in Derrida's translation]. On the contrary, receptivity must be regarded as the lowest level of activity" (*ibid.,* § 17, p. 83) [*Experience,* p. 79].

38. Besides, this only pushes the problem one stage back, because it becomes necessary to suppose the final sense of activity present *a priori* in the passivity.

39. *Ibid.,* § 11, pp. 47–48 [*Experience,* pp. 48–49].

40. *Ibid.,* § 11, pp. 47–48 [*Experience,* p. 49].

41. *Ibid.,* § 21, p. 93 ff. [*Experience,* p. 87 ff.]. He must do this because it is the most difficult stage of genesis. How can negation "modify" a certainty or an absolutely originary thesis?

42. *Ibid.,* § 21, p. 94 [*Experience,* p. 88].

43. *Ibid.,* pp. 94–95 [*Experience,* pp. 88–89].

44. *Ibid.,* p. 97 [*Experience,* p. 90].

45. *Ibid.,* p. 98 [*Experience,* p. 91].

46. *Ibid.*

47. Yet there is no room for this moment in the philosophy of Husserl. The latter, trying to describe the phenomenon of negation starting from a transcendental theoretical subject must, as soon as he is obliged to invoke a concrete and

existential attitude (the only one that saves negation from a logical and predicative origin), do so in terms of psychology. Failure, disappointment, etc. have no transcendental status. They are thus purely empirical.

This is the whole difference separating Husserl from Heidegger. The transcendental subject is originarily existential for the latter; which allows him to describe an origin of negation that is neither psychological nor logical. It is the very nothing which allows negation. The "genetic" regression of which Husserl speaks, the "reactualization" of the originary sense, will be more radical with Heidegger; anguish will place us back again "in front" of nothingness; paradoxically, it is because Husserl starts from a passive doxa—that is, from an originarily thetic attitude of being—that he remains prisoner of the psychological attitude or of a theoretic-logical attitude; it is because he starts out from being that he does not get to the ontological.

In this sense, he is very far behind Hegel and Heidegger, who give an originary sense to negation and found it, not on an attitude or on an operation but on nothingness. It would remain to be seen if, in making of nothingness a dialectical "motor" of becoming, there is not given back to it a logical sense that would be the dissimulation of the originary nothingness and of anguish.

48. *Ibid.*, § 23, p. 117 [*Experience*, p. 107].

49. *Ibid.*

50. *Ibid.*, § 23, p. 119 [*Experience*, p. 108.]

51. *Ibid.* [The italics are the translator's into English, not Derrida's.]

52. *Ibid.*, § 35, p. 180 [*Experience*, p. 156].

53. *Ibid.*, § 39, p. 198 [*Experience*, p. 170].

54. *Ibid.*, § 36, p. 183 [*Experience*, p. 158].

55. Henceforth, we will use the expression "transcendental activity in general" to designate transcendental activity in its totality as covering activity and passivity.

56. *Ibid.*, § 39, p. 198 [*Experience*, p. 169].

57. *Ibid.*, § 36, p. 184 [*Experience*, p. 159].

58. *Ibid.*, § 38, p. 188 [*Experience*, p. 162].

59. *Ibid.*, § 38, p. 190 [*Experience*, p. 164].

60. Our analysis here follows § 38 very closely.

61. *Ibid.*, p. 194 [*Experience*, p. 166].

62. Moreover, we have seen how it was necessary to interpret this indefinite burying of the originary from a "philosophical" point of view.

63. Pp. 66–72 [*Experience*, pp. 64–68].

64. *Ibid.*, § 14, p. 67 [*Experience*, p. 64].

65. Husserl was thinking about the possibility of such an absolute synthesis more and more.

66. *Ibid.,* p. 67 [*Experience,* p. 65].

67. "not attempt[ing] to deal with either the perception of movement, which is much more difficult to analyze, or judgment concerned with moving things," *ibid.,* § 14, p. 70 [*Experience,* p. 67].

68. *Ibid.,* § 38, p. 189 [*Experience,* p. 163].

69. *Ibid.,* § 14, pp. 71–72 [*Experience,* p. 68].

70. *Ibid.,* p. 72 [*Experience,* p. 68].

71. *Ibid.,* § 23, p. 116 [*Experience,* p. 106]. See also a reservation of the same kind in § 38, p. 194 [*Experience,* p. 167].

72. The important group C of unpublished work, where Husserl's thought ranges over paths most foreign to traditional phenomenology.

73. The latter refuses to publish or to hand over all these texts.

74. Our intention was originally to work at length on the problem of the genesis of mathematics and, following the thesis of Cavaillès (*On Logic and the Theory of Science,* Paris, 1947), to confront it with precise texts from *Formal and Transcendental Logic.* Time was lacking, and we abandoned this project.

75. J. Cavaillès, *Sur la logique et la théorie de la science* [*On Logic and the Theory of Science*], p. 78.

76. *Ibid.,* p. 65.

77. This confusion, being *a priori* synthetic, is not only eidetic but ontological. Intentionality, being merged with the originary existence of time, is then no longer a theoretical gaze. It is human existence itself. This is the consequence that Husserl always wanted to escape from, by making an eidetic relation out of the relation of the intentional consciousness with temporality. But he could no longer then account for the absolute phenomenological identity of lived intentionality and lived temporality.

78. We allow ourselves this neologism to avoid making out of one or the other of its elements the epithet of a noun, the attribute of a substance. A little later, it will be necessary for the same reason to say consciousness-existence. Here it is enough to point this out.

79. On the one hand, if we sketch out a Husserlian response to the objections of Cavaillès, we do this in expliciting the phenomenological theme; but on the other hand, it must be admitted that this myth of an absolute consciousness was also that of Husserl, and stayed so.

80. See what he says on this subject [Cavaillès, *Sur la logique et la théorie de la science*], p. 44.

81. *Ibid.,* p. 78.

82. Cavaillès had not read *Experience and Judgment;* he never cites *Cartesian Meditations.*

83. This is what Husserl will not resign himself to; existence is for him always factitious reality, one constituted by a theoretical subject.

Chapter Seven

1. *Cartesian Meditations*. Series of lectures given at the Sorbonne in 1929. They were first of all published in their French translation by G. Peiffer and E. Levinas, in 1947, then by S. Strasser in an edition revised, corrected, and completed in German (1950). We will always give the double reference, to the original texts and to the translation, occasionally slightly modified. [This remark of J. D. does not apply here, where the English translation by Dorion Cairns is given; cited as *CM*.]

2. § 3, p. 49 (German edition only) [*CM*, p. 8].

3. *Ibid.*, our underlining. What is the mysterious sense of this "possession"?

4. *Ibid.* [*CM*, p. 9].

5. *Ibid.*, p. 50 [*CM*, p. 9].

6. *Ibid.*, p. 50 [*CM*, p. 9].

7. *Ibid.*, p. 51 [*CM*, § 4, pp. 9–10].

8. See the preceding chapter.

9. § 18, p. 81 [*CM*, pp. 42–43].

10. § 31, p. 100 [*CM*, p. 66].

11. *Ibid.*

12. *Ibid.*

13. § 33, p. 102 [*CM*, p. 68; Cairns's italics].

14. § 34, p. 103 [*CM*, p. 69].

15. § 34, pp. 105–6 [*CM*, p. 71].

16. § 36, p. 108 [*CM*, p. 74].

17. § 37, p. 109 [*CM*, p. 75].

18. § 37, pp. 110–11 [*CM*, pp. 76–77].

19. § 38, p. 111 [*CM*, p. 77].

20. § 35, author's note in the French translation, p. 61 ["eidos ego" is in Cairns's translation "the eidos psyche," *CM*, p. 73].

21. § 38, p. 112 [*CM*, p. 78].

22. This is the necessary condition of a distinction between a Platonic essentialism and a Husserlian essentialism.

23. Besides, formalism meets up with a materialism. Since it is purely passive, intentional movement becomes effect or reflection of a natural causality.

24. § 38, p. 112 [*CM*, p. 78].

25. Originarily it takes the form of a synthesis of time, the latter being the foundation of every ontological synthesis in general.

26. § 38, p. 112 [*CM*, pp. 78–79].

27. The absolute unity of intuition can only be the pure form of an intuition which, originarily, cannot be more than a "formal intuition"; this latter is not originarily intuition of something.

28. § 38, p. 112 [*CM*, p. 79].

29. *Sich in ihr selbst bekundende Geschichte:* the history which announces itself (manifests itself) in itself.

30. § 38, p. 113 [*CM*, p. 79].

31. § 38, p. 113; our emphasis, J. D. [*CM*, p. 79.]

32. *Ibid.*, our emphasis, J. D. [*CM*, pp. 79–80].

33. § 39, p. 114 [*CM*, p. 81].

34. Omnitemporality itself is submitted to a dialectic of "reproduction" (See *Cartesianische Meditationen*, § 55, p. 155) [*CM*, p. 127].

35. § 40, p. 114 [*CM*, p. 81].

36. § 40, p. 115 [*CM*, p. 81].

37. § 41, p. 118 [*CM*, p. 86].

38. *Ibid.*

39. *Ibid.*

40. We regret that the limits of this work do not allow us to analyze closely and at length the unpublished material whose sense we give schematically here. Putting this off to a later work, we will be content to indicate, in an appendix to the present chapter, the titles and the themes of the manuscripts that we were able to consult very attentively and which could have interested us directly here.

41. Unpublished work bearing the press mark C-17-IV, summer 1930. Trân Duc Thao resumes its sense and probes it very brilliantly [*Phénoménologie et matérialisme dialectique*], p. 139 n. 1.

42. Pp. 1 and 3 of the transcription (1930).

43. P. 4 of the transcription (1932).

44. P. 7 of the transcription (1932).

45. P. 8 of the transcription (1932).

46. C-13, 11–15 November 1934, p. 9 of the transcription.

47. C.7, mid-June 1932. (This last phrase was crossed out afterward; I no longer know why. J. D., 1990.)

48. *Ibid.*, pp. 1–2 of the transcription.

49. See the fifth *Cartesian Meditation.*

50. C.6 August 1930, p. 5 of the transcription.

51. § 41, p. 121 [*CM*, p. 88].

52. Among the many texts that we were able to look at, we will cite only those whose themes have never been explicitly taken up in the published work.

Chapter Eight

1. The "Vienna Lecture" given at the Vienna Kulturbund on 7 May 1935, under the title "Philosophy in the Crisis of European Humanity," is the first of the texts composing the great cycle called "Cycle of the *Krisis*," which comprises in particular a series of lectures to the Philosophical Circle of Prague for Research on Human Understanding. These lectures end in the essential text of the *Krisis*, entitled "The Crisis of European Sciences and Transcendental Phenomenology" (whose first two parts were published in 1936 by the revue *Philosophia*, Belgrade, and, in a bad translation, in French in *Etudes philosophiques*, 1949, trans. Gerrer) <see the preface of 1953/54, n. 8>.

The text of the Vienna Lecture, translated by P. Ricœur and with a preface by Dr. Strasser, has been published in *RMM*, 1950. [References to the Vienna Lecture are to Ricœur's translation. The page references in square brackets refer to David Carr's English translation, in *Crisis*, appendix 1]. The Husserl Archives are at this moment finishing publishing the whole edition of the *Krisis* cycle, which will comprise as well several important and numerous additional texts, collected and presented by W. and M. Biemel. <See the preface of 1953/54, n. 8.>

On the history of the *Crisis*, its development, and its composition, see Dr. Strasser's preface to the Vienna Lecture and the excellent article by P. Ricœur, "Husserl et le sens de l'histoire" [Husserl and the sense of history], in *RMM*, July-October, 1949, pp. 280–82.

Husserl's philosophy of history is the constant pretext for critics to utter psychological or even psychoanalytical considerations about the personal reasons that turned Husserl's thought in a direction which is claimed to be absolutely new (see, for example, P. Ricœur's article, pp. 280–83). Although these remarks are not merely anecdotal in sense, they often mask the deep continuity which links Husserl's philosophy of history to his preceding philosophy and stop us seeing how the one is required by the other, right from its beginning.

2. From the Vienna Lecture, p. 237 [*Crisis*, p. 276].

3. We still think that "human reality" is the contradiction itself. Simply put, it is that contradiction which appears and reveals itself to itself.

4. Text cited by P. Ricœur, ["Husserl et le sens de l'histoire"], p. 290. Unfortunately we were not able to have access to the numerous unpublished texts of the *Krisis*, which were then at Cologne, where W. Biemel was correcting the proofs of the future edition. But the essential of these texts is known to us by already published fragments. <This edition appeared in 1954, in *H*. 6. Its complete translation [into French] by G. Granel (J. Derrida for the *Origin of Geometry*, 1962) appeared in 1976 [in *La Crise des sciences européennes et la phénoménologie transcendentale*, Paris, Gallimard.]> [See the preface of 1953/54, n. 8; and chap. 8, n. 1.]

5. Vienna Lecture, pp. 235–36 [*Crisis*, p. 275.]

6. *Ibid.*

7. *Ibid.* [*Crisis*, p. 276].

8. 1. This finite existence is not the one Heidegger speaks of. For the latter, the possibility of a definitively authentic existence, assuming "being for death" in a "resolute decision," the possibility of an absolute purity of "anguish" suspends the dialectic of originary temporality. The latter must in fact force us to begin again indefinitely—and that is our finitude—the movement toward the originary that every constitution, in one and the same gesture, covers over in revealing it.

2. This dialectic is not the one Trân Duc Thao speaks of. For the latter, dialectic being purely "worldly" and being established by a matter that, as such, is not animated by dialectic, becomes "for-self" in a very mysterious way. We remain prisoners of a metaphysics.

Nor is it that of Hegel, which is brought to an end in Absolute knowledge, etc. <This note was crossed out afterward. J. D., 1990>.

9. *Ibid.*, p. 238 [*Crisis*, p. 278].

10. *Ibid.* [*Crisis*, p. 279].

11. *Ibid.*, p. 249 [*Crisis*, p. 292].

Chapter Nine

1. Quoted by Ricœur, ["Husserl et le sens de l'histoire"], pp. 289–90.

2. Husserl, in *Cartesian Meditations*, makes a very important distinction between the evidence of the existence (of the world) and apodictic evidence. In spite of [the degree] "to which this evidence is prior in itself to all the [other] evidences," it is very interesting to note that the existential evidence cannot "claim to be[ing] apodictic" [*CM*, p. 17]. This dissociation fully confirms what we say.

3. The Vienna Lecture, *passim*, especially p. 247 [*Crisis*, appendix 1, especially p. 291].

4. *Ibid.*, p. 241 [*Crisis*, p. 286].

5. The full title of this text is "The question of the origin of geometry as a historico-intentional problem."

6. *Ursprung der Geometrie*, p. 207, Husserl's emphases. <Henceforward, we will give in brackets the pages of the edition in *H. 6*. Here pp. 365–66.> [Followed by the corresponding pages of the translation of Husserl's text by David Carr, in *Geometry*.]

7. *Ibid.*

8. *Ibid.*, p. 208 <*H. 6*, p. 367> [*Geometry*, p. 159].

9. *Ibid.*, p. 214 <*H. 6*, p. 373> [*Geometry*, p. 166].

10. *Ibid.* My underlining, J. D.

11. <*H.* 1, p. 59> [From "La crise des sciences européennes et la phénoménologie transcendantale," French trans. R. Gerrer, in *Les etudes philosophiques* (1949), p. 256; *Crisis,* p. 58].

12. *Ursprung der Geometrie,* pp. 212–16 <*H.* 6, p. 372 ff.> [*Geometry,* p. 164]. <Sometime afterward, I noted: "No. Look at again!" opposite these lines. J. D., 1990.>

13. That would refer us to another insoluble form of the problem of gene- sis: How is a passive intentional and transcendental genesis continuous with a real and empirical subject? How can it have the same "content" as the factitious genesis?

14. *Ibid.,* p. 208 <*H.* 6, p. 367> [*Geometry,* p. 159].

15. *Ibid.,* p. 209 <*H.* 6, p. 367> [*Geometry,* p. 160; Carr translates by "entity" what Derrida translates as "étant."].

16. *Ibid.,* p. 209 <*H.* 6, pp. 368–69> [*Geometry,* p. 161].

17. *Ibid.* <*Ibid.*> It refers us to the difficulties we have already looked at.

18. *Ibid.,* p. 216 <*H.* 6, p. 374> [*Geometry,* p. 168].

19. *Ibid.,* p. 218 <*H.* 6, p. 377> [*Geometry,* p. 171]. (In the margin sometime later I put the following note: "No, misunderstanding." This was corrected in my translation of the *Origin,* p. 197. J. D., 1990).

20. *Expérience et jugement,* § 10, p. 42 [*Experience,* p. 45]. The image is taken up again in *Krisis.*

21. *Formale und tranzendentale Logik,* § 105, p. 245 [Edmund Husserl, *For- mal and Transcendental Logic,* trans. Dorion Cairns (1969; The Hague: Martinus Nijhoff, 1978), p. 278].

22. P. 221 <*H.* 6, p. 380> [*Geometry,* p. 174].

23. It seems that it is from Husserl that contemporary psychology has bor- rowed the concept of motivation, which gives back a dynamic, intentional sense to the psychological and natural classical "causality." At least, that is what Husserl says (*Ideas* I).

24. See p. 221. <*H.* 6, pp. 380–81> [*Geometry,* p. 174].

25. *Ibid.,* p. 220. <*H.* 6, p. 379> [*Geometry,* pp. 172–73].

26. About this technical genesis, see three important and very explicit texts whose length prevents us from quoting. *Krisis* II, pp. 150–51, p. 230, and p. 246 <*H.* 6, pp. 24–25, 32 ff., 49> [*Crisis,* pp. 26–27, 34 ff., 49].

27. *Ursprung,* p. 224 <*H.* 6, pp. 383–84> [*Crisis,* pp. 177–79].

28. *Ibid.,* see p. 221<*H.* 6, p. 379 ff. p. 179> [and J. Derrida's introduction, *Geometry,* p. 146 n. 6].

29. *Ibid.,* p. 225 <*H.* 6, p. 385> [*Geometry,* p. 180].

Chapter Ten

1. <That is to say, [*The Crisis of the Sciences as Expression of the Radical Life-Crisis of European Humanity*].>

2. *Krisis* II, p. 136 <*H*. 6, pp. 9–10> [*Crisis*, pp. 11–12].

3. *Ibid.*, p. 269 <*H*. 6, p. 71> [*Crisis*, p. 70].

4. *Ibid.*, p. 267 <*H*. 6, p. 69> [*Crisis*, p. 68, then pp. 72, 73].

5. *Ibid.*, p. 268 <*H*. 6, p. 71> [*Crisis*, p. 70; italics in the English, not the French translation.].

6. Paul Ricœur's expression.

7. *Ibid.*, p. 245 <*H*. 6, p. 49> [*Crisis*, pp. 48–49].

8. Quoted by Ricœur, ["Husserl et le sens de l'histoire"], p. 302.

9. *Krisis*, p. 250, Husserl's emphases. <*H*. 6, p. 53> [*Crisis*, pp. 52–53; German cited by Carr].

10. *Ibid.*, pp. 287–88 <*H*. 6, p. 90> [*Crisis*, p. 88; Derrida translates the last sentence as: "it is regrettable that a more elevated sense of his philosophical responsibility does not correspond to it."].

11. [Derrida makes the following remark on the French text he is using] Without having seen the original text, the deficiencies of the translation can be guessed. No doubt one should translate action by "production" *(Leistung)* of transcendental knowledge. [The German in *H*. 6, p. 98, l. 20 does indeed read *Leistung*].

12. *Ibid.*, p. 295 <*H*. 6, p. 98> [*Crisis*, p. 95].

13. *Ibid.*, p. 298 <*H*. 6, p. 101> [*Crisis*, p. 98].

14. *Ibid.*, pp. 299–300 <*H*. 6, p. 102> [*Crisis*, p. 99].

15. These are Husserl's words to his sister, Dr. Adelgundis Jägersschmidt, during a talk that he had with her during his last serious illness. Quoted by Walter Biemel, in the introduction to "La philosophie comme prise de conscience de l'humanité" [Philosophy as becoming aware of humanity], *Deucalion, Vérité et Liberté* 3 (1950), p. 113.

BIBLIOGRAPHY

For the French edition of 1990, Elisabeth Weber updated the references to Husserl's texts; her contributions are marked between angle brackets < >. For this edition, the translations into French have been removed, with the exception of those published by 1954–55 and available to Derrida at the time of writing.

WORKS OF HUSSERL

Published Works

Philosophie der Arithmetik, 1st part (only one published): *Psychologische und lo-gische Untersuchungen*, 1891 <reedited by Lothar Eley, in *Husserliana*, vol. 12, The Hague: M. Nijhoff, 1970>.

Psychologische Studien zur elementaren Logik (Phil. Monatshefte), Band 30, 1894, pp. 159–91 <reedited by Bernhard Rang, in *Husserliana*, vol. 22: *Aufsätze und Rezensionen (1890–1910)*, The Hague: M. Nijhoff, 1979, pp. 92–123>.

Logische Untersuchungen, 1st ed., vol. 1: 1900; vol. 2: 1901 <reedited Tübin-gen: Max Niemeyer, 1968>.

Vorlesungen zur Phänomenologie des inneren Zeitbewußtseins (1905), edited by M. Heidegger, *Jahrbuch für Philos. u. phänomen. Forschung*, 9, 1928, pp. 367–496, edited separately <reedited by Rudolf Boehm, in *Husserliana*, vol. 10: *Zur Phänomenologie des inneren Zeitbewußtseins (1893–1917)*, The Hague: Martinus Nijhoff, 1966>.

Philosophie als strenge Wissenschaft (Logos I, 1911, pp. 289–431) <reedited by Th. Nenon and H. R. Sepp, in *Husserliana*, vol. 25, The Hague: M. Nijhoff, 1987>.

Ideen zu einer reinen Phänomenologie und phänomenologischen Philosophie I (*Jahrbuch . . .* , 1913), 4th reedition by Biemel, in *Husserliana*, 1950;

translation into French by Ricœur (of the 3rd ed., which reproduces unchanged the 1st ed.), [Paris:] NRF, 1950.

Erfahrung und Urteil, Untersuchungen zur Genealogie der Logik, written and edited by L. Landgrebe, 1939, from manuscripts dating for the most part from 1919 <6th ed., Hamburg: Meiner, 1985>.

Formale und transcendantale Logik (Jahrbuch . . . , 1929), separately edited <*Formale und transzendentale Logik. Versuch einer Kritik der logischen Vernunft,* Halle (Saale): Max Niemeyer, 1929>.

Nachwort zu meinen "Ideen . . ." (Jahrbuch . . . , 1930), separately edited.

Cartesianische Meditationen und Pariser Vorträge, published in *Husserliana* by Dr Strasser, 1950; this had been translated from the manuscript by G. Peiffer and E. Levinas, 1931 <*Méditations cartésiennes. Introduction à la phénoménologie,* reedited by Vrin, 1980>.

La philosophie dans la crise de l'humanité européenne. Lecture in Vienna, 7 May 1935 [Philosophy in the crisis of European humanity; the Vienna lecture of 7 May 1935], text established and presented by Dr. Strasser, trans. Ricœur, in *RMM* [*Revue de métaphysique et de morale*], 1950, no. 3, pp. 229–58.

Die Krisis der europäischen Wissenschaften und die transzendantale Phänomenologie (1st part only published), Belgrade, revue *Philosophia,* vol. 1, 1936, pp. 77–176; trans. R. Gerrer, in *Les Etudes philosophiques,* 1949, pp. 126–57 <reedited by Walter Biemel, in *Husserliana,* vol. 6, The Hague: M. Nijhoff, 1954>.

Die Frage nach dem Ursprung der Geometrie als intentional-historisches Problem (*Revue intern. de Philosophie,* no. 2, January 1939, pp. 207–25) <reedited by Walter Biemel in *Husserliana,* vol. 6, *op. cit.* French trans. by Jacques Derrida, *L'origine de la géométrie,* Paris: PUF, 1962>.

Manuscripts Published in Fragments

M III, L I. 16, January 1913, published in French by W. Biemel, under the title Rapport entre la phénoménologie et les sciences [Relation between phenomenology and the sciences], in *Les Etudes philosophiques,* 1949, pp. 1–7.

La philosophie comme crise de conscience de l'humanité, text established and presented by W. Biemel, trans. Ricœur, in *Deucalion,* 3, *Vérité et Liberté,* [1950], pp. 109–27.

Unpublished (We cite here the titles of the transcriptions)

Group A. *Mundane Phänomenologie,* 4 Wissenschaftstheorie: 9, May–June 1932: Genesis der Wissenschaft aus der Lebenswelt; 4, November 1933: Genesis der wissenschaftlicher Weltanschauung aus dem Vorwissenschaftlichen; 13, 1931: Genesis der Wissenschaft.

Groups B, C, D. See the appendix to chapter 7. We will not cite here the other manuscripts we were able to consult but did not use directly in the present work.

— *Grundlegende Untersuchungen zum phänomenologischen Ursprung der Räumlichkeit der Natur* (7–9 May 1934), in *Phil. Essays in Memory of E. Husserl*, 1940.

CRITICAL WORKS

Berger G., *Le cogito dans la philosophie de Husserl*, Paris, 1941.

Berger G., Husserl et Hume, in *Revue internationale de Phil.*, no. 2, January 1939, p. 342.

Cairns D., An approach to phenomenology, in *Phil. Essays*, p. 3.

Cavaillès J., *Sur la logique et la théorie de la science*, PUF, 1947.

Chestov L., Memento mori—A propos de la théorie de la connaissance de Husserl, *Rev. phil.*, January-February, 1926, pp. 5–62.

Delbos V., Husserl—Sa critique du psychologisme et sa conception d'une logique pure, in *RMM* [*Revue de métaphysique et de morale*], 1911, pp. 685–98.

Dessoir M., La phénoménologie de Husserl, *Rev. int. de Phil.*, no. 2, January 1939, pp. 271–76.

Farber M., *The Foundation of Phenomenology*, Harvard, 1943.

Farber M., *Phenomenology, in Twentieth Century Philosophy*, 1943, p. 345.

Farber M., The ideal of a presuppositionless philosophy, in *Phil. Essays*, 1940, p. 44.

Fink E., Die Phänomenologische Philosophie E. Husserls in der gegenwärtigen Kritik, in *Kantstudien*, Band 38, 3/4, Berlin, 1933, pp. 319–83.

Fink E., Das Problem der Phänomenologie E. Husserls, in *Rev. int. de Phil.*, no. 2, January 1939, pp. 226–70.

Fink E., L'analyse intentionnelle et le problème de la pensée spéculative, in *Problèmes actuels de la phénoménologie*, p. 53.

Gill V. J. Mc., A materialist approach to Husserl's philosophy, in *Phil. Essays*, p. 231.

Gurvitch G., *Les tendances actuelles de la philosophie allemande*, chap. 1, 1930.

Gurwitsch A., On the intentionality of consciousness, in *Phil. Essays*, p. 65.

Kaufmann F., Phenomenology and logical empiricism, in *Phil. Essays*, p. 124.

Klein J., Phenomenology and the history of science, in *Phil. Essays*, p. 143.

Kattsoff L. O., The relation of science to philosophy in the light of Husserl's thought, in *Phil. Essays*, p. 203.

Kuhn H., The phenomenological concept of horizon, in *Phil. Essays*, p. 106.

Landgrebe L., Husserls Phänomenologie und die Motive zu ihrer Umbildung, *Rev. int. de Phil.*, no. 2, pp. 277–316.

Landgrebe L., Lettre à J. Wahl, in *Phénoménologie-Existence*, 1953, pp. 205–6.

Levinas E., *La théorie de l'intuition dans la phénoménologie de Husserl*, Paris, 1930.

Levinas E., *En découvrant l'existence avec Husserl et Heidegger*, Paris, 1949.

Merleau-Ponty M., *Les sciences de l'homme et la phénoménologie*, 1 (CDU).

Merleau-Ponty M., Le philosophe et la sociologie, in *Cahiers int. de Soc.*, 1951, p. 50.

Merleau-Ponty M., Sur la phénoménologie du langage, in *Problèmes actuels*, p. 89.

[*Phénoménologie-Existence, Recueil d'études*, Paris: Armand Colin, 1953; re-edited Paris: Vrin-Reprise, 1985.]

Picard Y., Le temps chez Husserl et Heidegger, in *Deucalion*, vol. 1, 1946, p. 93.

Pos H. J., Phénoménologie et linguistique, in *Rev. int. de Phil.*, no. 2, p. 354.

Pos H. J., Valeur et limites de la phénoménologie, in *Problèmes actuels*, p. 31.

Ricœur P., Husserl et le sens de l'histoire, in *RMM*, July-October 1949, p. 214.

Ricœur P., Analyses dans *Ideen* II, in *Phénoménologie-Existence*, 1953, p. 23.

Ricœur P., Méthodes et tâches d'une phénoménologie de la volonté, in *Problèmes actuels*, 1951, p. 111.

Schuetz A., Phenomenology and the social sciences, in *Phil. Essays*, p. 164.

Spiegelberg H., The "reality-phenomenon" and reality, in *Phil. Essays*, p. 84.

Trân-Duc-Thao, *Phénoménologie et matérialisme dialectique*, Paris, 1951.

Trân-Duc-Thao, Les origines de la réduction phénoménologique chez Husserl, in *Deucalion*, vol. 3, p. 128.

Trân-Duc-Thao, Existentialisme et matérialisme dialectique, *RMM*, July-October 1949, p. 317.

Thevenaz D., La question du point de départ radical chez Descartes et Husserl, *Problèmes actuels*, p. 9.

Van Breda H. L., Note sur Réduction et authenticité d'après Husserl, in *Phénoménologie-Existence*, p. 7.

Waelhens A. de, De la phénoménologie à l'existentialisme, in *Le choix–le monde–l'existence*, 1947, p. 37.

Wahl J., Note sur la première partie de *Erfahrung und Urteil*, in *Phénoménologie-Existence*, p. 77.

Wahl J., Note sur quelques aspects empiristes de la pensée de Husserl, in *Phénoménologie-Existence*, p. 107.

LIST OF HUSSERL TRANSLATIONS
USED IN THIS EDITION

Cartesian Meditations. Translated by Dorion Cairns. The Hague: Martinus Nijhoff, 1960.

The Crisis of European Sciences and Transcendental Phenomenology: An Introduction to Phenomenological Philosophy. Translated by David Carr. Evanston, Ill.: Northwestern University Press, 1970.

Experience and Judgment: Investigations in a Genealogy of Logic. Revised and edited by Ludwig Landgrebe. Translated by J. S. Churchill and Karl Ameriks. Evanston, Ill.: Northwestern University Press, 1973.

Formal and Transcendental Logic. Translated by Dorion Cairns. The Hague: Martinus Nijhoff, 1969.

The Idea of Phenomenology: A Translation of "Die Idee der Phänomenologie." Translated by Lee Hardy. *Husserliana* 2. Dordrecht: Kluwer Academic, 1999.

Ideas: General Introduction to Pure Phenomenology. Translated by W. R. Boyce Gibson. 1931. 4th impression, London: Allen & Unwin; New York: Humanities Press, 1967.

Ideas Pertaining to a Pure Phenomenology and to a Phenomenological Philosophy. Book 2: *Studies in the Phenomenology of Constitution.* Translated by Richard Rojcewicz and André Schuwer. In *Collected Works,* vol. 3. Dordrecht: Kluwer Academic, 1989.

Logical Investigations. Translated by J. N. Findlay from the 2d German edition. 2 vols. London: Routledge & Kegan Paul; New York: Humanities Press, 1970.

Origin of Geometry. In Jacques Derrida, *Edmund Husserl's Origin of Geometry: An Introduction,* edited by David B. Allison, translated by John P. Leavey. Husserl's text translated by David Carr (reprinted from *Crisis of European Sciences and Transcendental Phenomenology*). Stony Brook, N.Y.: Nicholas Hays; Sussex: Harvester Press, 1978.

The Phenomenology of Internal Time Consciousness. Edited by Martin Heidegger. Translated by James S. Churchill. Bloomington: Indiana University Press, 1964.

"Philosophy as Rigorous Science." Translated by Quentin Lauer. In *Phenomenology and the Crisis of Philosophy*, pp. 71–147. New York: Harper & Row, 1965. Also in *Husserl: Shorter Works*, edited by Peter McCormick and Frederick Elliston. Notre Dame, Ind.: University of Notre Dame Press, 1981.

INDEX